W9-AVS-028

TOKYO
ENCOUNTER

WENDY YANAGIHARA

Tokyo Encounter

Published by Lonely Planet Publications Pty Ltd
ABN 36 005 607 983

Australia	Head Office, Locked Bag 1, Footscray, Vic 3011 ☎ 03 8379 8000 fax 03 8379 8111 talk2us@lonelyplanet.com.au
USA	150 Linden St, Oakland, CA 94607 ☎ 510 893 8555 toll free 800 275 8555 fax 510 893 8572 info@lonelyplanet.com
UK	72–82 Rosebery Avenue, Clerkenwell, London EC1R 4RW ☎ 020 7841 9000 fax 020 7841 9001 go@lonelyplanet.co.uk

This title was commissioned in Lonely Planet's Melbourne office and produced by: **Commissioning Editor** Rebecca Chau **Coordinating Editor** Stephanie Ong **Coordinating Cartographer** Owen Eszeki **Layout Designer** Katie Thuy Bui **Managing Editor** Geoff Howard **Managing Cartographers** David Connolly, Julie Sheridan **Cover Designer** Pepi Bluck **Project Manager** Eoin Dunlevy **Series Designers** Nic Lehman, Wendy Wright **Thanks to** Ross Butler, Rebecca Dandens, Sally Darmody, Ryan Evans, Quentin Frayne, Josh Geoghegan, Margedd Helioz, Errol Hunt, Laura Jane, Wayne Murphy, Malisa Plesa, Lauren Rollheiser, Wibowo Rusli, Lyahna Spencer, Tashi Wheeler, Celia Wood

All images are copyright of the photographers unless otherwise indicated. Many of the images in this guide are available for licensing from **Lonely Planet Images**: www.lonelyplanetimages.com.

ISBN 978 1 74059 558 2

Printed through Colorcraft Ltd, Hong Kong.
Printed in China

HOW TO USE THIS BOOK

Colour-Coding & Maps

Colour-coding is used for symbols on maps and the text that they relate to (eg all eating venu on the maps and in the text are given a green f symbol). Each neighbourhood also gets its ov colour, and this is used down the edge of the pa and throughout that neighbourhood section.

Shaded yellow areas on the maps denc 'areas of interest' – for their historical signi cance, their attractive architecture or their gr bars and restaurants. We encourage you to he to these areas and just start exploring!

Prices

Multiple prices listed with reviews (eg ¥10/5 ¥10/5/20) indicate adult/child, adult/concessi or adult/concession/child.

Send us your feedback We love to hear from readers – your comments help make our books better. We read every word you send us, and we always guarantee that your feedback goes straight to the appropriate authors. The most useful submissions are rewarded with a free book. To send us your updates and find out about Lonely Planet events, newsletters and travel news visit our award-winning website: *lonelyplanet .com/contact*

Note: We may edit, reproduce and incorporate your comments in Lonely Planet products such as guidebooks, websites and digital products, so let us know if you don't want your comments reproduced or your name acknowledged. For a copy of our privacy policy, visit *lonelyplanet.com/privacy*

WENDY YANAGIHARA

Wendy first toured Tokyo perched on her mother's hip at the age of two. Beyond childhood summers spent with relatives in Japan, she has spent time over the past several years diligently eating, drinking and dancing her way across Tokyo in the name of research. She has contributed to several Lonely Planet titles including *Japan, Tokyo, Vietnam, The Asia Book* and *Southeast Asia on a Shoestring*. Before pitching herself into writing for Lonely Planet in 2003, she taught English in Vietnam and worked as a designer for publishers (including Lonely Planet) in the San Francisco Bay Area, Santa Barbara and Lake Tahoe. When not in Japan she continues a self-directed study of Japanese language and literature, and contemplates following in her mother's footsteps in the study of the *koto* (a Japanese 13-stringed instrument).

WENDY'S THANKS

Many thanks go to the 'five families' – the Maekawas, Takahashis, Yanagiharas and the two branches of Yamamotos. Thanks to Kenichi-san, Yamada-san, and most especially Mariko Matsumura for the excellent photos and help on the ground. To Marie, Miguel, Alberto, Midori and Naoya, *muchas gracias* for *shabu-shabu* and midnight strolls.

THE PHOTOGRAPHERS

Growing up in Melbourne, Anthony Plummer unearthed a nest of travel bugs. He has since dedicated years to soothing those itches, but neither bitter Kyrgyz kumiss nor smooth Belizean Beliken beer could cure his hankering for a peripatetic life. Perhaps even stronger than the call of the road is Anthony's fondness for photography. His work has appeared in various magazines and publications including Lonely Planet.

Mariko Matsumura also contributed photos for the local interviews.

Our Readers Many thanks to the travellers who wrote to us with helpful hints, useful advice and interesting anecdotes, especially Jean-Louis Fragnay.

Cover Photograph Young Japanese girls in gothic dress posing in Harajuku, Tokyo, Iain Masterton/Photolibrary. **Internal Photographs** p180 Arco Images/Alamy; p17 Bernard O'Kane/Alamy; p33 David Coll/OnAsia; p169 Haruyoshi Yamaguchi/Corbis; p84, p172 Iain Masterton/Alamy; p53, p70, p114 by Mariko Matsumura; p32, p34 Peter Usbeck/Alamy; p30 Photo Japan/Alamy; p157 Richard T. Nowitz/Corbis; p29 Steve Vidler/Imagestate Ltd/Photolibrary; p109 Tom Wagner/TWPhoto/Corbis; p31 Toru Yokota/OnAsia. All other photographs by Lonely Planet Images, and by Anthony Plummer except pp10-1 Antony Giblin; p6 (bottom), p12, p13, p24, p25, p27, p36 (top right), p38, p59, p65, p69, p72, p77, p78, p90, p173, p175, p181 Greg Elms; p164, p168 John Ashburne; p165 Michael Taylor.

A local busker strikes a chord with the crowd in Inokashira Park, Kichijōji (p92)

CONTENTS

THIS IS TOKYO

Life in Tokyo moves at a well-oiled clip, with an energy that borders on mania and an obsession with newness that seems to make all ideas quickly obsolete. Fashions begin to fade almost as soon as they are plucked from clothes hangers, and *keitai* (mobile phones) are traded up for each latest technological advancement. But even while throngs of tech-savvy, smartly styled Tokyoites trot through subway stations, there is a traditional side to this hyperurban cosmopolis, which may not be immediately evident.

Beneath the conspicuous consumption of its shopping districts and shiny façades of the latest architectural achievement, Tokyo throws out unexpected glimpses of its cultural core. At a Shintō shrine across town, a young man purchases a fortune and, after reading it, ties it to a strung frame whose many paper fortunes rustle like leaves in a breeze. In a neighbourhood *sentō* (public bath) in Asakusa, an old woman bathes with her tiny granddaughter, much as she once did with her own grandmother.

Tokyo's unique vitality springs from this intertwining of the new with the time-honoured old. While it's the wellspring of Japanese pop culture, it is also a place where the patrilineage of its imperial family is a tightly held institution. It's the city to which Japanese nonconformists flee but where individuality is often linked to an older form of small-group identity. It's a metropolis where the pressure cooker of traditional societal mores and expectations explodes into cutting-edge art, music and inventions like the 'boyfriend's arm pillow'. Even pop culture like manga, as it takes the world by storm, is rooted in the tradition of Edo-period ukiyo-e (woodblock prints from the 'floating world'). And so, as its modern gears keep turning, the basic machinery of this intriguing city remains true to its origins.

Top left A traditional wedding at Meiji-jingū-gyoen (p103) **Top right** Tokyo's fashionable youth culture lets its hair down **Bottom** School kids tie their fortunes at Sensō-ji Temple (p77)

>HIGHLIGHTS

Through the spidery legs of *Maman* looms the Roppongi Hills tower (p143)

>1 THE BIG BOYS

ENJOY THE RITUALISTIC DISPLAY OF ATHLETIC PROWESS THAT IS SUMŌ

Highly ritualistic and more athletic than initial appearances may imply, sumō is a stunning, charged spectacle that you cannot miss if you're in Tokyo at tournament time. Linked with the rituals of Shintōism, sumō probably originated about 2000 years ago, but only became a popular sporting event in its own right in the 17th century. Sumō's whole visual vocabulary is infused with Shintōist motifs and ideas, from the scattering of salt to the structure and embellishments of the sumō *dōyō* (wrestling ring).

The rules are simple: the *rikishi* (wrestler) who causes any part of his opponent's body other than his feet to touch the ground inside the *dōyō*, or pushes him outside the *dōyō*, wins. Although *rikishi* may look like infants on steroids, those prodigious amounts of flesh conceal some very powerful muscle.

The action during the Tokyo tournaments, or *bashō*, takes place at the green-roofed Ryōgoku Kokugikan (p64) in January, May and

September. Although the best ringside seats are bought up by those with the right connections, box seats accommodating up to four people are a great way to watch sumō in style. Attendees in box seats can order food and tea from servers dressed smartly in *happi* (half-coats) and straw sandals.

RITUALS OF THE RING

It begins with the victor of the last match offering a wooden ladle of water to the incoming *rikishi* (wrestler), in order to perform a symbolic cleansing. Before entering the *dōyō*, each *rikishi* takes a handful of coarse salt to scatter before him to purify the ring. Then squatting, facing each other from opposite ends of the *dōyō*, they stretch theirs arms out to their sides, palms raised, to signify their intentions for a fair fight. Several minutes of false starts – in which they both slap their thighs and bellies in an intimidating manner – usually precede the final stare down as the *rikishi* settle into squats. Only when both *rikishi* have put both fists to the ground does the match officially begin, at which point the opponents will suddenly charge.

>2 HARAJUKU GIRLS

PLAY PAPARAZZO TO THE SUNDAY SUBCULTURE CELEBRITIES AT JINGŪ-BASHI

You don't have to show up on weekends, but then you'll miss out on Harajuku's most famed populace: the flamboyant and outrageously-clad *cosplay-zoku* (costume-play gang). It's an organic rather than organised group, a constantly evolving conglomeration of mostly teenage girls, often those who are bullied in school. By inhabiting alter egos, they find freedom and acceptance in subcultures whose 'official' garb is wildly creative.

Some of the *cosplay-zoku* are fans of *visual-kei* (visual-type) bands, or of *anime* characters, which is reflected in their choice of costume; many others simply dress as a subculture's aesthetic dictates, like the vampy, black-on-black Goth-loli (Gothic Lolita). The resulting kaleido-scope of costumes ranges from *anime* superhero garb, bloody-eyed nurse outfits, blonde ringlets and Victorian bustles or over-the-top platform heels paired with postmodern kimonos. Although their get-ups run the gamut, they're united in a sense of pride in their alienation.

Weekends draw the *cosplay-zoku* from the suburbs of Tokyo to Jingū-bashi, the bridge linking Meiji-jingū (p103) with Omote-sandō (p102), – which, in turn, draw hordes of tourist-paparazzi excitedly snapping away as the girls pose, sulk and preen resplendent in all their crazy finery.

>3 TSUKIJI MARKET

**DODGE FLYING FISH AT TOKYO'S WORLD FAMOUS
SEAFOOD MARKET**

Come for the tuna auctions, stay for the sushi breakfast. After it's
been fished from the sea and before it turns up on a sashimi platter,
most of Tokyo's seafood transits through Tsukiji Market (p51). This
gigantic pulsating hub of Tokyo's gastronomic system pumps at a
frenetic, fish-fuelled pace. Workers yell, slice blocks of ice, haul massive bluefin tuna, spit, stop for a smoke, laugh, bone an eel and yell
some more. Watching the rough-and-ready, hardworking market
men and women of Tsukiji, you can imagine the massive creative,
communal energy that allowed Tokyo to rise, in less than 200 years,
from riverside swamp to one of the world's greatest cities.

You'll have to trundle out here early to see the predawn arrival of
fish and its wholesale auctioning, but even around 7am there's still
some good market bustle and seafood slinging going on. Slicks of
wet muck cover the floor, so don't wear your party shoes, and watch
out for the electric carts zipping around the narrow aisles.

After poking around the market, move out to the nearby alleys
of the external market, where hundreds of little stalls sell pottery,
cooking equipment, cutlery and packaged foods for a fraction of the
prices charged at department stores. Then top it all off with melt-in-
your-mouth fresh sushi as another morning winds down in Tsukiji.

>4 GOLDEN GAI

DRINK AT DUSK IN THE NARROW ALLEYS OF THE GOLDEN GAI

Tenaciously hanging on in the shadow of the skyscrapers surrounding it, the narrow alleys of the Golden Gai are a stubborn anomaly in a city relentlessly obsessed with making the old new. Filled with tiny, eccentric drinking establishments, some so small that they can only fit a few patrons at a time, these alleys come to life as dusk settles and the lights of the city begin to glow. Wandering into this little maze at this witching hour feels like walking into a time warp.

But as the keepers of older bars retire, many spots are being turned over by a new generation who are remaking them with their own creative style while honouring the spirit of these small watering holes. While it's true that some bars in the Golden Gai do not welcome foreigners, or even nonregulars, those that do are an intriguing and unique venue for a drink.

See also p97.

>5 KICHIJŌJI

ESCAPE THE URBAN JUNGLE AND TAKE REFUGE IN THIS HIP SUBURBAN HAVEN

Tokyo's enormity and nonstop energy can make you want to run for the hills. Luckily, even this megalopolis has some surprisingly quiet quarters within easy fleeing distance. One such suburban oasis is Kichijōji, about 10km west of Shinjuku and centred on Inokashira Park (p92), which itself surrounds a large pond.

The road leading from station to park is packed with hip little cafés, bohemian boutiques and cool, cosy bars, making it a wonderful getaway for a just few hours or an entire day and evening. Buy an ice cream and wander down to the shady park. On weekends there's usually an arts-and-crafts market where artists will paint your portrait, as you listen to a local band playing at the water's edge. If you have a ticket to the Ghibli Museum (p91), you could arrive at the park early and meander through on your way to the museum; allow at least 20 minutes for the walk.

>6 ROPPONGI HILLS

ROAM ROPPONGI HILLS AND GET LOST IN THIS ULTRAMODERN MINI-CITY

Although it's a metropolis that's larger than life with a population to match, Tokyo sprang from villages within towns that now make up the greater city of Tokyo. But ultramodern Roppongi Hills is something else entirely, an artificial microcosm of the city, containing metropolitan elements from luxury housing to the impressively curated 52nd-floor Mori Museum of Contemporary Art (pictured above). The angular architecture and sinuous curves of this constructed landscape are accented with Japanese gardens and eye-catching public art.

It took developer Mori Minoru 17 years to buy up the real estate he envisioned developing into an urban mini-city where the centralisation of home, work and leisure could improve its dwellers' quality of life. Whether the vision triumphs or not seems immaterial, as it's been a smashing success as a destination. Monumental Roppongi Hills attracts millions of visitors a month, with its weekend all-night movie screenings, multilevel shopping nirvana, international restaurants from low budget to high calibre, and the fundamental wonder of its immense, glittering scale. Come take a whirl.

See also p143.

>7 EDO-TOKYO MUSEUM

EXPLORE THE CAPTIVATING EXHIBITS DETAILING EDO-ERA LIFE AT THE EDO-TOKYO MUSEUM

The oddly modern, tradition-inspired exterior of the Edo-Tokyo Museum (p65) both belies and reflects what's inside – exhibits illustrating Tokyo's rise from the humble riverside origins of Edo (the Eastern capital) to today's futuristic megalopolis. The museum's layout is imaginatively designed, with a full-size replica of the bridge at Nihombashi dividing the vast display into recreations of Edo-period and Meiji-period Tokyo.

Large, life-size reconstructions of typical wooden homes and workshops depict scenes from everyday living; these are outdone only by the intricately assembled scale models of the riverside near Nihombashi, the market and the residence compound of a *daimyō* (feudal lord). Examples of the wooden wells and water pipes that made up Edo's first waterworks system bring to life the more quotidian underpinnings of Edo infrastructure, while displays of the gorgeously made kimonos worn by style-setting courtesans capture the more glamorous aspects of its culture. Don't miss the miniature animated model of a kabuki theatre, showing how special effects were cleverly created.

Meiji-period displays trace the influence of international culture on Tokyo, with photographs, models and multimedia presentations, and there's a detailed exhibit on the Great Kantō Earthquake of 1923.

While you're out here, consider poking your head into the Sumō Museum (p64) and taking a self-guided tour of the local sumō *beya* (sumō stable).

>8 GINZA
WINDOW-SHOP WITH THE LADIES WHO LUNCH ALONG THE GINZA BOULEVARDS

Ginza is classic glam, Tokyo's parallel to New York City's Fifth Avenue. With some of the priciest real estate on this planet, the boulevards are lined with serious contenders, such as Chanel, Tiffany, Hermès and the big-in-Japan Louis Vuitton. Ginza is not shy about showing off its status, nor are the ladies who shop here, displaying designer label shopping bags on delicately crooked forearms.

Shopping here is not the exclusive domain of the elite; nestled along with the purveyors of *haute couture* are wonderful stationery shops carrying fountain pens and hand-dyed handkerchiefs, Japan's department store heavies with their heavenly *depachika* (basement food halls) and handicraft shops that carry Japanese goods befitting Tokyo's traditional roots.

Neither is Ginza only about material consumption – sumptuous eye candy fills the many art and photography galleries scattered about, and restaurants here live up to the high expectations of those who haunt the neighbourhood.

Weekends in Ginza are particularly pleasant, when Chūō-dōri and some smaller cross-streets are closed to vehicles, allowing kimono-clad ladies and toddlers alike to meander peacefully in the middle of the crowded boulevard.

See also p52.

>9 ELECTRIC TOWN

GEEK OUT ON THE MANGA AND ELECTRONICS IN AKIHABARA

Don't drink too much caffeine before beginning a foray into sensory-overloaded Akihabara, otherwise known as Denki-gai (Electric Town) or Akiba. It's something akin to the maddest Asian market you've ever been in, but instead of selling mangosteens they're hawking manga and motherboards – and the sellers are not only pushy, they're prerecorded.

Once Tokyo's dominant centre for discount cameras, then videos, then computers, Akihabara's role as discount central is declining due to increased competition from huge stores in denser hubs like Shinjuku and Ikebukuro. Nowadays, Akihabara has begun to turn to the booming market in games and manga, particularly of the porno-graphic variety. Deals on electronics may be competitive with those of your home country, but it's unusual to find prices matching those of Hong Kong or Singapore. Still, Akihabara has a massive range of electrical appliances and remains the place to find a robotic dog, wireless mouse or the most megapixels for your money.

Browse the bargain bins of games, electronics and manga and let your inner geek run wild.

See also p52.

>10 MEIJI-JINGŪ

TAKE IN THE MAGNIFICENCE OF MEIJI-JINGŪ, TOKYO'S SHRINE FOR ALL SEASONS

No doubt about it – Meiji-jingū (p103) is Tokyo's, if not Japan's, most splendid Shintō shrine. Passing under each majestic *torii* (shrine gate) takes you further into the muffled, green temple grounds to the symbolic domain of the *kami* (gods). Completed in 1920 Meiji-jingū was constructed in honour of Emperor Meiji and Empress Shōken, under whose rule Japan ended its long isolation from the outside world. Unfortunately, like much of Tokyo, it was obliterated by WWII incendiary bombing, but up it sprang again in 1958 next to Yoyogi-kōen (p28). It might be a reconstruction of the original, but it was rebuilt with all the features of a Shintō shrine preserved: the main building with Japanese cypress, and the huge *torii* with cypress from Taiwan.

On many weekends you have a fair chance of catching the striking yet subdued wedding proceedings of couples in full-on, kimono-clad regalia at Meiji-jingū. Spring brings a burst of pink when the cherry blossoms come into season, while June and July mean that the purple irises are in bloom at the adjacent Meiji-jingū-gyoen (p103), the tranquil, shaded park that was formerly an imperial garden. The one time of the year you're guaranteed not to be alone here is at New Year's and the few days thereafter, when throngs (as in millions) of people come to celebrate in Shintō style.

>11 KABUKI-ZA

SEE AND HEAR THE HIGH DRAMA OF KABUKI AT KABUKI-ZA

Men in drag and dramatic make-up, stylised movements and elaborate staging characterise colourful kabuki, the most accessible of Japanese performing arts for non-Japanese. Performances are accompanied by distinctive *shamisen* (three-stringed lute), flute and drum music called *nagauta*.

Kabuki began in the early 17th century and caught on after a troupe of women dancers put on a performance to raise funds for the Izumo Taisha shrine in Shimane prefecture. It was soon being performed with prostitutes playing the lead roles, and as performances plumbed ever-greater depths of lewdness, women were banned from kabuki. Scandalised authorities eventually decreed that all roles be played by older men – today, the tradition of an exclusively male cast remains in effect.

The best place to catch a kabuki performance in Tokyo is at the venerable, atmospheric Kabuki-za (p63) in Ginza. Kabuki performances can be quite a marathon, lasting from four to five hours. You can follow the action using earphone guides (¥650, plus ¥1000 deposit) that provide commentary in English. Check the Kabuki-za website for details on current performances and show times; performances generally start at around 11am and 4pm. Be sure to buy a *bentō* (boxed meal) between acts so you don't run out of steam before the actors do.

If you're not up for the long haul, you can ask for *hitomakumi* (one-act balcony seats; ¥600 to ¥1000) on the day of the performance, but earphone guides are not available.

>12 UENO-KŌEN & TOKYO NATIONAL MUSEUM

TAKE IN TEMPLES AND NATIONAL TREASURES AT UENO-KŌEN AND TOKYO NATIONAL MUSEUM

Expansive Ueno-kōen is one of those parks where Tokyo comes to unwind, date, have illicit encounters, busk and hone hip-hop moves. But aside from the usual attractions for relaxation, Ueno-kōen is also the place where you can coo over the pandas at Ueno Zoo, take a paddleboat for two to view the giant lotuses covering Shinobazu Pond, look in on the latest Dalí or Matisse exhibition at the National Museum of Western Art (p68) or roam around its many temples and shrines. And then there is the National Science Museum (p68), the Tokyo Metropolitan Museum of Art (p69) and the magnificent Tokyo National Museum (p69). The park packs a cultural punch.

Ueno Hill was the site of a last-ditch defence of the Tokugawa Shōgunate by about 2000 Tokugawa loyalists in 1868. They were duly dispatched by the imperial army and the new Meiji government decreed that Ueno Hill would become one of Tokyo's first parks. It's now home to these major museums and is a big destination for *hanami* (cherry-blossom viewing) in the spring.

At the park's northern end is the Tokyo National Museum, established in 1872. Comprised of five buildings, this is unquestionably

BASE CAMP

Tokyo's homeless population is estimated at more than 30,000, although government figures peg it significantly lower. Although homeless encampments exist along Tokyo riverbanks, under bridges and in isolated corners of the city's larger parks, for visitors the city's most visible homeless settlement is in Ueno-kōen. The disenfranchised population of this blue-tarp-and-cardboard tent city keeps its presence discreet during the daytime, when the park is full of visitors.

Most of these people are middle-aged and aging men who hit the skids during Japan's long economic slump. Despite their marginalised circumstances, they fastidiously hang their laundry on plastic clotheslines and line up their shoes outside their makeshift shelters, and continue to *gaman* (endure).

the museum of choice if a gallery stroll figures into your Ueno-kōen plans. The Honkan (Main Gallery) is the most important, with an awe-inspiring collection of art from the Jōmon period to the Edo. To the right of the ticket booth is the Tōyōkan (Gallery of Eastern Antiquities), housing art and archaeological finds from all of Asia, with an emphasis on China. To the left of the ticket booth is the cupola-capped Hyōkeikan (Hyōkei Gallery), used for special exhibitions, while the Heiseikan (Heisei Gallery) at the back of the complex features Japanese archaeological artefacts. Most impressive of all is the Hōryū-ji Hōmotsukan (Gallery of Hōryū-ji Treasures), featuring 300 Buddhist antiquities once belonging to Hōryū Temple in Nara. As some of these exhibits are more than a thousand years old, this wing remains closed during humid or wet weather.

The park exit from the Ueno JR station will put you directly across from the museum area, but if you take the Shinobazu exit instead, you can take in a few temples on your way to the museums.

>13 SHIBUYA

EXPLORE WHAT MAKES YOUTH CULTURE TICK IN SHIBUYA

Schlep in any direction across Shibuya's six-way intersection for a rush of youth culture – this is *the* spot for people-watching and prime shopping. Hip *gyaru* ('gals' identifiable by their big hair, fake tans and exaggerated white eyeshadow) and their male counterparts travel in packs around Center-gai and the department stores that cater to their fast-forward fashion trends.

Leave the JR station via the Hachikō exit and you'll get an eyeful of moving images flashing across the buildings looming over Shibuya Crossing, notably the several-storeys-high screen of the Q-Front Building. Don't forget to say hello to the Hachikō statue (p120) before joining the timed tide across Shibuya Crossing.

From Hachikō exit head to the right of Shibuya 109 (p123), the streets between Bunkamura-dōri and Jingū-dōri are full of excellent youth-oriented department stores for the knee-high pink boots or vinyl micromini you covet. If you seek vinyl of a different groove, you'll hit a cluster of record shops in Udagawachō, specialising in everything from Motown to Japanese hip-hop. Also, Shibuya stays up late, and the streets between Bunkamura-dōri and Dōgenzaka are covered with clubs, bars and love hotels, so soak it up as long as you please.

>14 SUMIDA-GAWA

TAKE A LEISURELY RIDE DOWN THE SUMIDA RIVER

Travelling by *suijo-bus* (water bus; see p196) down the Sumida River not only gets you a face full of fresh air, but brings you closer to Tokyo's riverborne heritage, showing off a more home-grown perspective of the city than a subway spin will. When you're hemmed in by concrete and glass, it's easy to forget that Tokyo's vibrant river systems are the arteries through which its commerce has traditionally flowed, from the Edo period to the present day.

Down at water level, you see the huge timber- and landfill-hauling barges, the occasional lone fisherman and the *yakata-bune* – floating restaurants where, traditionally, customers seated on tatami (woven-floor matting) eat *ayu* (sweet fish) washed down with sake. Redevelopment schemes are slowly changing the face of the riverfront, but as you pass beneath the dozen colourful bridges on your journey, you'll continue to spy the hanging laundry drying on the apartment blocks of regular Tokyo folk, as well as some prime riverfront encampments of Tokyo's more down-at-heel inhabitants.

The best way to work in a river cruise is to travel between Asakusa (p74) and Hama-rikyū-teien (p48), the lovely waterfront garden near Ginza. Consider taking in a walking tour of Asakusa sights, then catching the *suijo-bus* for a stroll through Hama-rikyū-teien. Alternatively, you could cruise across Tokyo Bay to travel from old-fashioned Asakusa out to the modern amusements of the manmade island of Odaiba (p154).

>15 SENSŌ-JI

EXPERIENCE THE MODERN LIFE OF AN ANCIENT TEMPLE

The grand old temple Sensō-ji (p77) may attract millions of tourists annually, but it is still very much a living, working temple for the people of working-class Asakusa.

Indeed, Sensō-ji's very origins are intertwined with the history of the local people. Legend has it that a golden image of Kannon, the Goddess of Compassion, was fished out of the nearby Sumida-gawa by two fishermen in AD 628. In time, a temple was built to house the image, which has remained on the same spot ever since, giving it its alternative name, Asakusa Kannon-dō. Whether the ancient image of Kannon actually exists inside is a secret. Not that this stops a steady stream of worshippers making their way up the stairs to the temple, where they cast coins, clap ceremoniously and bow in a gesture of respect.

When approaching Sensō-ji from the Asakusa subway stations, enter through Kaminarimon (Thunder Gate) between the scowling protective deities: Fūjin, the god of wind, on the right; and Raijin, the god of thunder, on the left. Near Kaminari-mon, you'll probably be wooed by jinrikisha (people-powered rickshaw) drivers in traditional dress with gorgeous lacquer rickshaws; these energetic, fit guides

THE MERRY *MATSURI*

You might inadvertently stumble onto a *matsuri* (festival) around Tokyo, hearing first the rhythmic chanting, *taiko* (drums) and *yokobue* (flutes) nearby, or coming across a crowd dressed in *happi* (half-coats) carrying a *mikoshi* (portable shrine) on their shoulders. If you follow the *mikoshi*, you'll eventually end up at a temple where you'll find people of all ages dressed in colourful *yukata* (cotton kimonos); stalls selling plastic toys and masks; shallow trays of goldfish to catch with a net; and, best of all, tasty *matsuri* morsels such as *takoyaki* (fried balls of octopus on a stick) and *okonomiyaki* (stuffed Japanese pancakes).

The *matsuri* is an integral part of Japanese culture, dating back to the early days of communal rice cultivation, when townships would gather to pacify the gods. Call the Tokyo Tourist Information Center (TIC; p202) for *matsuri* information.

will cart you around the temple and neighbourhood, giving you the scoop on architecture and history in English or Japanese.

Straight on through the gate is Nakamise-dōri, a busy pedestrian shopping street set within the actual temple precinct. Everything from tourist trinkets to genuine Edo-style crafts are sold here; there's even a shop selling the elaborate wigs that are worn with kimonos.

Nakamise-dōri leads to the main temple compound. In front of the temple is a large incense cauldron, whose smoke is said to bestow health. If any part of your body – modesty permitting, naturally – is giving you trouble, do as the locals do and fan some smoke your way, rubbing it through your clothes into the area that ails you.

>16 YOYOGI-KŌEN

WANDER INTO YOYOGI-KŌEN ON WEEKENDS FOR A MIXED BAG OF FREE ENTERTAINMENT

Amazing but true: those Japanese rockabilly cats with their greaser pompadours or nouveau poodle skirts still cut a rug on Sundays at Yoyogi-kōen (p107), the 54-hectare city park. Bring a *bentō* and have yourself a picnic – take your pick of background music, whether it's *shamisen* (three-stringed lute) practice or a punk rock set. You never know what you'll get for entertainment – it might be anything from fire-eaters to pavement theatre, J-hop dance troupes to drum circles.

Officially the authorities put the kibosh on live music and dancers, but on most fair-weather Sundays you'll find a healthy sampling of both. The park isn't in itself all that remarkable, although walking the lovely tree-lined paths is pleasantly punctuated by little tykes zipping by on rented bikes. Cherry blossoms do bloom here in the spring, but autumn is the time to come, when the gingko leaves go golden.

An afternoon at Yoyogi park could easily round out a Sunday visiting Meiji-jingū (p20), snapping pics of *cosplay* kids at Jingū-bashi (p12) and browsing teenybopper fashion down Takeshita-dōri (p108).

>TOKYO DIARY

As one of the brighter stars of Asia's constellation of cities, Tokyo plays host to many international festivals and events. Festivities across the city can be as humble as the neighbourhood *matsuri* (p26) to huge anime trade fairs, gay-and-lesbian film festivals and singularly Japanese holidays when it seems the entire population of Tokyo is converging all at once on its most famous shrines. The larger holidays celebrate auspicious ages and the turning of seasons, reconnecting Tokyoites to their roots and allowing visitors a chance to mingle with locals at their most traditional.

Smiling faces and bright kimonos celebrate Shichi-go-san (7-5-3), a festival for these milestone ages (p34)

JANUARY

Shōgatsu

From 1–3 January people turn out in droves to shrines and temples such as Sensō-ji (p77) and Meiji-jingū (p103) to celebrate the New Year.

Seijin-no-Hi (Coming-of-Age Day)

Also at Meiji-jingū (p103), traditional archery displays are held on 15 January to mark the move into adulthood.

FEBRUARY

Setsubun

At home and at temples such as Sensō-ji (p77), beans are thrown outside as people shout, 'Oni wa soto! Fuku wa uchi!' ('Devils out! Fortune in!'), to mark the first day of spring on 3 or 4 February.

MARCH

Hina Matsuri (Girls' Day)

On 3 March a doll festival is held near Azumabashi and *hina* (princess) dolls are displayed in homes and public spaces.

Tokyo International Anime Fair

www.tokyoanime.jp/en

Held in late March or early April, this huge trade fair is held at Tokyo Big Sight (p157) for *anime* fans and industry pros alike.

Hina (princess) dolls are displayed for the 'princess' in every family on the annual Girls' Day

Get as close as you dare to the tattooed flesh and tense stares of a *yakuza* gang during Sanja Matsuri

APRIL

Hanami

In late March and early April, *hanami* (cherry-blossom) viewing parties (p91) take place day and night in parks across the city.

Art Fair Tokyo

www.artfairtokyo.com

Held at the appropriately innovative Tokyo International Forum (p51), this young fair showcases cutting-edge art from Japan, Asia and beyond. Artists and collectors meet here in mid-April.

MAY

Otoko-no-Hi (Boys' Day)

Family homes honour their sons by flying *koinobori* (banners in the shape of a carp) on 5 May.

Sanja Matsuri

Hundreds of *mikoshi* (portable shrines) are carried through the thronged streets around Sensō-ji (p77) over three days in mid-May.

Design Festa

www.designfesta.com

In mid-May a wide showcase of work from budding designers and artists is displayed at Design Festa, held at Tokyo Big Sight (p157).

Two men pout, preen and pose for the Tokyo Pride Parade

JUNE

Iris Viewing

The inner garden at Meiji-jingū (p103) is
a favoured spot for viewing irises – most
vibrant in June, when these flowers are in
full bloom.

JULY

Fuji Rock Festival

http://fujirockfestival.com

This outdoor concert in late July draws
international acts and thousands of fans to
its beautiful woodland surroundings.

Tokyo International Lesbian & Gay Film Festival

www.tokyo-lgff.org

Check the website to see where screenings
are held for this queer film festival, growing
steadily into its second decade. Held in
mid-July.

Sumida River Fireworks

On the last Saturday of July, *hanabi* (fireworks) over the Sumida River are the year's
most popular.

AUGUST

Asakusa Samba Festival
The highlight of this festival is the parade down Kaminarimon-dōri, drawing half a million spectators and samba troupes from Tokyo to Rio. On the last Saturday of August.

Tokyo Pride Parade
http://parade.tokyo-pride.org
It's on again, off again, but come mid-August, the parade may be taking to the streets in Harajuku (p102). Check the website.

SEPTEMBER

Ningyō-kujō
Dolls are offered to Kannon (the Buddhist goddess of mercy) at Kiyomizu Kannon-dō (p68) by childless couples who wish to conceive. The dolls are ceremonially burned there on 25 September.

OCTOBER

Tokyo International Film Festival
www.tiff-jp.net
This festival lasts about 10 days and begins in late October. Although featured films focus on Asia, most are subtitled in English.

Kōyō
Autumn foliage-viewing season (p175) begins in mid-October or early November. As this colourful season is longer, the crowds are more low-key than for *hanami* (p31).

Crowding for a glimpse of their idols at the opening ceremony of the Tokyo International Film Festival

TOKYO DIARY

A sea of fluttering white-and-red flags greet the Emperor of Japan on his birthday

NOVEMBER

Shichi-Go-San (Seven-Five-Three Festival)

On 15 November this festival celebrates these milestone ages, and parents in turn bring their traditionally clad little ones to temples and shrines to mark the occasion on the nearest weekend.

Design Festa

www.designfesta.com

Returning to Tokyo Big Sight (p157) for its second annual stint (see p31).

DECEMBER

Emperor's Birthday

On 23 December, this is one of only two days per year that the *Kōkyo* (Imperial Palace; Map pp46–7) is opened to the public; the other is 2 January.

>ITINERARIES

Admire the glass walls and open spaces of Tokyo International Forum (p51)

ITINERARIES

Don't be daunted by Tokyo's enormity. Taken in small bites you can get your fill of a thousand of the city's unique flavours. Pick a few must-do experiences and appealing neighbourhoods to explore. If your time is limited, use these itineraries as suggestions and customise according to your own tastes.

ONE DAY

Start before dawn at Tsukiji Market (p13) to check out the catch of the day. Breakfast on the freshest tuna at Daiwa Sushi (p59), and then walk up to Ginza (p45) for window-shopping and gallery-hopping. Go underground to one of the *depachika* (department-store food basements; p57) to marvel at the gourmet goods, then play with high-tech gadgets at the Sony Building (p50). Stop for lunch at the Tokyo International Forum (p51). Stroll through the Imperial Palace East Garden (p48) and exit from the garden's northeast to wander through Kitanomaru-kōen. Continue west on to Yasukuni-jinja (p51). Catch a train from Ichigaya Station to Shinjuku (p88) for an extravagant dinner at New York Grill (p96).

SUNDAYS

Pick up a *bentō* (boxed meal) and hop the JR Yamanote line to Harajuku (p102) when the *cosplay-zoku* (costume-play gang; p12) come out in force. After you've taken your 100 photos, head across Jingū-bashi to magnificent Meiji-jingū (p103). Exit the temple grounds and head west until you reach the entrance to Yoyogi-kōen (p107). Have a picnic lunch in the park. Afterwards, head back out and backtrack to Omote-sandō (p108) to while away an afternoon shopping on the boulevard and in the alleys. Treat yourself to a fusion dinner at stylish Fujimamas (p112), and end with a cocktail with the locals at Tokyo Apartment Café (p116).

THREE DAYS

Follow the one-day itinerary and then, if your visit doesn't fall on a Sunday, spend your second day on the Sunday sights but skip Yoyogi-kōen. On your third day start at Hama-rikyū-teien (p48) before catching

Top left Take to the streets on a rickshaw (p74) ride in Asakusa **Top right** Ornate doorways at Meiji-jingū Shrine (p103) **Bottom** Soak up serenity with a foot bath at Ōedo Onsen Monogatari (p159)

a Sumida River cruise to Asakusa (p76). Visit Sensō-ji (p77), take a *jinrikisha* (rickshaw) tour (p74) and bang on a few drums at Taikokan (p77). Then walk westward to Kappabashi-dōri (p78) to check out plastic food and kitchenware before catching the metro from Tawaramachi to Ueno (p66). Walk through the south end of Ueno-kōen (p68) taking in the temples and parklife. Wind up at the Tokyo National Museum (p69). In the evening, take the Yamanote line to Ebisu (p130) for dinner and a drink.

A FIVE-DAY WEEK

After three days you should gear up for a Friday or Saturday night all-nighter in Roppongi (p138). Then take it easy and immerse yourself in crowd culture with a roll around Shinjuku (p90). Shop for records, trinkets and manga in Shibuya (p121). Make sure to get to a *sentō* (public bath) or *onsen* (hot spring; p176), and then take the monorail out to Odaiba (p154) for a look at Tokyo over the bay. Take the time to check out one of Tokyo's outlying neighbourhoods, such as Kichijōji (p92) and Ryogoku (p65). Save Friday or Saturday night to do an all-nighter.

Roppongi's bright lights keep the night at bay in the district that doesn't sleep

FORWARD PLANNING
Two to three months before you go Book an appointment for the Ghibli Museum (p91); reserve a table at L'Osier (p60) to sweep your date off their feet with a fancy French supper, or at Kisso (p147) for a memorable *kaiseki* (elegant, multicourse meal) experience.
One month before you go Find out what holidays (p29) will be in swing during your visit, like *hanami* (cherry-blossom viewing) in spring, Asakusa's Sanja Matsuri in May and *hanabi* (fireworks) over the Sumida River in July.
One week before you go Check *Metropolis* online (p199) for current goings-on and concert listings.
One day before you go Reconfirm your flight and review the names of your favourite sushi.

RAINY DAY

It's wet, but this doesn't have to dampen your mood as there's lots to do indoors. Hole up in one of Tokyo's mega-malls for the day. At Roppongi Hills (p143) take in a movie in the plush Virgin Toho Cinemas (p153). Have lunch and window-shop in the shopping complex before seeing the latest exhibition at Mori Art Museum (p139). End with a cocktail at Maduro (p150).

Otherwise, pretend you're in Hong Kong at Daiba Little Hong Kong (p158) and then trick your senses on the virtual-reality rides at Sega's Tokyo Joypolis (p159). Let your day end in Edo times at Ōedo Onsen Monogatari (p159) with a soul-reviving soak.

FOR FREE

The budget can quickly be exceeded on unplanned expenditures like that must-have, one-off shirt you found in Ura-Hara (p108). But with the exception of Shinjuku-gyōen (p91), Tokyo's large parks are free – take your bentō to Ueno-kōen (p68) or the Imperial Palace East Gardens (p48) and have a picnic. Showrooms like the Sony Building (p50) and Toyota Amlux (p84) offer up their wares for playing and testing. Roaming Tsukiji Market (p13) is a pleasure you won't pay for, as are the temples and shrines (p177) of Tokyo.

>NEIGHBOURHOODS

View from Tokyo Tower, Central Tokyo

NEIGHBOURHOODS

Less a chaotic urban jungle than a massive, neatly manicured garden, Tokyo is more navigable than first glances at the skyscrapers and subway maps may have you believe. Think of its various districts as smaller villages within the bigger metropolis, for this is how Tokyo evolved and how its neighbourhoods are organised.

Most of Tokyo's action takes place around the loop of the JR Yamanote line, which encircles the central area of this sprawling city. As defined here, Central Tokyo encompasses several districts surrounding Tokyo station, a transport hub near the Imperial Palace and the upscale commercial district of Ginza. North of Central Tokyo is Ueno, where Tokyo's largest park contains several museums and temples. Off the Yamanote orbit, to the east of Ueno, lies Asakusa, the heart of old Shitamachi (Edo's low town) with its famous temple. Out west, Ikebukuro has its intriguing corners, while further south the neon glows and skyscrapers of Shinjuku stand tall. Next stop, Harajuku, where role-play is a living art, just up the boulevard from elegant Aoyama, where high fashion reigns. But youth culture rules another stop south at Shibuya, a neighbourhood that serves up disposable style-of-the-moment. To the south, a refined but relaxed vibe prevails in stylish Ebisu and Daikanyama. Moving west, just inside the Yamanote loop, Roppongi has long been the place to party but has also gained a measure of respectability with the addition of its city-within-a-city, Roppongi Hills. Its neighbour, Akasaka, stands slightly aloof to this decadence, as the serious business of the national government is based here. Meanwhile, the loop swoops north again to Ginza via Shimbashi. It's forgivable to forget that Tokyo is a seaside city, but a visit to Odaiba, an artificial island in Tokyo Bay, makes an excellent reminder.

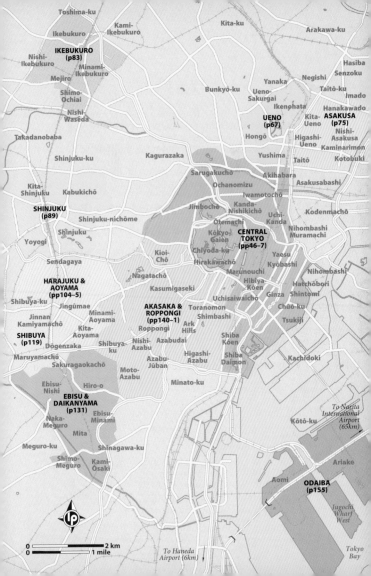

>CENTRAL TOKYO

Central Tokyo is rooted to the location of the Imperial Palace, where the imperial family resides today and the outer garden on which visitors can stroll. Just across the moat is the business district of Marunouchi, where salarymen busily power the banks, communications and big businesses lining these streets. To the east of Marunouchi is the hub that is Tokyo Station, and still eastward is Nihombashi and its commerce. South of Tokyo Station lies the upscale shopping district of Ginza, whose Western architecture was once the pinnacle of modernity and now provides a stately backdrop to conspicuous consumption. Further southeast of Ginza you'll find the seafood-trading bustle of Tsukiji Market, and the revitalised commercial district of Shiodome, with its luxury hotel-and-dining complexes. The core of Central Tokyo is fringed with sights worth the walk or extra subway stop, such as the Yasukuni-jinja war memorial and Tokyo Dome for sports-mad fans, as well as speciality neighbourhoods such as Jimbōchō with its bookshops, and Akihabara for manga and electronics.

CENTRAL TOKYO

Please see over for map

SEE

CRIMINOLOGY MUSEUM OF MEIJI UNIVERSITY
明治大学博物館刑事

☎ 3296 4431; 3F, Daigaku Kaikan, 1-1 Kanda Surugadai, Chiyoda-ku; admission free; ⏰ 10am-4.30pm Mon-Fri, 10am-12.30pm Sat; 🚇 Chūō & Sōbu lines to Ochanomizu (Ochanomizu exit), 🚇 Marunouchi line to Ochanomizu (exit B1); ♿

Covering centuries of crime and punishment in Japan, this museum will fascinate both the criminally minded and the morbidly curious. While there isn't much English signage, the wood-block prints and torture devices are self-explanatory. From the stations, walk downhill on Meidai-dōri. The Daigaku Kaikan building will be on your right, on the corner just before the huge Meiji University building.

GINZA GRAPHIC GALLERY
ギンザグラフィックギャラリー

☎ 3571 5206; www.dnp.co.jp/gallery /ggg/index_e.html; 1F, DNP Ginza Bldg, 7-7-2 Ginza, Chūō-ku; admission free; ⏰ 11am-7pm Mon-Fri, 11am-6pm Sat; 🚇 Ginza, Hibiya & Marunouchi lines to Ginza (exits A1 & A2); ♿

WORTH THE TRIP

Nestled just above Central Tokyo but seemingly from another decade, **Kagurazaka** (🚉 Chūō line to Iidabashi (east exit), 🚇 Namboku, Tōzai, Yūrakuchō & Toei Ōedo lines to Iidabashi (exit B3)) is a formerly vibrant geisha quarter, whose local residents are attempting to preserve its old-fashioned integrity. Before WWII the alleys here – many of them still cobbled – saw steady foot traffic to the many traditional, exclusive restaurants called *ryotei*. Nowadays, the slope is looking almost as modern as other low-scale Tokyo neighbourhoods, with the addition of convenience stores and a few high-rise apartment buildings. But these narrow, winding alleys still hide small temples and shrines, tiny old-fashioned bars, atmospheric restaurants and its inherent, abundant charm.

Kagurazaka-dōri leads uphill from Iidabashi Station, leaving behind the canal that was formerly the outermost moat of the Imperial Palace grounds. Walking uphill, the street is lined with shops selling *geta* (wooden sandals worn with kimono), kitchen wares and old-fashioned *wagashi* (sweets). On your left is a red temple called **Bishamonten** (its formal name is Zenkoku-ji). Once you arrive at the temple, duck into the alleys on the other side of Kagurazaka-dōri to roam the winding back streets. If you continue up Kagurazaka-dōri past the main intersection, you'll eventually hit Kagurazaka station on the Tōzai subway line, which can take you back to Central Tokyo. Alternatively, you could head back down the slope and enjoy a drink along the green canal at the **Canal Café** (☎ 3260 8068; 1-9 Kagurazaka, Shinjuku-ku; ⏰ 11am-10.30pm Tue-Sun; 🚇 Namboku, Tōzai, Yūrakuchō & Toei Ōedo lines to Iidabashi, exit B3) before leaving from Iidabashi Station.

Excellent exhibitions with an emphasis on graphic design are this gallery's forte. The gallery also hosts workshops and talks by visiting artists, covering everything from tiny typography to monumental architecture.

☺ HAMA-RIKYŪ-TEIEN 浜離宮庭園

☎ 3541 0200; admission ¥300/150; ☽ 9am-5pm; ☺ Toei Ōedo line to Tsukiji-shijō (exit A2); ♿

The shōguns used to have this magnificent place to themselves when it was Hama Rikyū, 'the beach palace'. Now mere mortals can enjoy this wonderful garden, one of Tokyo's best. Sometimes known as the Detached Palace Garden, it is impossibly elegant and a must for garden aficionados. Consider approaching it from Asakusa via the Sumida-gawa cruise (p25).

☺ IDEMITSU ART MUSEUM 出光美術館

☎ 3213 9402; 9F, Teigeki Bldg, 3-1-1 Marunouchi, Chiyoda-ku; admission ¥800/500; ☽ 10am-5pm Tue-Thu, Sat & Sun, 10am-7pm Fri; ☺ Chiyoda & Toei Mita lines to Hibiya (exits A1 & B3); ♿

Most famous for its collection of work by the Zen monk Sengai, this superb, eclectic collection of Chinese and Japanese art is brought

to you courtesy of a petroleum zillionaire. There are also lovely views of the Imperial Palace from the museum, which is next to the Imperial Theatre.

☺ IMPERIAL PALACE EAST GARDEN 皇居東御苑

☎ 3213 2050; admission free; ☽ 9am-4.30pm Tue-Thu, Sat & Sun Mar-Oct, closed from 4pm Nov-Feb; ☺ Chiyoda, Hanzōmon, Marunouchi & Tōzai lines to Ōtemachi (exits C10 & C13b); ♿

One of the nearest emergency exits from Ginza street chaos, this garden (known as the Kōkyo Higashi Gyoen) is the only quarter of the palace proper that is open to the public. The Edo-period watchtower, Fujimi-yagura, was designed to provide the aristocracy with a handy view of Mt Fuji. The store inside the garden sells a good map for ¥150.

RUN AWAY

Runners, rejoice – there are parks aplenty in Tokyo for jogs and power walks. Our favourite is the 5km route around the Imperial Palace East Garden (above), but other great places to run include Yoyogi-kōen (p107), Jingū-gaien (p103), and Shinjuku-gyōen (p91).

Of course, for a different kind of runner's high, those top-end hotel treadmills have the most pulse-racing views.

Rippling waters add to the quiet charm of the Imperial Palace East Garden

◎ KITE MUSEUM
凧の博物館

☎ 3271 2465; www.tako.gr.jp/eng
/museums_e/tokyo_e.html; 5F, Taimeikan
Bldg, 1-12-10 Nihombashi, Chūō-ku;
admission ¥200/100; 🕑 11am-5pm
Mon-Sat; ◎ Ginza, Tōzai & Toei Asakusa
lines to Nihombashi (exit C5); 🚼

This unusual little museum feels
like a kitemaker's store cupboard,
with everything crammed in tight
(and not much explanatory material). But the kites are wonderful, especially the vintage ones
depicting folk tales and kabuki
(stylised Japanese theatre). Made
of bamboo and *washi* (handmade
paper), the kites for sale make
beautiful souvenirs.

◎ KOISHIKAWA KŌRAKUEN
小石川後楽園

☎ 3811 3015; 1-6-6 Kōraku,
Bunkyō-ku; admission ¥300/free;
🕑 9am-5pm; ◎ Namboku, Tōzai,
Yūrakuchō & Toei Ōedo lines to
Iidabashi (exits C3 & 6); 🚼

A beautiful amalgam of Japanese
and Chinese landscape design,
this mid-17th-century garden is
left off most tourist itineraries.
That's a shame, because it's one
of Tokyo's best gardens; but then
again, it's also a blessing, since
you'll be far from the maddening
crowds. You can buy an excellent
English map at the garden's
entrance.

WORTH THE TRIP

The poets' favourite, **Rikugien** (☎ 3941 2222; 6-16-3 Hon-Komagome, Bunkyō-ku; admission ¥300; ☽ 9am-5pm Tue-Sun; ☒ JR Yamanote line to Komagome, south exit) is a 10-hectare Edo-style *kaiyū* (many-pleasure) garden, built around a tranquil, carp-filled pond. It's another garden ideal for strolling, with land-scaped views unfolding at every turn of the pathways that crisscross the grounds. The design is said to evoke famous scenes from Chinese literature and Japanese *waka* (31-syllable poetry).

◉ LEICA GINZA SALON
ライカ銀座店

☎ 6215 7070; www.leica-camera.us /culture/galeries/gallery_tokyo; 1F & 2F, Tokaido Bldg, 6-4-1 Ginza, Chūō-ku; admission free; ☽ 11am-7pm Tue-Fri; ⊙ Ginza, Hibiya & Marunouchi lines to Ginza (exit C2)

Exhibiting the outstanding work of up-and-coming photographers and long-time professionals, this clean, minimalist salon remains one of the best photography galleries in the area.

◉ NATIONAL MUSEUM OF MODERN ART
国立近代美術館

☎ 5777 8600; www.momat.go.jp /english/; 3-1 Kitanomaru-kōen, Chūō-ku; admission ¥420/130/70; ☽ 10am-5pm Tue-Thu, Sat & Sun; 10am-8pm Fri; ⊙ Tōzai line to Takebashi (exit 1a); ♿

The National Museum of Modern Art has a magnificent collection of Japanese art from the Meiji period onwards. Your ticket (hold on to the stub) gives you free admission to the nearby Crafts Gallery, which houses ceramics, lacquerware and dolls.

◉ SHISEIDO GALLERY
資生堂ギャラリー

☎ 3572 3901; www.shiseido.co.jp/e /gallery/html; B1F, Tokyo Ginza Shiseido Bldg, 8-8-3 Ginza, Chūō-ku; admission free; ☽ 11am-7pm Tue-Sat, 11am-6pm Sun; ☒ JR Yamanote line to Shimbashi (Ginza exit), ⊙ Ginza line to Shimbashi (exits 1 & 2)

Open since 1919, this gallery is one of the oldest in the neigh-bourhood. Showing an ever-changing selection of art, its exhibitions lean more towards the experimental and are well worth a look.

◉ SONY BUILDING
ソニービル

☎ 3573 2371; www.sonybuilding.jp; 5-3-1 Ginza, Chūō-ku; admission free; ☽ 11am-7pm; ⊙ Ginza, Hibiya, Marunouchi line to Ginza (exit B9)

Although essentially a Sony show-room, this place has fascinating hands-on displays of Sony's latest gizmos and gadgets – some that have yet to be released. There's often a bit of a wait, but kids (and gamer types) will love the free video and virtual-reality games on the 6th floor.

⊙ TOKYO INTERNATIONAL FORUM 東京国際フォーラム
☎ 5221 9000; www.t-i-forum.co.jp /english; 3-5-1 Marunouchi, Chiyoda-ku; admission free; ☽ 8am-11pm; ☒ JR Yamanote line to Yūrakuchō (main exit), ⊙ Yūrakuchō line to Yūrakuchō (exit A4b); ♿
Designed by architect Rafael Viñoly, the Tokyo International Forum looks like a fantastic glass ship plying the urban waters of central Tokyo. Largely used for conventions and meetings, the cantilevered spaces and plaza also house a library, art gallery, cafés and shops.

⊙ TSUKIJI MARKET 築地市場
☎ 3541 2640; www.tsukiji-market.or .jp; 5-2 Tsukiji, Chūō-ku; ☽ closed 2nd & 4th Wed most months, Sun & public holidays; ⊙ Toei Ōedo line to Tsukiji-Shijō (exits 1 & 2)
Tsukiji keeps market hours, so come early for the best action – 3am is when it opens and the fish are hauled in, but even around 8am you can still get a feel for the sheer scale and energy of this phenomenal fish market.

⊙ YASUKUNI-JINJA 靖国神社
☎ 3261 8326; www.yasukuni.or.jp /english; 3-1-1 Kudan-kita, Chiyoda-ku; admission free; ☽ 9.30am-5.30pm Mar-Oct, 9.30am-5pm Nov-Feb; ⊙ Hanzōmon, Tōzai & Toei Shinjuku lines to Kudanshita (exits 1 & 2); ♿
Yasukuni-jinja, the perennial fly-in-the-chardonnay in Japan-Asia

WORTH THE TRIP
The **Museum of Contemporary Art Tokyo** (☎ 5245 4111; www.mot-art-museum.jp; Kiba Park, 4-1-1 Miyoshi, Kōtō-ku; admission ¥500/250-400/free; ☽ 10am-6pm Tue-Sun; ⊙ Hanzōmon & Toei Ōedo lines to Kiyosumi-Shirakawa, exit B2) is a must for architecture buffs as well as art fans. Constructed from wood, stone, metal and glass, it creates an oasis of pure light. The museum houses a permanent collection of significant modern Japanese art, and each work has its own interpretive postcard with photo, title and artist biography written in both Japanese and English.
Back towards the station and the Sumida River, there's also a newish industrial space housing more than a half-dozen **art galleries** (5F-7F, 1-3-2 Kiyosumi, Kōtō-ku; ☽ noon-7pm Tue-Sat; ⊙ Hanzōmon & Toei Ōedo lines to Kiyosumi-Shirakawa, exit A3). Representing innovative contemporary artists spanning multiple styles and media, these galleries are well worth a detour.

WORTH THE TRIP

Tokyo Disneyland (☎ 045-683 3777; www.tokyodisneyresort.co.jp; 1-1 Maihama, Urayasu-shi, Chiba; one-day passport ¥5800/5000/3900; ☷ varies, see website; ☷ Keiyō line to Maihama (main exit); ☷ ☷), much beloved by the Japanese, is a near-perfect replica of the California original…making it the second-happiest place on earth? Adjacent to Tokyo Disneyland is Tokyo DisneySea, the more maritime- and futuristic-themed sibling of these twin amusement parks, which will probably appeal more to adults. One-day passports give you unlimited access to rides and shows at either Disneyland or DisneySea. Opening hours for both vary seasonally, so phone ahead or check the website before you set out. Parking costs ¥2000 per day.

relations, is the 'Peaceful Country Shrine' and a memorial to Japan's victims of war. No wonder it invites controversy. Politics aside, it has a beautiful, contemplative inner sanctum in the style of ancient Ise shrines – a stark contrast to the *uyoku* (right-wing activists) shouting their rhetoric outside.

🛍 SHOP

North of the Marunouchi business district is the Kanda neighbourhood, which holds little of interest to travellers other than for bookworms. Jimbōchō is famous for its bookshops, serving all sorts of special-interest readers, from manga maniacs to collectors of antique maps. Northeast of Jimbōchō across the Kanda River is even more manga, and electronics, in Akihabara (Electric Town). But the most famous shopping Mecca in Central Tokyo is glittery Ginza, its snob value still holding sway.

📷 APPLE STORE
アップルストア
Cameras & electronics
☎ 5159 8200; 3-5-12 Ginza, Chūō-ku; ☷ 10am-9pm; ☷ Ginza & Marunouchi lines to Ginza (exit A13)
This sleek retail cube takes up five floors, with the Genius Bar on the 2nd floor (some staff speak English), theatre on the 3rd and internet café on the 4th. There's another branch in Shibuya.

📷 HAIBARA はいばら
Stationery
☎ 3272 3801; 2-7-6 Nihombashi, Chūō-ku; ☷ 9.30am-6.30pm Mon-Fri, 9.30am-5pm Sat; ☷ Ginza, Tōzai, Toei Asakusa lines to Nihombashi (exits B8 & C3)
Even Haibara's business cards are made from exquisite paper. Find gorgeous, high-quality *washi* and tiny treasures such as wallets, hand mirrors and mobile phone accessories made from printed paper in this jewellery box of a paper shop.

Makiko Suda
Apparel designer at Indian Motorcycle Co, Inc

How would you describe Tokyo style? Tokyoites are always looking for something new, original and high quality. They care about the small details that can't be easily found elsewhere, like the design of pockets or the lining. For Tokyoites, fashion defines their own identity. **Who are your favourite Japanese designers?** When I was younger I was impressed by Yohji Yamamoto (p112) and his collection of exclusively black clothes. Nowadays I'm more interested in those anonymous fashion designers who work for Muji (p56) or Uniqlo (p58). Their designs are revolutionary in the Japanese fashion market, even though we don't know the designers' names. **Your personal design influences?** The fashions of young people around town always give me great inspiration. I often go people-watching in Shinjuku and Harajuku – when I see somebody *oshare* (stylish), I ask her where she bought her clothes.

Interview by Mariko Matsumura

HAKUHINKAN TOY PARK
博品館 *Toys*

☎ 3571 8008; www.hakuhinkan.co.jp;
8-8-11 Ginza, Chūō-ku; ⏰ 11am-8pm;
🚉 JR Yamanote line to Shimbashi (Ginza
exit), Ⓜ Ginza & Toei Asakusa lines to
Shimbashi (exits 1 & 3)

One of Tokyo's most famous toy
stores, this 'toy park' is crammed to
the rafters with dolls, action figures,
squawking video games, seas of
colourful plastic and the softest
plush toys ever. Hakuhinkan also
harbours child-friendly restaurants
and even a theatre in this huge children's attention-deficit paradise.

HASHI GINZA NATSUNO
箸銀座夏野 *Handicrafts*

☎ 3569 0952; www.e-ohashi.com in
Japanese; 1F & 6F, Ginza Takahashi Bldg,
6-7-4 Ginza, Chūō-ku; ⏰ 10am-8pm
Mon-Sat, 10am-7pm Sun; Ⓜ Ginza, Hibiya
& Marunouchi lines to Ginza (exit B3)

Look out for this narrow shopfront
in Ginza if you'd like to add some
hashi (chopsticks) to your stash of
souvenirs. Ginza Natsuno stocks
a staggering array of *hashi*, from
inexpensive, colourful children's
sets to hand-carved pairs costing
thousands of yen. Lovely chop-
stick rests, ceramics and decora-
tions fill out every other corner of
usable space.

ITŌYA 伊東屋 *Stationery*

☎ 3561 8311; 2-7-15 Ginza, Chūō-ku;
⏰ 9.30am-7pm Mon-Sat, 9.30am-6pm
Sun; Ⓜ Ginza, Hibiya & Marunouchi lines
to Ginza (exits A12 & A13)

Nine floors of stationery-shop
love await paper (and paperclip)
fanatics at Itōya. In addition to
a comprehensive collection of
washi, there are Italian leather
agendas, erasable pens in the
season's coolest hues and even

CHOPSTICK TIPS

Although foreigners will be forgiven most dining faux pas, remember this basic *hashi* (chop-
stick) etiquette:
> As anywhere in Asia, never leave chopsticks upright in your rice bowl; this is only done
  at funerals.
> Don't pass food from one set of chopsticks to another, as this is associated with another
  funereal ritual.
> Use the other end of your chopsticks when picking up food from a shared plate, so as
  not to use the ends that go in your mouth.
> It's considered rude to gesture with or point at anyone with chopsticks; when you're not
  using them to eat, it's best to lay them on the table in front of you.
> If you must resort to stabbing your food rather than picking it up with your chopsticks,
  consider requesting a fork and knife.

COLD BREWS & WARM BREEZES

During the summer many large department stores open up rooftop beer gardens. While not actual gardens, they're great, casual places to hoist a few beers outdoors with the salarymen knocking off work early. There's usually a good assortment of European and Japanese pub-style food on the menu, and many places offer *tabehōdai* (all-you-can-eat) and *nomihōdai* (all-you-can-drink) deals for around ¥2500 (with a two-hour limit, usually). Check out the rooftops of Takashimaya (p57) in Nihombashi, Matsuya (below) in Ginza, or the pleasant gardenlike setting of **Kudan Kaikan** (☎ 3261 5521; 1-6-5 Kudan-Minami, Chiyoda-ku; ☽ 5-10pm; ◉ Hanzōmon, Tōzai & Toei Shinjuku lines to Kudanshita, exit 4).

tenugui – beautifully hand-dyed, all-purpose traditional handkerchiefs.

☐ LAOX ラオックス
Cameras & electronics
☎ 3253 7111; 1-2-9 Soto-Kanda, Chiyoda-ku; ☽ 10am-9pm, closing hours vary at end of month; ☒ JR Sōbu & Yamanote lines to Akihabara (Electric Town exit)

The multilingual staff at this duty-free Laox will help you figure out whether the voltage on your new superjuicer is compatible with your home voltage before you lug it on the plane. This huge chain, selling discounted electrical equipment, has very competitive prices. There's another duty-free Laox nearby.

☐ MARUZEN 丸善 *Books*
☎ 5288 8881; 1F-4F, Oazo Bldg, 1-6-4 Marunouchi, Chiyoda-ku; ☽ 9am-9pm; ☒ JR Yamanote line to Tokyo (Marunouchi north exit)

Based in the curvy Oazo Building just across from Tokyo Station's Marunouchi exit, Maruzen boasts a satisfyingly wide selection of English-language books and magazines. The 4th floor is where you'll find the foreign-language material, a stationery shop and a café. Maruzen's revamped original branch, near exit B1 of Nihombashi Station, is expected to reopen in late 2007.

☐ MATSUYA 松屋
Department store
☎ 3567 1211; 3-6-1 Ginza, Chūō-ku; ☽ 10.30am-7.30pm; ◉ Ginza, Hibiya, Marunouchi lines to Ginza (exits A12 & A13)

A boon for foreign visitors, Matsuya offers the works with packaging and international shipping service, tax-exemption assistance and useful, if haphazard, in-store English-speaking guides. Don't forget to take a peek at Matsuya's art gallery on the 7th floor, and in the summer, the rooftop beer garden.

☐ MIKIMOTO PEARL ミキモト真珠
Jewellery & accessories

☎ 3535 4611; www.mikimoto.com/jp/; 4-5-5 Ginza, Chūō-ku; ⏱ 11am-6.30pm; ⊕ Ginza, Hibiya & Marunouchi lines to Ginza (exit B5)

Founded in 1899, Mikimoto Pearl was founded by the self-made Mikimoto Kokichi. At an early age he became fascinated with pearl divers and later developed the cultured pearl, building Mikimoto into the most famous of Tokyo's pearl shops. The store is located right next door to Wakō department store in Ginza.

☐ MITSUKOSHI 三越
Department stores

☎ 3562 1111; 4-6-16 Ginza, Chūō-ku; ⏱ 10am-7.30pm Mon-Sat, 10am-7pm Sun, closed occasional Mon; ⊕ Ginza, Hibiya, Marunouchi lines to Ginza (exits A7 & A11)

Tokyo's oldest department store was originally modelled on that London bastion of commerce, Harrods. Mitsukoshi is a posh and polished leviathan filled to the gills with tempting wares. Look for the Mitsukoshi lion at the corner entrance, which is a popular meeting spot for locals. There's also the original store in Nihombashi.

☐ MUJI 無印良品 *Clothing & homewares*

☎ 5208 8241; 2F & 3F, 3-8-2 Marunouchi, Chiyoda-ku; ⏱ 10am-8pm; ⊕ JR Yamanote line to Yūrakuchō (main exit), ⊕ Yūrakuchō line to Yūrakuchō (exit A4b)

Mujirushi Ryōhin – literally, 'no-name brand' – is the paradoxical designer label that took Japan, then Paris, London and Hong Kong by storm. Everything is reasonably priced and simply designed, from tea sets to toddler clothing and travel gear. This is the flagship store, but you'll find other branches all over Tokyo.

☐ OHYA SHOBŌ 大屋書房
Books

☎ 3291 0062; www.ohya-shobo.com; 1-1 Kanda Jimbōchō, Chiyoda-ku; ⏱ 10am-6pm Mon-Sat; ⊕ Hanzōmon, Toei Mita & Toei Shinjuku lines to Jimbōchō (exit A7)

You could lose yourself for hours in this splendid, musty old bookshop specialising in ukiyo-e ('floating world' prints) and ancient maps. The friendly staff can help you find whatever particular piece of antiquated trivia your heart desires.

☐ SOFMAP ソフマップ
Cameras & electronics

☎ 3253 9255; 1-10-8 Soto-Kanda, Chiyoda-ku; ⏱ 11am-9pm; ⊕ JR Sōbu & Yamanote lines to Akihabara (Electric Town exit)

Crafty marketing, ruthless discounting and a staff of tech geeks have helped Sofmap sprout more than a dozen branches within Akihabara alone. This company rules the cut-price computer world with a fist of silicon. Each shop specialises in new and used Macs, PCs and other cybergoodies; this one's the duty-free branch.

🏠 TAKASHIMAYA 高島屋
Department stores
☎ 3211 4111; 2-4-1 Nihombashi, Chūō-ku; 🕐 10am-7.30pm; 🚇 Ginza, Tōzai, Toei Asakusa lines to Nihombashi (exit B1 & B2)
In Nihombashi Takashimaya is one of the more venerable old establishments with palatial architecture. Primly-dressed, white-gloved attendants operate the old-fashioned lifts and bow demurely as you arrive and depart; take the lift to the rooftop patio, where you can bring your *bentō* (boxed meal). There's another branch in Ginza and the

enormous Takashimaya Times Square complex in Shinjuku.

🏠 TAKUMI HANDICRAFTS
たくみ *Handicrafts*
☎ 3571 2017; www.ginza-takumi.co.jp in Japanese; 8-4-2 Ginza, Chūō-ku; 🕐 11am-7pm Mon-Sat; 🚇 JR Yamanote line to Shimbashi (Ginza exit)
Takumi carries an elegant selection of toys, textiles, ceramics and other traditional folk crafts from around Japan. The shop also thoughtfully encloses information detailing the origin and background of any pieces you purchase.

🏠 TORA-NO-ANA
とらのあな *Books*
☎ 5294 0123; www.toranoana.co.jp; 4-3-1 Soto-Kanda, Chiyoda-ku; 🕐 10am-10pm; 🚇 JR Sōbu & Yamanote lines to Akihabara (Electric Town exit)
Keep your eyes up and look for the cute illustrated tiger-girl on

DOING THE DEPACHIKA
Tokyo's department stores are marvels unto themselves, not least because in their underground levels *depachika* (basement food halls) rule. Sure, there's the high-end grocery aspect to it, and the takeaway that takes your breath away — but they are an epicure's wet dream. This is where discriminating OLs (office ladies) and *obāsan* (grannies) purchase those archetypical hundred-dollar gift melons, the highest-grade, first-harvest tea and hand-rolled, bittersweet, Belgian-style truffles. Gourmet gifts abound, as well as sit-down counters where you can lunch on tempura or take away some *onigiri* (rice balls) for a picnic in the park. They're like every other Asian market in the world, except you could eat your *bentō* (boxed meal) off the immaculate floor — though, to be polite, we don't recommend it.

the top of this building, which has seven floors of manga and anime. Tora no Ana has other branches in Shinjuku and Ikebukuro.

🛍 UNIQLO ユニクロ *Fashion*
☎ 3569 6781; 5-7-7 Ginza, Chūō-ku; 🕙 11am-9pm; 🚇 Ginza, Hibiya & Marunouchi lines to Ginza (exit A2 & A3)
Like Muji and the Gap, Uniqlo has made a name for itself by sticking to the basics. Offering inexpensive clothing with simple lines, this chain has opened over 80 stores in Tokyo. A convenient place to pop in for an extra set of cheap jeans or plain shirts.

🛍 YODOBASHI AKIBA ヨドバシアキバ
Cameras & electronics
☎ 5209 1010; 1-1 Kanda-Hanaokachō, Chiyoda-ku; 🕙 9.30am-10pm; 🚆 JR Sōbu & Yamanote lines to Akihabara (Electric Town exit)
This megalith of a discount store is located on the east side of Akihabara Station, with a whopping nine floors of cameras, computer equipment and enough electronics for the most hardcore geek.

🍴 EAT
Ginza is a great place to splash out on a quality Japanese dinner, at one of its classic establishments. For lunch there are heaps of excellent traditional *soba* (buckwheat

noodle) shops around less-pretentious Kanda, while the must-do sushi breakfast should be taken in Tsukiji, naturally.

For *yakitori* (skewers of grilled chicken) in the most atmospheric spot in the neighbourhood, try Yūrakuchō Yakitori Alley, a conglomeration of simple *yakitori* stalls beneath the JR tracks just south of Yūrakuchō station. It's noisy, smoky and convivial; sit yourself down and wash down your *yakitori* with some cold beer.

🍴 BIRDLAND バードラン *Yakitori* ¥¥
☎ 5250 1081; B1F, Tsukamoto Sozan Bldg, 4-2-15 Ginza, Chūō-ku; 🕙 5-9pm Tue-Sat; 🚇 Ginza, Hibiya & Marunouchi lines to Ginza (exits C6 & C8)
Who knew Gewürztraminer went so well with skewered chicken hearts? Birdland does. Before said hearts are set aflame, they belong to free-range chickens so pure that they can be ordered as sashimi. Upscale and in demand, Birdland limits your dinner to two hours and only takes same-day reservations (from noon) for its famous *yakitori*.

🍴 BOTAN ぼたん *Traditional Japanese* ¥¥¥
☎ 3251 0577; 1-15 Kanda-Sudachō, Chiyoda-ku; 🕙 11.30am-8.30pm Mon-Sat; 🚇 Marunouchi line to Awajichō (exits A3 & A5) or Toei Shinjuku line to Ogawamachi (exits A3 & A5); 🍴

Botan has been making flawless *torisuki,* an Edo-period pot-stew, in the same buttonmaker's house for more than 100 years. Savouring a meal here will be a culinary highlight of a visit to Tokyo. Reservations are recommended.

🍴 DAIWA SUSHI 大和寿司
Sushi & sashimi   ¥¥

☎ 3547 6807; 5-2-1 Tsukiji, Chūō-ku; ⏱ 5am-1.30pm Mon-Sat, closed 2nd Wed of the month; Ⓜ Toei Ōedo line to Tsukiji-shijō (exit A2); ♿ Ⓥ ⚐

Lines are unavoidable at Tsukiji's famed sushi bar, but once your first piece of sushi hits the counter gratification is inevitable. The sushi sets are a good bet if you're not comfortable ordering in Japanese, and though they'll be too polite to say so, you're expected to eat without wasting time and then give up your seat.

🍴 EDOGIN 江戸銀
Sushi & sashimi   ¥¥¥

☎ 3543 4401; 4-5-1 Tsukiji, Chūō-ku; ⏱ 11am-9.30pm Mon-Sat; Ⓜ Hibiya line to Tsukiji (exit 2); ♿ Ⓥ ⚐

Reeling them in to the alleys northwest of Tsukiji Market with its fresh, oversized, but reasonably priced Edo-style sushi, Edogin has a functional feel that showcases its quality fish. At dinnertime it's worth shelling out for the *toku-jōnigiri* sushi set. There's no

Watch expert sushi chefs cut loose on your dinner at Daiwa Sushi, Tsukiji Market

English sign outside, but it's easily identified by the plastic sushi in the window.

🍴 KANDA YABU SOBA
神田やぶそば
Soba ¥

☎ 3251 0287; 2-10 Kanda-Awajichō, Chiyoda-ku; ⏱ 11.30am-8pm; Ⓜ Marunouchi line to Awajichō (exits A3 & A5) or Toei Shinjuku line to Ogawamachi (exits A3 & A5); ⚹

A Kanda stalwart, this restaurant's authentic surroundings and sung-out orders heighten the experience. Yet, fittingly, it's the smooth *soba* (buckwheat noodles) that make the day. Look for queues of customers in front of the traditional Japanese building, its small garden surrounded by a wooden fence.

🍴 KYŪBEI 久兵衛
Sushi & sashimi ¥¥¥¥

☎ 3571 6523; 8-7-6 Ginza, Chūō-ku; ⏱ 11.30am-2pm & 5-10pm Mon-Sat; ☒ JR Yamanote line to Shimbashi (Ginza exit), Ⓜ Ginza line to Shimbashi (exits 1 & 2)

It's not just high-end fish you're paying for at Kyūbei, but the wonderful surroundings in a sushi restaurant widely considered to be one of Tokyo's best. Discreet to the point of being almost impossible to find, look for the minimalist Japanese façade with a small path

leading to the left. It's one street west of Chūō-dori.

🍴 L'OSIER
レストランロオジェ
French ¥¥¥¥

☎ 3571 6050; www.shiseido.co.jp/e/losier/top.htm; 7-5-5 Ginza, Chūō-ku; ⏱ noon-3pm & 6-10pm Mon-Sat; Ⓜ Ginza, Hibiya & Marunouchi lines to Ginza (exit B6); ⚹

Add to your extravagant expenditures in Ginza by reserving a table (well in advance) at L'Osier, considered by many to be one of Tokyo's finest French restaurants. The modern interpretations of classic cuisine are exquisite and complemented by an imposing wine list. And if dinner seems too rich for your blood, lunch is a superb deal.

🍴 MATSUYA まつや
Soba ¥

☎ 3251 1556; 1-13 Kanda-Sudachō, Chiyoda-ku; ⏱ 11.30am-8pm Mon-Sat; Ⓜ Marunouchi line to Awajichō (exits A3 & A5) or Toei Shinjuku line to Ogawamachi (exits A3 & A5)

Rival to Kanda Yabu Soba and located almost next door, Matsuya is just as bustling and feels a notch more casual. Try plain *zaru soba*, then follow it up with the *kamo nanban*, *soba* with slices of roast duck. Soak it all up along with the merry crowd.

🍴 MEIDI-YA 明治屋
International groceries

☎ 3563 0221; 2-6-7 Ginza, Chūō-ku; ⏱ 10am-9pm Mon-Sat, 11am-9pm Sun; ⊚ Yūrakuchō line to Ginza-itchōme (exits 8 & 9)

Meidi-ya specialises in high-end groceries for foreign palates, carrying cheeses, wines, cookies and other titbits you might crave in this foreign land. Note, there are other locations throughout the city, including branches in Akasaka and Ginza.

🍴 ROBATA 炉端
Izakaya   ¥¥

☎ 3591 1905; 1-3-8 Yūraku-chō, Chiyoda-ku; ⏱ 5.30-11pm Mon-Sat; ⊚ Hibiya & Chiyoda lines to Hibiya (exit A4)

Back near the railway tracks, this is one of Tokyo's most celebrated *izakaya* (Japanese-style pub). A little Japanese language ability is helpful here, but the point-and-eat method works just fine. It's hard to spot the sign, even if you can read Japanese; better to look for the rustic, weathered façade.

🍴 SAKATA さか田
Udon   ¥

☎ 3563 7400; 2F, 1-5-13 Ginza, Chūō-ku; ⏱ 11.30am-2pm & 5.30-10pm Mon-Fri, 11.30am-2pm Sat; ⊚ Yūrakuchō line to Ginza-itchōme (exit 4)

You may have to wait for a seat at peak hours at Sakata, widely recognised as Tokyo's best noodle spot. Apart from the sublime *udon* (thick wheat noodles), Sakata-san is incredibly gracious and will go out of his way to serve you. There's no English menu, but the divinely silky *sanuki udon* is recommended.

🍴 TEN-ICHI 天一
Tempura   ¥¥¥

☎ 3571 1949; 6-6-5 Ginza, Chūō-ku; ⏱ 11.30am-9.30pm; ⊚ Ginza, Hibiya, Marunouchi lines to Ginza (exits A1, B3 & B6)

One of Tokyo's oldest and best tempura restaurants, the refined and gracious Ten-Ichi is where one should go to experience tempura the way it's meant to be: light, airy and crispy. You'll find several branches elsewhere in Tokyo, but the distinguished Ginza original is the smartest. Reservations are recommended.

🍴 YONEHANA 米花
Traditional Japanese   ¥¥

☎ 3541 4670; 5-2-1 Tsukiji, Chūō-ku; ⏱ 5am-1pm; ⊚ Toei Ōedo line to Tsukiji-Shijō (exits 1 & 2)

This family-run *unagi* (eel) restaurant in Tsukiji Market is now in the hands of its third generation, and the friendly, English-speaking chef is happy to make recommendations. It's an excellent spot to try *unagi* if you're not up for a sushi breakfast.

NEIGHBOURHOODS

CENTRAL TOKYO

▼ DRINK

▼ 300 BAR *Bar*

☎ 3571 8300; www.300bar-8chome.com
in Japanese; B1F, No 2 Column Bldg, 8-3-12
Ginza Chūō-ku; ⏱ 5pm-2am Mon-Sat,
5-11pm Sun; ⒭ JR Yamanote line to
Shimbashi (Ginza exit)

One of the few places in Ginza that
can truthfully say it offers a bargain, the 300 Bar charges ¥300 for
everything – cocktails, snacks and
all. There's no cover, and it's a fun
place to stand around with a few
drinks after some Ginza window-
shopping.

▼ AUX AMIS DES VINS
オザミ デバン *Bar*

☎ 3567 4120; www.auxamis.com/desvins
in Japanese; 2-5-6 Ginza, Chūō-ku;
⏱ 5.30pm-2am Mon-Fri & noon-midnight
Sat; ⒪ Yūrakuchō line to Ginza-itchōme
(exits 5 & 8)

Both the informal indoor and a
small outdoor seating area at
this wine bar feel welcoming in
all seasons. A solid selection of
mostly French wines comes by
the glass (¥800) or by the bottle.
You can also order snacks to go
with your wine, or full prix-fixe
dinners; lunch is served only on
weekdays.

▼ TAKARA 宝 *Izakaya*

☎ 5223 9888; B1F, Tokyo International
Forum, 3-5-1 Marunouchi, Chiyoda-ku;
⏱ 11.30am-2.30pm & 5-11pm Mon-Fri,
11.30am-2.30pm & 5-10pm Sat & Sun;
⒭ JR Yamanote line to Yūrakuchō (main
exit), ⒪ Yūrakuchō line to Yūrakuchō
(exit A4b)

Those seeking to sample some
sake should do themselves a
favour and wander on into
Takara, which has a dizzying sake
selection and an English *izakaya*
menu. This is a wonderfully
unpretentious and classy spot
for a sip.

MAID CAFÉS

Where *cosplay* (costume-play) culture and *otaku* (geeks; see p123) intersect, Akihabara
would seem the obvious crux. This collision of subcultures results in a new iteration of an old
game, with Tokyo's uniquely modern twist: maid cafés. This is master-slave role-playing as
above-board commercial service, where young waitresses dressed in cartoonish French maid
outfits serve the Akiba geeks who love them. Variations on the theme abound, with cafés
employing women in drag playing slender, spiky-haired *anime* heroes, and even nun(!) cafés
for those with Catholic fetishes. Look out for flyers and costumed touts, luring customers to
the dozens of maid cafés that have set up shop in Akihabara.

PLAY

⭐ KABUKI-ZA 歌舞伎座
Theatre

☎ 5565 6000; www.shochiku.co.jp/play
/kabukiza/theater/index.html; 4-12-5
Ginza, Chūō-ku; admission ¥2500-17,000;
🕐 11am-9pm; Ⓜ Hibiya & Toei Asakusa
lines to Higashi-Ginza (exit 3)
Originally opened in 1889, Kabuki-
za has been rebuilt several times
following the Great Kantō Earthquake in 1923 and WWII bombing
in 1951. These days, its dramatic
and imposing architecture pops
out amid the modern edifices of
Higashi-Ginza, worth a walk-by
even if you don't plan on attend-
ing a performance.

⭐ KŌRAKUEN AMUSEMENT
PARK 後楽園 遊園地
Amusement park

☎ 5800 9999; Tokyo Dome City, 1-3-61
Kōraku, Bunkyō-ku; one-day pass/after
5pm ¥4000/3000, individual rides ¥200-
1000; 🕐 10am-10pm Jun-Aug, 10am-6pm
Dec-Feb, 10am-8pm rest of year; 🚇 Chūō
line to Suidōbashi (east exit) Ⓜ Marunouchi line to Kōrakuen (main exit)
Adrenaline junkies of all ages
will enjoy the exciting old-school
rollercoasters at this amusement
park, as well as the newer, high-
tech Geopolis side of the park that
includes the Geopanic indoor roll-
ercoaster. Once your equilibrium

has been well and truly scrambled,
head next door to the contemplative spaces of the Koishikawa
Kōrakuen (p49) park for a dose of
serenity.

⭐ NATIONAL FILM CENTRE
フィルムセンター *Cinema*

☎ 5777 8600; 3-7-6 Kyōbashi, Chūō-ku;
cinema ¥500/300/100, gallery ¥200/70/40/
free; 🕐 cinema 3-10pm Tue-Fri, 1-7pm
Sat & Sun, gallery 11am-6.30pm Tue-Sat;
Ⓜ Ginza line to Kyōbashi (exit 2) or Toei
Asakusa line to Takarachō (exit A3)
The third arm of the National
Museum of Modern Art (p50), this
centre shows tremendous film
series on a range of subjects,
from the history of Japanese
animation to the masterpieces of
Cuba's film tradition. The centre
also houses a library and a gallery that includes a permanent
collection of antique cinematic
equipment.

⭐ NATIONAL THEATRE
国立劇場 *Theatre*

☎ 3230 3000; www.ntj.jac.go.jp/english
/index.html; 4-1 Hayabusachō, Chiyoda-ku;
admission ¥1500-9200 🕐 reservations
10am-6pm, performances 11.30am &
5pm; Ⓜ Namboku & Yūrakuchō lines to
Nagatachō (exit 4)
Otherwise known as Kokuritsu
Gekijō, this theatre features

WORTH THE TRIP

On the east bank of the Sumida River, Ryōgoku is akin to a sumō village. Because the sumō stadium is located here, so too are the sumō *beya* (wrestling stables) that train and house *rikishi* (wrestlers).

During Grand Tournament time at **Ryōgoku Kokugikan** (☎ 3623 5111; www.sumo .or.jp; 1-3-28 Yokoami, Sumida-ku; ⌚ 10am-4.30pm; 🚉 JR Sōbu line to Ryōgoku (west exit), 🚇 Toei Ōedo line to Ryōgoku (exit A4)), non-reserved seats in back sell for as little as ¥1500 and standing-room-only tickets are a meagre ¥500. Simply turn up on the day you'd like to attend, but get there early as keen punters start queuing the night before. Only one ticket is sold per person to foil scalpers, so come with your entire entourage.

When tournaments aren't in season, you can pick up a handbook at the stadium and take a self-guided walking tour of the neighbourhood and some of the local *beya*. Be sure to also take a peek into the **Sumō Museum** (☎ 3622 0366; www.sumo.or.jp/eng/museum/index

astonishingly lifelike, bunraku puppets are half to two-thirds life-size and are each operated by three hooded, visible puppeteers. A single narrator, standing on a dais to one side, intones the story using a different voice for each character. Performances take place in Tokyo in February, May, September and December.

⭐ **SESSION HOUSE**
セッションハウス *Theatre*
☎ 3266 0461; 158 Yaraichō, Shinjuku-ku; admission varies; ⌚ performances 7pm; 🚇 Tōzai line to Kagurazaka (exit 1)
Dance aficionados consider Session House one of the best traditional, folk and modern dance spaces in the city. The theatre seats only 100 people, ensuring an intimate feel for all performances. Exit right from Kagurazaka Station,

make a right into the first narrow alley, and turn left where it dead-ends. Session House will be a few metres on your right.

⭐ **TOKYO DOME**
東京ドーム *Spectator sports*
☎ 5800 9999; www.tokyo-dome.co.jp/e; 1-3-61 Kōraku, Bunkyō-ku; from ¥1800; 🚉 Chūō, Sōbu lines to Suidobashi (west exit), 🚇 Marunouchi & Namboku lines to Kōrakuen (Kōrakuen exit)
A trip to a Japanese ballpark is truly a cultural experience in baseball-mad Japan. Fans in matching *happi* (half-coats) perform synchronised cheers, and entire sections of the extremely well-mannered crowd often wind up singing in unison. Tokyo Dome is the home turf of Japan's most popular team, the Yomiuri Giants.

.html; 1F, 1-3-28 Yokoami, Sumida-ku; admission free; ☻ 10am-4.30pm Mon-Fri; 🚇 Sōbu line to Ryōgoku, west exit, ☻ Toei Ōedo line to Ryōgoku, exit A4), located inside Ryōgoku Kokugikan. Although there's little English explanation, exhibits are visually interesting enough to be worth a look. Note that during tournaments, the museum is open only to ticket-holding attendees.

Just behind Ryōgoku Kokugikan is the superb **Edo-Tokyo Museum** (☎ 3626 9974; www.edo-tokyo-museum.or.jp; 1-4-1 Yokoami, Sumida-ku; admission ¥600/300-480/free; ☻ 9.30am-5.30pm Tue-Fri & Sun, 9.30am-7.30pm Sat; 🚇 JR Sōbu line to Ryōgoku, west exit, ☻ Toei Ōedo line to Ryōgoku, exit A4). Offering a fascinating view into Edo-era life, this museum is highly accessible by wheelchair, fun for kids and even has volunteers who give free tours in English (and other languages). Call ahead to confirm availability of such tour guides.

For more information on Sumo see p11.

Home-run hype hits Tokyo Dome

☆ TOKYO TAKARAZUKA GEKIJŌ 東京宝塚劇場
Theatre

☎ 5251 2001; http://kageki.hankyu.co.jp /english; 1-1-3 Yūrakuchō, Chiyoda-ku; admission ¥3500-10,000 ☻ times vary; ☻ Chiyoda, Hibiya & Toei Mita lines to Hibiya (exits A5 & A13)

Kabuki kicked women out of the tradition, but the ladies have taken the ball and run with it at the Takarazuka Revue, founded in 1913. The extensively trained, all-female cast puts on an equally grand – if drastically different – show. These musical productions tend toward the soap-operatic and attract a disproportionate percentage of swooning female fans.

>UENO

Ueno-kōen (Ueno Park), the preeminent attraction to this Shitamachi neighbourhood, is a feast of culture with its numerous museums, temples and shrines. While most people enter the park at the museum plaza, another pleasant way to see the park before museum-fatigue sets in is to start at the south end. From the Shinobazu exit of the Ueno JR station, cross the road and go up the stairs to the left of the Keisei Ueno station entrance, up to the small pavilion where the Takamori Saigō statue stands. From there, continue uphill to the temple complex before heading out, near the zoo, into the museum area.

Also near the south end of the park is Shinobazu-ike, a large pond where lotuses proliferate and where you can rent small **boats** (☎ 3828 9502; rowboats per hr ¥600; paddle boats 30min ¥600; ☉ 9am-5pm Mar-Nov) for a serene stint on the water's surface. This pond also has its own temple, Benten-dō, on an island.

UENO

👁 SEE

Benten-dō	1	B4
Kiyomizu Kannon-dō	2	C4
National Museum of Western Art	3	C3
National Science Museum	4	C3
Shitamachi History Museum	5	C5
Tokyo Metropolitan Museum of Art	6	C3
Tokyo National Museum	7	C3
Tōshōgū	8	B3
Ueno Zoo	9	B3
Yayoi Museum & Takehisa Yumeji Museum	10	A3

🛍 SHOP

Ameyoko Arcade	11	C5

🍴 EAT

Echikatsu	12	B5
Hantei	13	A3
Izu-ei	14	C5
Sasa-no-Yuki	15	D1
Ueno Yabu Soba	16	C5

A B C D

1

Nippori

Yanaka Cemetery
谷中霊園

Negishi
根岸

Yanaka
谷中

2

Kototoi-dōri 言問通り

Uguisudani
鶯谷

Uguisudani
鶯谷

Hibiya Line

Heiseikan

Ueno-
Sakuragi

Gallery of Hōryū-ji
Treasures
Hakubutsukan
Dōbutsuen

Hyōkeikan

Tōyōkan (Gallery Of
Eastern Antiquities)

3

Nezu
根津

Ikenohata

Rinnō-ji

Shuto Expwy No 1

Kita-Ueno
北上野

Ueno-
kōen
上野公園

Monorail

Aesop
Bridge

9

8

Suijōdōbutsu-
ike

Bōto-
ike

Tokyo Metropolitan
Festival Hall
東京文化会館

Ueno
Ueno-no
Mori Art
Museum

Hirokō-
ji Exit

Ueno

Keisei

Taito-ku
Ward Office
Asakusa-dōri 浅草通り

4

Dōbutsuen-dōri

2

Shitamachi
History Museum

Keisei

Ueno

Ueno

Higashi-Ueno
東上野

Shinobazu-dōri

Hongō
本郷

Shinobazu-ike

1

Okachimachi
御徒町

Kasuga-dōri 春日通り

5

Tokyo Regional Cr

Nakamachi-dōri

5

Chūō-dōri 中央通り

Ueno Nakamachi
Okachimachi

Ameyoko
Arcade

16

Naka
Okachimachi

Okachimachi

Taito
台東

Shin-
okachimachi
新御徒町

Yushima

12

Ueno-
Okachimachi

Ueno Okachimachi Chuodo

Ueno-hirokōji
Matsuzakaya
Miyamoto

6

Yushima
湯島

Suehirochō

Showa-dōri

◉ SEE

◉ BENTEN-DŌ 弁天堂

☎ 3821 4638; 2-1 Ueno-kōen, Taitō-ku; admission free; ☾ 9am-5pm; 🚃 JR Yamanote line to Ueno (Shinobazu exit)

Take a stroll down the causeway leading to the island on which Benten-dō stands. The temple is dedicated to Benzaiten, the Buddhist goddess of the arts, wisdom, the sea and the protector of children (she covers a lot of territory). More interesting than the temple itself is its location and the opportunity to see the birds and botany that thrive around the pond.

◉ KIYOMIZU KANNON-DŌ 清水観音堂

1-4 Ueno-kōen, Taitō-ku; admission free; ☾ 9am-5pm; 🚃 JR Yamanote line to Ueno (Shinobazu exit)

This red temple, up the path from the Takamori Saigō statue, was modelled after Kiyomizu-dera in Kyoto. During Ningyō-kuyō (p33), women wishing to conceive a child leave a doll here for Senjū Kannon (the 1000-armed goddess of mercy), and the accumulated dolls are ceremonially burnt each 25 September.

◉ NATIONAL MUSEUM OF WESTERN ART 国立西洋美術館

☎ 3828 5131; www.nmwa.go.jp; 7-7 Ueno-kōen, Taitō-ku; admission ¥420/130/70; ☾ 9.30am-5pm Tue-Thu, Sat & Sun, 9.30am-8pm Fri; 🚃 JR Yamanote line to Ueno (Park exit); ♿

It may seem odd coming all this way just to check out Rodin sculptures and Le Corbusier architecture, but the Museum of Western Art can be well worth a stop during its frequent visiting exhibits. Check local listings for what's on during your visit; there are often extra admission fees for special exhibitions.

◉ NATIONAL SCIENCE MUSEUM 国立科学博物館

☎ Mon-Fri 3822 0111, Sat & Sun 3822 0114; www.kahaku.go.jp/english; 7-20 Ueno-kōen, Taitō-ku; admission ¥500/free, additional ¥500 for special exhibitions; ☾ 9am-4.30pm Tue-Sun 🚃 JR Yamanote line to Ueno (Park exit); ♿ 👶

Renovations in recent years have made this museum more user-friendly for foreigners, with interpretive English signage throughout. The interactive exhibits are great fun for kids, especially those that allow clambering. Between the dinosaur displays here and the animals at Ueno Zoo (p71), this is an excellent outing for children.

◉ SHITAMACHI HISTORY MUSEUM 下町風俗資料館

☎ 3823 7451; 2-1 Ueno-kōen, Taitō-ku; admission ¥300/100; ☾ 9.30am-4.30pm Tue-Sun; 🚃 JR Yamanote line to Ueno (Hirokōji exit); ♿ 👶

Learn some games and try on clothes in the style of Edo's Shitamachi, the plebeian downtown quarter of old Tokyo. Hands-on or walk-in exhibits include a sweet shop, the home and business of a copper-boiler maker and a tenement house (don't forget to take off your shoes).

TOKYO METROPOLITAN MUSEUM OF ART
東京都美術館
☎ 3823 6921; www.tobikan.jp; 8-36 Ueno-kōen, Taitō-ku; admission varies; ⏱ 9am-5pm Tue-Sun, closed 3rd Mon of each month; 🚃 JR Yamanote line to Ueno (Park exit); ♿
The Tokyo Met has several galleries that run temporary displays of contemporary Japanese art. Galleries feature all manner of Western-style art and Japanese-style works such as *sumi-e* (ink-brush painting) and ikebana. Apart from the main gallery, the rental galleries are curated by the artists and collectives who rent them, so exhibitions are a mixed bag.

TOKYO NATIONAL MUSEUM 東京国立博物館
☎ 3822 1111; www.tnm.jp; 13-9 Ueno-kōen, Taitō-ku; admission ¥420/130, free on 2nd Sat; ⏱ 9.30am-5pm Tue-Thu, Sat & Sun, 9.30am-8pm Fri; 🚃 JR Yamanote line to Ueno (Park exit); ♿

Armed to the teeth at Tokyo National Museum

This showcase of Japanese and Asian art and artefacts is the crown jewel of Ueno Park museums. Mull over your visit with a stroll in the peaceful Tokugawa Shōgun Cemetery, located just behind the museum.

TŌSHŌGŪ 東照宮
☎ 3822 3455; 1-9 Ueno-kōen, Taitō-ku; admission ¥200; ⏱ 9am-4.30pm; 🚃 JR Yamanote line to Ueno (Shinobazu exit)
Established in 1627, this shrine has the distinction of being one of the few extant early Edo

Masahiro Tatematsu
Bicyclist-musician playing in Ueno Park (p22) and Tokyo International Forum (p51)

How did you start performing in public? In 2002 the Tokyo Metropolitan Government launched the `Heaven Artist' programme which licenses artists to perform in designated public places, and I was selected after a rigorous audition. I started performing in March 2003 and now play 15 to 20 days per month, mostly in Ueno. **What instruments do you play?** The wooden xylophone, bongo, cymbal, *pandeiro* (Brazilian tambourine), *chajchas* (Andean rattle), Indian bells, *kalimba* (African thumb piano)... **Any instruments of your own invention?** The folding xylophone. **What music do you enjoy listening to?** Haydn's string quartets, Tchaikovsky's symphonies, jazz and African music. I'd like to travel to West Africa, as I'm very interested in their music. **Top spots for visitors to Tokyo?** Tokyo National Museum (p69) is always showing some interesting exhibition. Outside Tokyo, the city of Kawagoe (in Saitama-ken) has old-fashioned streets with traditional wooden houses and is still relatively unknown to tourists.

Interview by Mariko Matsumura

structures, having survived the Great Kantō Earthquake of 1923, WWII destruction and other historical disasters. The intricate decoration and the architecture of the shrine, typical to other Tōshōgū shrines throughout Japan, and the atypical copper lanterns lining the path, are well worth the price of admission.

UENO ZOO 上野動物園
☎ 3828 5171; 9-83 Ueno-kōen, Taitō-ku; admission ¥600/200/free; ⏰ 9.30am-5pm Tue-Sun; ⓜ Chiyoda line to Nezu (south exit), ⛍ JR Yamanote line to Ueno (Park exit); ♿ ⛁

Established in 1882, Ueno Zoo was the first of its kind in Japan. It makes a good detour if you're travelling with kids; otherwise, it can be safely dropped from a busy itinerary. The zoo is very popular with Japanese visitors, for its

charming pandas (who are not on view on Fridays).

YAYOI MUSEUM & TAKEHISA YUMEJI MUSEUM
☎ 5689 0462; www.yayoi-yumeji -museum.jp in Japanese; 2-4-3 Yayoi, Bunkyō-ku; admission ¥800/700/400; ⏰ 10am-5pm Tue-Sun; ⓜ Chiyoda line to Nezu (exit 1)

These two charming brick museums focus mostly on illustrations from popular art, books and other precursors to Japan's manga tradition. The work represents graphic art from the Meiji, Taishō and Shōwa periods, including some Japanese-style Art Deco illustrations. The museums are on a side street facing the northeastern end of Tokyo University.

SHOP

AMEYOKO ARCADE アメ横 Market
⛍ JR Yamanote line to Okachimachi (north exit) or Ueno (Hirokōji exit), ⓜ Ginza line to Ueno-Hirokōji (exit A5) or Hibiya line to Naka-Okachimachi (exit A5)

Ameya-yokochō, or Ameyoko for short, is one of the only old-fashioned outdoor markets in Tokyo. It was famous as a post-WWII black market, and even now it retains that throwback feel, with merchants calling out to attract customers and open-air stalls displaying dried seafood, herbs and mushrooms. The Ameyoko Center

---

GOT GRUTT?

Museum-crawlers planning on visiting several museums during a Tokyo visit should grab a Grutt Pass (¥2000) at the Tokyo Tourist Information Center (p202). The pass is a book of tickets entitling the bearer to free or discounted entry to nearly 50 Tokyo museums and zoos. It's valid for two months after the first visit and is a fabulous deal as it pays for itself in a few visits. The Grutt Pass is also available at participating museums.

Monster sales and shopping in Ameyoko Arcade

Within the exquisite environs of a grand old Japanese house, take in the beautiful ambience with your sukiyaki (thinly sliced beef, vegetables and tofu cooked in broth at your table) and *shabu-shabu* (thinly sliced beef and vegetables cooked in broth and dipped in vinegar and citrus sauces). Many of the tatami rooms overlook small gardens. The staff don't speak English but will make a genuine effort to communicate; reservations are recommended.

HANTEI はん亭
Traditional Japanese ¥¥
☎ 3828 1440; 2-12-15 Nezu, Taitō-ku; noon-2pm & 5-10pm Tue-Sat, noon-2pm & 4-9.30pm Sun; Chiyoda line to Nezu (Shinobazu exit)
The procession of *kushiage* (deep-fried meat, fish and vegetables on skewers) comes to your table in groups of threes, as you dine in this lovely wooden-walled, traditional restaurant that was spared from WWII bombing. They'll keep the various dishes coming until you've had enough. Reservations are recommended.

Building contains stalls that sell imported spices, produce and herbs from mainland Asia, and there are a few bargains on clothing and shoes around the market area.

EAT

ECHIKATSU 江知勝
Sukiyaki ¥¥¥
☎ 3811 5293; 2-31-23 Yushima, Bunkyō-ku; 5-9.30pm Mon-Sat, closed Sat in Aug; Chiyoda line to Yushima (exit 5);

IZU-EI 伊豆栄
Traditional Japanese ¥¥
☎ 3831 0954; 2-12-22 Ueno, Taitō-ku; 11am-9.30pm; Chiyoda line to Yushima (exit 2), JR Yamanote line to Ueno (Shinobazu exit)

Beautifully presented, authentic Japanese eel meals make this an excellent spot to take Japanese friends or colleagues to dinner. The Izu-ei *unagi bentō* (eel boxed dinner) includes tempura and is best eaten near the window for a lovely view of the giant lilypads on Shinobazu-ike. There's a limited picture menu.

🍴 **SASA-NO-YUKI** 笹乃雪
Traditional Japanese   ¥¥
☎ 3873 1145; 2-15-10 Negishi, Taitō-ku; 🕙 11am-9pm Tue-Sun; 🚉 JR Yamanote line to Uguisudani (north exit); Ⓥ ⑤

Sasa-no-Yuki, or 'snow on bamboo', opened in Edo over 300 years ago. Staying true to its roots, this establishment continues to serve tofu in dozens of forms and in *tōfu-ryōri* (multi-course, tofu-based meals). Strict

vegetarians should note that many dishes include chicken and fish stock; ask the friendly staff for advice if the English menu doesn't provide you with enough information.

🍴 **UENO YABU SOBA**
上野やぶそば
Soba   ¥
☎ 3831 4728; 6-9-16 Ueno, Taitō-ku; 🕙 11.30am-9pm Thu-Tue; 🚉 JR Yamanote line to Ueno (Hirokōji exit); ⑤

Near the arcade, this busy, famous place rustles up top-class *soba*, from the simple *zaru soba* – plain, cold buckwheat noodles to dip in broth – to the richly filling *tenseiro* (noodles topped with shrimp and vegetable tempura). There's a picture menu to help you choose. Look for the black-granite sign in front that says in English 'Since 1892'.

>ASAKUSA

While Asakusa does draw significant tourist traffic, it carries on with the rough-around-the-edges Shitamachi spirit that powered the low city of old Edo. With its bustling centrepiece the temple Sensō-ji drawing devotees as well as photo-snapping visitors, the streets, temples and shrines of Asakusa imbue this area with a historical feel. So too do the neighbourhood's working artists busily keep customs alive by labouring over traditional handicrafts.

The neighbourhood, with kitchenware district Kappabashi-dōri to the west and the Sumida River to the east, is compact enough to take in with a walking tour. But near Kaminarimon you'll probably also be wooed by *jinrikisha* (rickshaw) drivers in traditional dress, who can cart you around on tours (per person ¥2000/5000/9000 for 10/30/60 minutes), stopping at sights to provide insightful commentary in English, Japanese or other languages. Asakusa runs at a steady hum throughout the day, but tends to shut down after night falls.

ASAKUSA

Imado

A
B
C
D

Kokisai-dōri

Kototoi-dōri

Taitō-ku

Asakusa

Kototoi-dōri

Sumida-kōen

Asakusa
View
Hotel

Hisago-dōri

Hanayashiki
Amusement
Park

Asakusa-
Kōen

Kototoi-bashi

Yoshino-dōri

Kappabashihon-dōri

Dembō-in

Hōzō-
mon

Hanakawadokōen

Umamich-dōri 馬道通り

Hanakawado

Nishi-
Asakusa
西浅草

Asakusa
Engei Hall

Shin-Nakamise-dōri

Tōbu
Asakusa
Tōbu
Asakusa

Shuto Expwy No 6 首都高速6号

Tokyo
Hongan-ji

Kappabashi-dōri かっぱ橋道具街通り

Orange-dōri オレンジ通り

Chiyoko-dōri

Nakamise-dōri

Edo-dōri

Kaminarimon-dōri

Kaminarimon

Asakusa

Suijo Bus Pier

Asahi
Super Dry
Building

Azuma-bashi 吾妻橋

Tawaramachi

Asakusa-dōri

Honjo-
Azumabashi

Kokusai-dōri 国際通り

Metro-dōri

Kotobuki

Komagata-bashi 駒形橋

Sumida River (Sumida-gawa) 隅田川

Kasuga-dōri

Shuto Expwy No 6 首都高速6号

Kuramae

Mitsume-dōri

Asakusabashi

⊙ SEE
⊙ ASAKUSA-JINJA 浅草神社
2-3-1 Asakusa, Taitō-ku; admission free; ⊕ **Ginza & Toei Asakusa lines to Asakusa (exits 1 & A5)**

Buddhist Sensō-ji sits just in front of its Shintō neighbour, Asakusa-jinja, in silent architectural testament to the peaceful coexistence of these two religions in Japan. Also known as Sanja-sama, this shrine is the site of one of Tokyo's most important *matsuri* (p31).

⊙ CHINGODŌ-JI 鎮護寺
2-3-1 Asakusa, Taitō-ku; admission free; ⊕ **Ginza & Toei Asakusa lines to Asakusa (exits 1 & A5)**

This quiet, odd little shrine on the banks of Dembō-in (right) pays tribute to *tanuki* – the 'raccoon dog' tricksters who figure in Japanese mythology. Shape-shifting *tanuki* are normally depicted with enormous testicles on which they can fly.

⊙ DEMBŌ-IN 伝法院
☎ **3842 0181; 2-3-1 Asakusa, Taitō-ku; admission free;** ⏱ **9am-4.30pm, closed for ceremonies;** ⊕ **Ginza & Toei Asakusa lines to Asakusa (exits 1 & A5)**

Adjacent to the Sensō-ji precinct is Dembō-in, a temple with an attached garden. Inside this secret sanctuary there's a picturesque pond and a replica of a famous Kyoto teahouse. Although it's not open to the public, you can make an appointment to visit by calling a few days ahead to the temple office (left of the Five-Storeyed Pagoda).

⊙ EDO SHITAMACHI TRADITIONAL CRAFTS MUSEUM 江戸下町伝統工芸館
☎ **3842 1990; 2-22-13 Asakusa, Taitō-ku; admission free;** ⏱ **10am-8pm;** ⊕ **Tsukuba Express to Asakusa (exit A1) or Ginza line to Tawaramachi (exit 3)**

This hall is a wonderful place to view the handicrafts that continue

---

VISITING A SHRINE
Just past the *torii* (shrine gate) is a *chōzuya* (water trough), with long-handled ladles perched on a rack above. This is for purifying yourself before entering the sacred precincts of the shrine. If you choose to purify yourself, take a ladle, fill it with fresh water from the spigot, pour some over one hand, transfer the spoon and pour water over the other hand. Then pour a little water into a cupped hand and rinse your mouth, spitting the water onto the ground beside the trough.

Head to the *haiden* (hall of worship), which sits in front of the *honden* (main hall) enshrining the *kami* (shrine god). Toss a coin into the offerings box, ring the gong by pulling on the thick rope in order to summon the deity, pray, then clap your hands twice, bow and then back away from the shrine.

Sensō-ji Temple illuminates the sky at dusk

to flourish in Shitamachi. The gallery on the 2nd floor of this museum displays a rotating selection of works (such as fans, lanterns, knives, intricate woodcarvings and glass) by neighbourhood artists, and crafts demonstrations take place around noon on most weekends.

SENSŌ-JI 浅草寺
☎ 3842 0181; 2-3-1 Asakusa, Taitō-ku; admission free; ◎ Ginza & Toei Asakusa lines to Asakusa (exits 1 & A5)

With its pagoda and shrines nearby, Sensō-ji is one of Tokyo's most popular sights. It lies in the heart of Asakusa and serves as a community temple. As you reach Hōzōmon, the second gate leading into the temple itself, have a look at the Five-Storeyed Pagoda to the left, the second-tallest in Japan.

TAIKOKAN (DRUM MUSEUM) 太鼓館
☎ 3842 5622; 2-1-1 Nishi-Asakusa, Taitō-ku; admission ¥300/150; ⏰ 10am-5pm Wed-Sun; ◎ Ginza line to Tawaramachi (exit 3)

It's tellingly human that the vast majority of us can't resist the temptation to bang a gong, given half the chance. Luckily for our percussive tendencies, this drum museum makes its instruments fair game unless they're marked with a red dot. From *taiko* (traditional Japanese drums) to African finger-harps, this museum displays examples of drums from around the world.

🛍 SHOP

Nakamise-dōri, the lively pedestrian street leading to Sensō-ji, is chock-a-block with shops selling tourist wares like *geta* (wooden sandals worn with kimonos), lacquer combs, purses and cigarette cases made from kimono fabric and Edo-style toys and trinkets. Look out for stalls selling *sembei* (savoury rice crackers), *anko* (azuki-bean paste) sweets and freshly made *mochi* (sticky-rice cakes). But don't just stick to the main drag; the alleys off to both sides of Nakamise-dōri, and the streets around Sensō-ji are full of small shops selling *tenugui* (traditionally dyed hand towels) or accessories to be worn with kimonos and other fine handicrafts.

🛍 KAPPABASHI-DŌRI
かっぱ橋通り
Homewares & novelties
On the west side of Asakusa is this kitchenware shopping strip, which supplies restaurants and locals with items such as ceramic ware, woven bamboo trays, iron teapots, *noren* (doorway curtains) and best

These plastic food models go down a treat on Kappabashi-dōri, Asakusa's kitchenware shopping strip

of all, those excellent plastic food models. They don't come cheap though – a couple pieces of sushi will set you back about ¥2500.

☐ YOSHITOKU 吉德
Specialist store

☎ 3863 4419; 1-9-14 Asakusabashi, Taitō-ku; ⏰ 9.30am-6pm; 🚇 Sōbu or Toei Asakusa lines to Asakusabashi (main exit or exit A2)

Dollmaker to the emperor, Yoshitoku has been in business since 1711. The dolls here are exquisitely crafted in silk and porcelain, dressed in sumptuous replicas of elaborate kimonos and accessories. It's possible to buy a small piece for around ¥2000. For the larger and more elaborate ones, unlace the purse strings.

🍴 EAT
🍴 DAIKOKUYA 大黒家
Tempura ¥¥

☎ 3844 1111; 1-38-10 Asakusa, Taitō-ku; dishes ¥1500-3000; ⏰ 11.30am-8.30pm Mon-Fri, 11.30am-9pm Sat; 🚇 Ginza & Toei Asakusa lines to Asakusa (exits 1 & A5); ♿

Near Nakamise-dōri, this famous place serves great, authentic tempura, a speciality in Asakusa. The line out the door usually snakes around the corner at lunchtime, but if it looks unbearably long, try your luck at the branch on the next block.

🍴 EDOKKO 江戸っ子
Tempura ¥¥

☎ 3841 0150; 1-40-7 Asakusa, Taitō-ku; ⏰ 11.30am-9pm Wed-Mon; 🚇 Ginza & Toei Asakusa lines to Asakusa (exits 6 & A5); ♿ ♿

Just outside the Senjō-ji complex is this well-known restaurant named after the local folk. And in honour of Edo, this place serves the neighbourhood speciality – tempura (try the *tendon*, shrimp tempura on rice) – in a very authentic atmosphere. Edokko has a traditional wooden façade and a white *noren* outside.

🍴 IROKAWA 色 *Unagi*
¥¥

☎ 3844 1187; 2-6-11 Kaminarimon, Taitō-ku; ⏰ 11.30am-1.30pm & 5-8.30pm; 🚇 Ginza & Toei Asakusa lines to Asakusa (exits 2 and A1)

Irokawa serves some of the best, most beautifully grilled *unagi* (eel) around. Try the *unaju* (broiled eel on rice). It has a humble, traditional-looking exterior, with plants flanking the entrance, and is a friendly neighbourhood spot to try *unagi* with the locals.

🍴 KOMAGATA DOZEU 駒形どぜう
Traditional Japanese ¥¥

☎ 3842 4001; 1-7-12 Komagata, Taitō-ku; ⏰ 11am-9pm; 🚇 Ginza & Toei Asakusa lines to Asakusa (exits 2 & A5); ♿

The 6th-generation chef running this marvellous restaurant continues the tradition of elevating the simple *dojō* (a small, eel-like river fish) to a thing of delicious wonder. You can try it 10 different ways, and there's an English menu. Floor seating at the shared, low wooden plank tables heightens the traditional flavour, but ladies: don't wear a skirt for this dining expedition.

🍴 VIN CHOU 萬鳥
Yakitori   -¥¥

☎ 3845 4430; 2-2-13 Nishi-Asakusa, Taitō-ku; ⏰ 5pm-11pm Thu-Sat, Mon & Tue, 4-10pm Sun; Ⓜ Ginza & Toei Asakusa lines to Asakusa (exits 1 & A5)

Tucked away in this corner of Asakusa, Vin Chou is an odd bird: a French-style *yakitori* joint, offering foie gras with your *tori negi* (chicken and spring onion). With cheeses and fowl imported from Europe, it's chic and unique. It's just round the corner one block west of the Taikokan (p77).

🍸 DRINK

Asakusa is another of those neighbourhoods without a compelling nightlife, but you can certainly throw back a few at these local bars.

🍸 ASAHI SKY ROOM
アサヒスカイルーム *Bar*

☎ 5608 5277; 22F, Asahi Super Dry Bldg, 1-23-1 Azumabashi, Sumida-ku; ⏰ 10am-10pm; Ⓜ Ginza & Toei Asakusa lines to Asakusa (exits 4 & A5)

Spend the day at religious sites and end at the Asahi altar, on the 22nd floor of the golden-tinged Asahi Super Dry Building. Directly adjacent to the infamous *Flamme d'Or* sculpture (aka 'The Golden Turd') on the east bank of the Sumida River, the venue itself isn't noteworthy, but serves up Asahi brews and a spectacular view, especially at sunset.

🍸 KAMIYA BAR 神谷バー
Bar

☎ 3841 5400; 1-1-1 Asakusa, Taitō-ku; ⏰ 11.30am-10pm Wed-Mon; Ⓜ Ginza & Toei Asakusa lines to Asakusa (exits 3 & A5)

Once popular with the Tokyo literati, this smoky old place hasn't changed much since it was founded in 1880. The 1st floor is a beer hall where you pay for drinks as you enter. Its best-known offering is the brandy-based cocktail *denki-bran*. The restaurants upstairs serve Japanese and Western food, but that's not the reason to come here.

⭐ PLAY

ASAKUSA KANNON ONSEN
浅草観音温泉 *Hot spring*

☎ 3844 4141; 2-7-26 Asakusa, Taitō-ku; admission ¥700; ⏰ 6.30am-6pm Thu-Tue; Ⓣ Ginza & Toei Asakusa lines to Asakusa (exits 1 & A5)

Look for the ivy-covered exterior of this large, traditional bath-house. The water here is a steamy 40°C, and Asakusa's historic ambience makes this a great place for a soul-soothing soak.

⭐ JAKOTSU-YU 蛇骨湯
Hot spring

☎ 3841 8645; www.jakotsuyu.co.jp in Japanese; 1-11-11 Asakusa, Taitō-ku; admission ¥400; ⏰ 1pm-midnight Wed-Mon; Ⓣ Ginza line to Tawaramachi (exit 3)

Jakotsu-yu is a wonderful little neighbourhood *onsen* (hot spring) with mineral-rich dark

TATTOO BLUES

Long the mark of the *yakuza* (mafia), *irezumi* (tattoos) are still largely taboo in Japan. Although body art is becoming more popular with younger people, tattoos are still not as commonplace as in the West. If your skin bears a tattoo or a few, be discreet when visiting a *sentō* (public bath) or *onsen* (hot spring). They usually post signs prohibiting entry to tattooed individuals, ostensibly to keep out the *yakuza*. In reality, if the *yakuza* want in, they'll get in – and in all likelihood you won't be mistaken for one. Keep in mind, however, that your ink may get you ejected.

water at a hot-hot-hot 45°C. This *onsen* has a small *rotemburo* (outdoor bath) with a garden setting. From Kokusai-dōri, make a right into the second alley north of Kaminarimon-dōri, then slip into the first narrow alley on the right and you're there.

>IKEBUKURO

Ikebukuro's former claim to fame was having Japan's hugest department stores, Asia's tallest building and the world's longest escalator. While those days are well and truly behind it, Ikebukuro's very unpretentiousness gives it a humble appeal, and there are some fabulous places to take kids. East Ikebukuro has also become a haven for the quietly burgeoning fringe population of *otome* (literally 'maidens'; colloquially 'girl geeks'), the female counterparts of their more famous brethren, the *otaku* (colloquially 'geek boys'). Although these fangirls themselves are not as colourful as the *cosplay-zoku* (costume-play gangs), this fascinating subculture exemplifies Ikebukuro's less-obvious cultural appeal.

Most of the entertainment is on the east side, where the small alleys contain karaoke bars, *pachinko* (a type of pinball game) parlours, a few maid cafés and love hotels. Follow Sunshine 60-dōri to Sunshine City. On the west side, have a look at the folk arts on display at the Japan Traditional Crafts Center or grab some cheap eats at a local *kaiten-sushi* (conveyor-belt sushi bar) or *rāmen* (egg noodles) shop.

IKEBUKURO

A | B | C | D

1

Kita-ikebukuro 北池袋

0   200 m
0   0.1 miles

Shuto Expwy No 5

2

Ikebukuro 池袋

Gekijō-dōri

Kami-Ikebukuro 上池袋

Sakashita-dōri

Tokiwa-dōri

Bunka-dōri

13

Higashi-Ikebukuro 東池袋

Kasuga-dōri 春日通り

Meiji-dōri 明治通り

3

Azalea-dōri

12   Ikebukuro

3   Mitsukoshi

254

Nishi-Ikebukuro kōen 西池袋

9
10

Ikebukuro Nishi-guchi-kōen

Ikebukuro

Metropolitan Exit

M   Ikebukuro

6

Metropolitan-dōri メトロポリタン通り

5

Ikebukuro

Seibu

Green-dōri

8

7   11
World Import Mart Building

4

Nishi-Ikebukuro 西池袋

Minami-Ikebukuro kōen 南池袋公園

Shuto Expwy No 5 首都高速5号

Higashi-ikebukuro 東池袋

Minami-Ikebukuro 南池袋

305

Satomi Building

Toshima-ku 豊島区

Zōshigaya (Streetcar Stop)

5

Meiji-dōri 明治通り

Zōshigaya Rei-en (Zōshigaya Cemetery) 雑司ヶ谷公園

Mejiro

Kishibojin-mae (Streetcar Stop)

6

Shimo-ochiai 下落合

Mejiro-dōri 目白通り

Mejiro 白

Kishimonjinmae

NEIGHBOURHOODS

IKEBUKURO

👁 SEE

👁 SUNSHINE INTERNATIONAL AQUARIUM
サンシャイン国際水族館

☎ 3989 3466; 10F, World Import Mart Bldg, 3-1-3 Higashi-Ikebukuro, Toshima-ku; admission ¥1800/900; ⏱ 10am-6pm; 🚇 JR Yamanote line to Ikebukuro (east exit); ♿ 🚼

Boasting the distinction of being the highest aquarium in the world, this high-rise water world has tanks full of electric eels, sharks and other intriguing sea life. Also living here are some incongruous land-lubbin' critters as well, like lemurs. The building is full of stimulating stuff for kids, such as a planetarium, shopping mall and food-themed amusement park.

👁 SUNSHINE STARLIGHT DOME サンシャインスターライトドーム

☎ 3989 3475; 10F, World Import Mart Bldg, 3-1-3 Higashi-Ikebukuro, Toshima-ku; admission ¥800/500; ⏱ noon-5.30pm Mon-Fri, 11am-6.30pm Sat & Sun; 🚇 JR Yamanote line to Ikebukuro (east exit); ♿ 🚼

We may be in down-to-earth Ikebukuro but some of us are looking at the stars. Alas, the planetarium's show is narrated in Japanese, but the visuals are spectacular enough to lift you out of this earthly end of Tokyo.

👁 TOYOTA AMLUX トヨタアムラックス

☎ 5391 5900; www.amlux.jp/english /access; 3-3-5 Higashi-Ikebukuro,

You don't need a drivers' licence to get behind the wheel in the Toyota Amlux showroom

OTOME ROAD

'Maiden Road', as it's called, is like alternate-universe Akihabara for the *otome* (geek girls), the female equivalent of *otaku* (p123). Most *otome* – some of whom are actually grown women in their 40s – hang here at the local manga shops to browse 'boys' love' manga (exactly what it sounds like). They even have their own versions of role-play cafés featuring butlers instead of maids…with women in drag waiting tables as butlers.

Toshima-ku; admission free;
☺ 11am-7pm Tue-Sun; 🚉 JR Yamanote line to Ikebukuro (east exit); ♿ 🚻
Toyota's Auto Salon features concept cars and virtual-reality driving experiences, which are only two aspects of this fascinating showroom for the mechanically minded. It's a six-storey multimedia extravaganza, with short movies, aerodynamic architecture and visions of vehicular beauty everywhere. There's an English-language floor guide available.

🛍 SHOP

📷 BIC CAMERA
ビックカメラ
Cameras & electronics
☎ 5396 1111; 1-41-5 Higashi-Ikebukuro, Toshima-ku; ☺ 10am-9pm; 🚉 JR Yamanote line to Ikebukuro (east exit)
Bic Camera may or may not be, as it claims, the cheapest camera store in Japan, but its ubiquity cannot be contested. Bic has other branches in **Ikebukuro** (☎ 3590 1111; 1-11-7 Higashi-Ikebukuro, Toshima-ku; ☺ 10am-9pm; 🚉 JR Yamanote line to Ikebukuro (east exit)), as well as in Shibuya (p121) and Shinjuku (p92). Deals are very competitive, but as always, shop around.

📷 BIC CAMERA (PC STORE)
Cameras & electronics
☎ 5956 1111; 1-6-7 Higashi-Ikebukuro, Toshima-ku; ☺ 10am-9pm; 🚉 JR Yamanote line to Ikebukuro (east exit)
Another branch of Bic Camera specialising in PCs.

📷 JAPAN TRADITIONAL CRAFTS CENTER
全国伝統的工芸品
Handicrafts
☎ 5954 6066; www.kougei.or.jp/english /center.html; 1F & 2F, Metropolitan Plaza Bldg, 1-11-1 Nishi-Ikebukuro, Toshima-ku; ☺ 11am-7pm; 🚉 JR Yamanote line to Ikebukuro (Metropolitan exit)
Apart from being a wonderful place to find high-quality souvenirs such as weavings, regional ceramics, *washi* (handmade paper) and wood work, this centre is a destination in its own right as a showcase for traditional crafts from all over Japan. Temporary exhibitions, demonstrations and classes are held on the 2nd floor.

🏠 LOFT ロフト
Homewares & novelties

☎ 5949 3880; 1-28-1 Minami-Ikebukuro,Toshima-ku; ⏰ 10am-9pm Mon-Sat, 10am-8pm Sun; 🚃 JR Yamanote line to Ikebukuro (east exit)
Loft stocks all sorts of fun and sometimes functional homewares, stationery and gift items. It has another store located in Shibuya (p122).

🏠 SUNSHINE CITY サンシャインシティ
Department store

☎ 3989 3331; 3-1-1 Higashi-Ikebukuro, Toshima-ku; observation deck ¥620; ⏰ 10am-10pm; 🚃 JR Yamanote line to Ikebukuro (east exit)
Billed as a 'city in a building', Sunshine City is another sprawling shopping centre, where for a small fee you can get catapulted in a speeding elevator to peer out across the Tokyo skyline. If you're lucky, you might catch a glimpse of Mt Fuji beyond the haze.

🏠 TŌKYŪ HANDS 東急ハンズ
Homewares & novelties

☎ 3980 6111; 1-28-10 Higashi-Ikebukuro, Toshima-ku; ⏰ 10am-8pm; 🚃 JR Yamanote line to Ikebukuro (east exit)
Not only does this branch of Tōkyū Hands sell all the fabulous

booty for which it's famous, it also houses Nekobukuro (opposite). Other stores can be found in Shinjuku (p94) and Shibuya (p124).

🍴 EAT

AKIYOSHI 秋吉 *Yakitori* ¥¥

☎ 3982 0601; 3-30-4 Nishi-Ikebukuro, Toshima-ku; ⏰ 5-11pm; 🚃 JR Yamanote line to Ikebukuro (west exit); ♿
Akiyoshi is the establishment to try for tasty *yakitori* (skewers of grilled chicken) in approachable, noisy and laid-back surroundings. This *yakitori* specialist certainly knows its stuff, while the picture menu is also a boon for non-Japanese speakers.

🍴 MALAYCHAN マレーチャン *Malaysian* ¥

☎ 5391 7638; www.malaychan.jp/New Files/contents_E.html; 3-22-6 Nishi-Ikebukuro, Toshima-ku; ⏰ 5-11pm Mon, 11am-2.30pm & 5-11pm Tue-Sat, 11am-11pm Sun; 🚃 JR Yamanote line to Ikebukuro (west exit); ♿
With its great location on a corner across from Nishi-Ikebukuro Park, Malaychan is Ikebukuro's most pleasant place to eat. Its Malaysian cuisine is also a rarity in Tokyo, serving a tasty breadth of dishes representing the country's multi-ethnic background.

¶ NAMCO NAMJATOWN
ナムコナンジャタウン
Food-themed park   ¥

☎ 5950 0765; 2F & 3F, World Import Mart Bldg, 3-1-3 Higashi-Ikebukuro, Toshima-ku; admission ¥300/200; ⏰ 10am-10pm; 🚊 JR Yamanote line to Ikebukuro (east exit)

Namco Namjatown houses three food-themed parks, specialising variously in *gyōza* (dumplings), cream puffs and ice cream. Is your mouth watering yet? Maybe it's just us. Admission fees only get you in; you pay for any goodies you eat.

Y DRINK

Y SASASHŪ 笹周 *Izakaya*
☎ 3971 6796; 2-2-6; Ikebukuro, Toshima-ku; ⏰ 5-10pm Mon-Sat; Ⓜ Marunouchi line to Ikebukuro (exit C5); ♿

Serving delicacies such as *ka-monabe* (duck stew), Sasashū is a highly respected sake specialist maintaining a dignified old façade amid west Ikebukuro's strip joints. If you lack Japanese language ability, trust the master to guide your culinary experience by asking for *omakase* (chef's choice).

Y TONERIAN 舎人庵 *Izakaya*
☎ 3985 0254; 1-38-9 Nishi-Ikebukuro, Toshima-ku; ⏰ 5-11.15pm; Ⓜ Marunouchi & Yūrakuchō lines to Ikebukuro (exit 12)

DRINKING ETIQUETTE
When you're out for a few drinks, remember that you're expected to keep the drinks of your companions topped up. But don't fill your own glass, as this implies your guests aren't taking care of you; wait for someone to pour yours. It's polite to hold the glass with both hands while it's being filled. And most importantly, remember to say, *'Kampai!'* – cheers!

One of Ikebukuro's many *izakaya* (pub/eateries), this is a busy place with friendly staff. Turn up here to learn about good *jizake* (regional sake) from the master, who speaks English. He'll be glad to make recommendations on what to eat and drink. Look for all the empty sake bottles piled up outside.

★ PLAY

★ NEKOBUKURO
ねこぶくろ *Petting zoo*
☎ 3980 6111; 8F, Tōkyū Hands, 1-28-10 Higashi-Ikebukuro, Toshima-ku; admission ¥600; ⏰ 10am-8pm; 🚊 JR Yamanote line to Ikebukuro (east exit)

For Tokyoites who may not have the time or space to keep their own pets, Nekobukuro provides a venue for short-term cuddling with surrogate cats. Creep up to the 8th floor of the Ikebukuro branch of Tōkyū Hands (p94) to get in on the kitten action.

>SHINJUKU

Shinjuku immediately immerses you into the sheer scale and manic energy of Tokyo, and thus makes the perfect introduction to the city. Shinjuku Station is Tokyo's largest hub, serving several major rail lines with an average of 3.5 million commuters each day. Getting from A to B within the station can be akin to negotiating the levels of a chaotic videogame you've never played before – keep your eyes on the signs and you'll get where you need to go.

Above the station are the requisite gigantic department stores owned by big rail lines such as Odakyū and Keiō, and the Takashimaya Times Square complex to the south. Based in Nishi-Shinjuku (the west side) are the Tokyo Metropolitan Government Offices and a spate of luxury hotels catering to business folk, while Shinjuku's east side shows off a seedier angle in Tokyo's red light district. The most well-known landmark on the east side is the Studio Alta building, an easy target for a meet-up in this lively quarter that many would consider downtown Tokyo.

SHINJUKU

👁 SEE
Hanazono-jinja 1 C3
Kabukichō 2 C2
Shinjuku-gyōen 3 D4
Tokyo Metropolitan
Government Offices......4 A3

🛍 SHOP
Beams...........................5 C3
Bic Camera....................6 B3
Disk Union.....................7 C3
Don Quijote...................8 C3
Isetan............................9 C3
Journal Standard.........10 C4
Kinokuniya 11 C3
Kinokuniya 12 C4
Marui Young................13 C3
Odakyū........................14 B3

Sakuraya Camera 15 B4
Sekaido........................16 D4
Tōkyū Hands................17 C4
Yodobashi Camera 18 B4

🍴 EAT
Daidaiya 19 C3
Ibuki 20 C3
Keika Kumamoto
Rāmen 21 D3
Kinkantei 22 D3
New York Grill 23 A4
Tokyo Dai Hanten 24 C3
Tsunahachi 25 C3

🍸 DRINK
Advocates Bar 26 D3
Arch 27 D3

Arty Farty 28 D3
Bar Plastic Model 29 C3
Bon's 30 C3
Kinswomyn 31 D3
La Jetée 32 C3
New York Bar............. (see 23)

⭐ PLAY
Finlando Sauna 33 C2
Green Plaza Ladies
Sauna 34 C2
Loft..............................35 C2
National Nō Theatre
(Kokuritsu Nō-
Gakudō).....................36 D6
Shinjuku Pit Inn...........37 D3

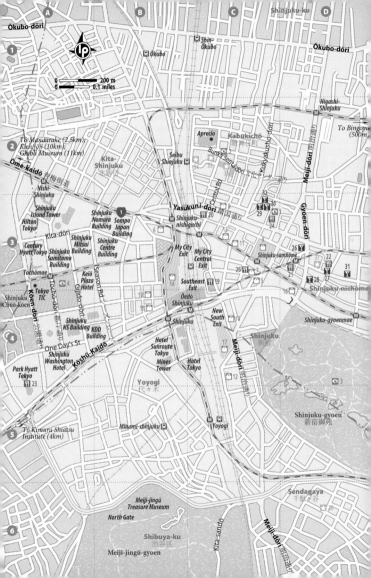

👁 SEE

📷 HANAZONO-JINJA
花園神社

☎ 3200 3093; 5-17-3 Shinjuku, Shinjuku-ku; admission free; 🕐 dawn-dusk; 🚇 Marunouchi & Toei Shinjuku lines to Shinjuku-sanchōme (exits B3 & B5)
Nestled in ultra-urban, high-rise Shinjuku is this quiet, unassuming shrine. Hanazono-jinja is particularly pleasant when it's lit up in the evening, but it also makes for a quick escape from the Kabukichō seediness. Sundays bring a flea market (open 8am to 4pm) to the shrine grounds, a good place to hunt for various vintage wares.

📷 KABUKICHŌ 歌舞伎町
🚃 JR Yamanote line to Shinjuku (east exit)
Kabukichō is Tokyo's red-light district, and it wears its gaudy neon bling on its sleeve. It's home to 'date clubs' and Soaplands ('massage' parlours) that the authorities are attempting to clean up, and *Yakuza* (mafia) and wannabes do maintain a visible presence in the area. However, while Japanese people may warn you that it's a dangerous neighbourhood, never fear, taking the usual precautions after dark should suffice.

Beyond the golden sign, Tokyo's red-light district, Kabukichō, beckons with bright lights and bling

WORTH THE TRIP

If you plan on visiting *anime* master Hayao Miyazaki's wondrous, imaginative **Ghibli Museum** (☎ 057-0000 777; www.ghibli-museum.jp/ticket/overseas.html; 1-1-83 Shimo-Renjaku, Mitaka-shi; adult ¥1000, child ¥100-700; 🕙 10am-6pm Wed-Mon; 🚉 JR Chūō line to Mi-taka, south exit), you *must* procure a reservation in advance of your trip (see the website for detailed information). Admittance is limited to provide the best, uncrowded experience for all visitors, and tickets can be purchased up to three months before you wish to go. While the mu-seum is geared towards children, anyone who fell in love with a Miyazaki film will be charmed. Each ticket even contains an original animation cell from a Studio Ghibli film.

There's a cute shuttle bus (one-way ¥300/150) from Mitaka Station to the museum if you'd prefer not to walk. But it's a flat 15-minute walk from Mitaka, or a pleasant 20-minute walk from Inokashira Park (p92) in Kichijōji.

🇬 SHINJUKU-GYŌEN
新宿御苑

☎ 3350 0151; www.shinjukugyoen.go.jp /english/english-index.html; 11 Naitochō, Shinjuku-ku; admission ¥200/50/free; 🕙 9am-4.30pm Tue-Sun; 🚉 Marunouchi line to Shinjuku-gyōenmae (exit 1)

Dating back to 1906, this down-town park provides the perfect escape from winter cold, as it boasts a hothouse full of exotic tropical plants, allegedly even including peyote! There's also a French garden and a pond full of giant carp. Keep this park in mind when you're exhausted by all that busy Shinjuku has to offer.

🇬 TOKYO METROPOLITAN GOVERNMENT OFFICES
東京都庁

☎ 5321 1111; 2-8-1 Nishi-Shinjuku, Shinjuku-ku; admission free; 🕙 observatories 9.30am-11pm, north

tower closed 2nd & 4th Mon, south tower closed 1st & 3rd Tue; 🚉 Toei Ōedo line to Tochōmae (exits A3 & A4); 🚹

Known as Tokyo Tochō, these colossal towers designed by Kenzō Tange comprise Tokyo's

AWESOME BLOSSOMS

Around April *sakura* (cherry blossom) fever grips the country with the pink-petalled flower emblazoning every sur-face that can be decorated: umbrellas, sake cups, hair accessories. The whole of Japan excitedly waits for the first buds to appear on cherry trees, and *hanami* (cherry-blossom viewing) parties pop up day and night to celebrate the flowers during their week-long flow-ering season. There's plenty of sake, singing and dancing at popular *hanami* spots, where the best sites are often taken by people who've camped out overnight for them. Good *hanami* spots include the Imperial Palace East Garden (p48) and Shinjuku-gyōen (left).

WORTH THE TRIP

On the western edge of Tokyo's 23 wards, **Kichijōji** is a short train ride from Shinjuku or Shibuya and makes an easy getaway for those suffering from urban overload. Kichijōji is one of Tokyo's most desirable neighbourhoods, with its university-town feel, understated hipness factor and high quality of living. Take a walk in the park, browse a few boutiques and finish off with a cocktail in one of the cool little local bars.

The centrepiece of Kichijōji is **Inokashira Park** (☎ 042-247 6900; Inokashira, Mitaka-shi; boat rentals ¥200; 🕙 24hr; 🚇 JR Chūō & Sōbu lines to Kichijōji, Park exit; 🚇 Keiō Inokashira line to Kichijōji, Park exit). The park is at its lively but low-key best on the weekends, when artists and musicians come out to play. Stroll the shaded edge of the small lake, visit the temple to Benzaiten (goddess of love and the arts), rent a paddle-boat and feel the urban tension melt away. However, cherry-blossom season is the exception to the peaceful rule.

From Kichijōji Station, take the park exit and look for the Marui department store. Walk down the road to the right of the building, which will lead you down the gentle slope to the park. Take your time on the way down, and poke around the cafés, bohemian-style shops and ethnic restaurants lining the road.

If you have arranged an appointment at the Ghibli Museum (p91), an alternative way to get there is walking through the park from Kichijōji. Allow at least 20 minutes for the walk.

---

bureaucratic heartland. From the amphitheatrelike Citizen's Plaza below, check out the architecture and complex symmetry of the towers. Then whiz up to the twin observation decks, over 200m above urban Shinjuku, for a look at Tokyo below.

🛍 SHOP
🛍 BEAMS *Fashion*
☎ 5368 7300; www.beams.co.jp; 3-32-6 Shinjuku, Shinjuku-ku; 🕙 11am-8pm; 🚇 JR Yamanote line to Shinjuku (south exit)

The Beams chain has spread across Japan and over to Hong Kong, but all the best of Beams – from basic to superstylish men's and women's clothes, accessories, cool housewares and a gallery – has been concentrated into the seven floors of this Shinjuku shop.

🛍 BIC CAMERA
Cameras & electronics
☎ 5326-1111; 1-5-1 Nishi-Shinjuku, Shinjuku-ku; 🕙 10am-9pm; 🚇 JR Yamanote line to Shinjuku (west exit)

One of the many branches of this cheap camera store. Other outlets are located in Ikebukuro (p85) and Shibuya (p121).

🔲 DISK UNION
ディスクユニオン *Music*
☎ 3352-2691; http://diskunion.net in Japanese; 3-31-4 Shinjuku, Shinjuku-ku; ⏰ 11am-9pm Mon-Sat, 11am-8pm Sun; 🚇 JR Yamanote line (east exit)
This seven-storey branch has an excellent selection of CDs, both new and used. It has another branch on Shibuya (p122).

🔲 DON QUIJOTE
ドンキホーテ
Homewares & novelties
☎ 5291 9211; www.donki.com; 1-16-5 Kabukichō, Shinjuku-ku; ⏰ 24hr; 🚇 JR Yamanote line to Shinjuku (east exit)
Meet Don Quijote, Tōkyū Hands' trashy cousin. In Kabukichō, the fluorescent-lit corner shop is filled to the brink with weird loot. Chaotic piles of knockoff electronics and designer goods sit alongside sex toys, fetish costumes and packaged foods. They have quite a presence in Tokyo, though not all shops are open 24 hours.

🔲 ISETAN 伊勢丹
Department store
☎ 3352 1111; 3-14-1 Shinjuku, Shinjuku-ku; ⏰ 10am-8pm 🚇 Marunouchi & Toei Shinjuku lines to Shinjuku-sanchōme (exit A1)
In addition to having a stunning food basement, Isetan offers a free service called I-club, match-ing English-speaking staff to visiting shoppers; the membership desk is on the 7th floor of the Isetan annexe building. While you're there take a peek at the current exhibition in the 5th-floor art gallery.

🔲 JOURNAL STANDARD
Fashion
☎ 5367 0175; http://journal-standard.baycrews.co.jp; 4-1-7 Shinjuku, Shinjuku-ku; ⏰ 11am-8pm 🚇 JR Yamanote line to Shinjuku (south exit)
Browsing the corners and surfaces of this hip shop turn up all sorts of items to add style to your wardrobe. Collections here are smart but bohemian, and sizes tend toward the Japanese figure (ie, small). This is also a great place to end a shopping spree, as there's a lovely rooftop café on the 3rd floor.

🔲 KINOKUNIYA
紀伊國屋書店 *Books*
☎ 5361 3301; Annexe Bldg, Takashimaya Times Square, 5-24-5 Sendagaya, Shibuya-ku; ⏰ 10am-8pm Sun-Fri, 10am-8.30pm Sat; 🚇 JR Yamanote line to Shinjuku (new south exit)
Kinokuniya's large annexe store in the Takashimaya Times Square complex surpasses the main **Shinjuku store** (☎ 3354 0131; 3-17-7 Shinjuku, Shinjuku-ku; ⏰ 10am-9pm; 🚇 JR Yamanote line to Shinjuku (east exit)),

with its variety and depth of titles in English. Find foreign-language books on the 6th floor, and a rainy day's worth of art books, magazines and manga everywhere else.

🏬 MARUI YOUNG
マルイヤング
Department store
☎ 3354 0101; 3-18-1 Shinjuku, Shinjuku-ku; ⏱ 11am-9pm; 🚉 JR Yamanote line to Shinjuku (east exit)
You can't swing a coat hanger in Shinjuku without hitting a Marui (look for the Marui logo: OIOI), as there's a large contingent of its speciality branches here. Marui Young is the place to begin shopping if you want to buy Goth-Lolita garb with the local whitest-shade-of-pale girls.

🏬 ODAKYŪ 小田急百貨店
Department store
☎ 3342 1111; 1-1-3 Nishi-Shinjuku, Shinjuku-ku; ⏱ shops 10am-8pm, restaurants 11am-10pm; 🚉 JR Yamanote line to Shinjuku
The 16-floor behemoth of a department store that sits atop Shinjuku Station, Odakyū contains several restaurant floors, high-end boutiques and low-budget accessories shops, as well as just about anything you'd need to live inside the station for the next 10 years.

🏬 SAKURAYA CAMERA
さくらやカメラ
Cameras & electronics
☎ 3346 3939; 1-16-4 Nishi-Shinjuku, Shinjuku-ku; ⏱ 10am-8.30pm; 🚉 JR Yamanote line to Shinjuku (west exit)
One of the big three camera emporiums, Yodobashi Camera offers many of the same inventory as the others, at similar prices. It has an incredible selection of long lenses and tiny digital cameras. You'll find some great deals here but like anywhere, comparison shopping is essential.

🏬 SEKAIDO 世界堂
Stationery
☎ 5379 1111; 3-1-1 Shinjuku, Shinjuku-ku; ⏱ 9.30am-9pm; Ⓜ Marunouchi & Toei Shinjuku lines to Shinjuku-sanchōme (exit C1)
Art supply junkies should only visit Sekaido on a preset budget, as they're otherwise doomed to blow a fortune on the blindingly broad array of art supplies, exquisite *washi* (handmade paper) and vast selection of manga.

🏬 TŌKYŪ HANDS
東急ハンズ
Homewares & novelties
☎ 5361 3111; Takashimaya Times Square, 5-24-2 Sendagaya, Shibuya-ku; ⏱ 10am-8.30pm; 🚉 JR Yamanote line to Shinjuku (new south exit)
Ostensibly a do-it-yourself store, Tōkyū Hands carries a compre-

WORTH THE TRIP

Psst – wanna score some high-quality handicrafts? **Bingoya** (☎ 3202 8778; www.quasar.nu/bingoya; 10-6 Waka-matsuchō, Shinjuku-ku; 🕙 10am-7pm Tue-Sun; 🚇 Toei Ōedo line to Waka-matsu-Kawada) may be just the ticket. It's only a couple of stops from Shinjuku to the sweet, unassuming neighbour-hood of Wakamatsuchō. Just a short stroll from the station (turn right from either exit), this friendly shop stocks regional ceramics, vibrant batik textiles, richly dyed *washi* (handmade paper), handmade glassware and *tatami* (woven-floor mats) in five compact floors. They also accept credit cards.

hensive collection of everything you didn't know you needed, from blown-glass pens to chainsaws, tofu tongs to party supplies. The Takashimaya Times Square branch is probably the least maddening to shop in, but there are others in Shibuya (p124) and Ikebukuro (p86).

📷 YODOBASHI CAMERA
ヨドバシカメラ
Cameras & electronics
☎ 3346 1010; 1-11-1 Nishi-Shinjuku, Shinjuku-ku; 🕙 9.30am-9.30pm; 🚇 Toei Shinjuku line to Shinjuku (exit 5), 🚉 JR Yamanote line to Shinjuku (west exit)
Yodobashi is Sakuraya's larg-est competitor and sits directly

across the street. This store stocks anything from digital camcorders to second-hand enlargers. Prices at Yodobashi are very competi-tive, and if you can't dig it up here then it probably can't be found in Japan.

🍴 EAT
Although it's rumoured to be razed in 2008, Omoide-yokochō (Memory Lane, or 'Piss Alley', as it's less politely known) might still be standing when you visit. Alongside the tracks just outside the west exit of Shinjuku station, this alley is lined with small stalls and rickety eateries. Round about evening rush hour, salarymen and labourers alike spill into these shops specialising variously in *rāmen*, *yakitori* or *nabe* to have a bite before braving their full-to-bursting trains home. It's a nostalgic taste of Occupation-era atmosphere – and it really isn't as pungent as its nickname might suggest.

🍴 DAIDAIYA 橙家
Asian fusion　　　　　　　¥¥
☎ 5362 7173; 3F, Shinjuku Nowa Bldg, 3-37-12 Shinjuku, Shinjuku-ku; 🕙 5pm-1am; 🚉 JR Yamanote line to Shinjuku (My City exit)
The happy fusion of neon with tatami in Daidaiya's décor paral-lels its deft commingling of both

modern international cuisine with traditional Japanese dishes. The prix-fixe meals are a better deal than ordering à la carte, although if you're tempted to order wine (just give in), the point is moot.

🍴 **IBUKI** 伊吹
Sukiyaki & shabu-shabu ¥¥
☎ 3352 4787; 3-23-6 Shinjuku, Shinjuku-ku; ⏰ 5pm-11.30pm; 🚆 JR Yamanote line to Shinjuku (east exit) 🚇 Marunouchi line to Shinjuku (Kabukichō exit); ♿ ♨
Ibuki is an excellent initiation into the pleasures of cooking your own sukiyaki (thinly sliced beef, vegetables and tofu cooked in broth at your table) and *shabu-shabu* (thinly sliced beef and vegetables cooked in broth and dipped in vinegar and citrus sauces). As they're accustomed to foreign visitors, they accept credit cards, have an English menu and host guests in a friendly and traditional atmosphere.

🍴 **KEIKA KUMAMOTO RĀMEN**
桂花熊本ラーメン
Rāmen ¥
☎ 3354 4591; 3-7-2 Shinjuku, Shinjuku-ku; ⏰ 11am-11pm; 🚇 Marunouchi & Toei Shinjuku lines to Shinjuku-sanchōme (exit C4); ♿ ♨
The Kyūshū-style *tonkotsu rāmen* (pork-broth-based noodles), is worth queuing for at this nation-

ally famous *rāmen* shop. You order and pay as you enter; try the *chāshū-men* (*rāmen* with sliced pork). There's no English sign, so look for the large, multicoloured cartoon mural of a chef and pigs on its exterior.

🍴 **KINKANTEI** きんかんてい
Soba ¥
☎ 3356 6556; 2-17-1 Shinjuku, Shinjuku-ku; ⏰ 7pm-4am Mon-Sat; 🚇 Marunouchi & Toei Shinjuku lines to Shinjuku-sanchōme (exit C7); Ⓥ ♨
Hemmed in by sex shops and serving the nocturnal life of Shinjuku-sanchōme, Kinkantei has been serving *soba* for over two centuries. There's always *zaru soba*, but adventurous eaters can try the deep-fried *nattō* (fermented soybeans). From the station, turn right at the first alley, continue to its end, turn right again and look for the green sign.

🍴 **NEW YORK GRILL**
ニュヨークグリル
American ¥¥¥
☎ 5323 3458; 52F, Park Hyatt Tokyo, 3-7-1-2 Nishi-Shinjuku, Shinjuku-ku; ⏰ 11.30am-midnight; 🚇 Toei Ōedo line to Tochōmae (exit A4); ♿ Ⓥ ♨
The drop-dead delicious view notwithstanding, this sky-high spot continues to earn its reputation as one of Tokyo's top restaurants with its slabs of steak and racks of

lamb. A treat worth waking for is the Sunday brunch (¥5800; open 11.30am to 2.30pm Sun), which includes a glass of champagne. On the first floor, the New York Deli is lovely for a more casual lunch, with a delectable selection of fine cheeses, olives and cured meats.

🍴 TOKYO DAI HANTEN
東京大飯店 *Yum cha*   ¥

☎ 3202 0121 4F, Oriental Wave Bldg, 5-17-13 Shinjuku, Shinjuku-ku; 🕙 11.30am-10pm; ⊕ Marunouchi & Toei Shinjuku lines to Shinjuku-sanchōme (exits B3 & C6)

Established in 1960, Tokyo Dai Hanten is one of your few possibilities for *yum cha* (dim sum) and the place of choice for Hong Kong expats. Especially brisk and fresh are weekend brunches, served in the customary manner, with *yum cha* rolling by on trolleys for you to flag down at will.

🍴 TSUNAHACHI つな八
Tempura   ¥¥

☎ 3352 1012; 3-31-8 Shinjuku, Shinjuku-ku; 🕙 11am-10pm; 🚃 JR Yamanote line to Shinjuku (east exit); ♿ ♨

Sit at the counter for the pleasure of watching the efficient chefs fry each perfect tempura and plate them one by one. From Shinjuku-dōri as you face Mitsukoshi depart-

ment store, go down the small street to its left; Tsunahachi will be on your left. There's another, airier branch on the 13th floor at Takashimaya Times Square.

🍸 DRINK

You won't find another low-lying cluster of bars like the Golden Gai elsewhere in Tokyo; the atmosphere of each reveals something of its proprietor's personality, with some only small enough to accommodate a few patrons at a time. Note that some bars will only serve regular customers, but those we've listed welcome strangers.

Nearby, the Shinjuku-nichōme (known simply as Nichōme) neighbourhood has a thriving gay and lesbian scene, with gay bars filling out the nooks of these alleys. Keep your eyes peeled for signs in the windows; the bars around here are jammed in everywhere.

🍸 ADVOCATES BAR
Gay & lesbian bar

☎ 3358 3988; 1F, Dai-7 Tenka Bldg, 2-18-1 Shinjuku, Shinjuku-ku; 🕙 6pm-5am Mon-Sat, 6pm-1am Sun; ⊕ Toei Shinjuku line to Shinjuku-sanchōme (exit C8)

Advocates Bar is just that – a bar, and a small one. As the crowd gets bigger over the course of

Start your night at Advocates Bar and watch the crowds multiply and the drinks flow

the evening, it overflows onto the street and becomes more like a block party. The staff here speak English, and it's another good venue to start off a night in Nichōme.

☎ ARCH *Gay & lesbian bar*
☎ 3352 6297; www.clubarch.net; B1F, Dai-2 Hayakawaya Bldg, 2-14-6 Shinjuku, Shinjuku-ku; cover varies; ⏱ 8pm-4am; ⊕ Toei Shinjuku line to Shinjuku-sanchōme (exits C7 & C8)
At this fun club, you can relax with a mixed crowd, groove to what the DJ's spinning or cheer on the campy drag queens. Some nights are men- or women-only, so check the website before heading out.

☎ ARTY FARTY
アーティファーティ
Gay & lesbian bar
☎ 5362 9720; www.arty-farty.net; 2F, 2-11-7 Shinjuku, Shinjuku-ku; ⏱ 5pm-5am Mon-Sat, 4pm-5am Sun; ⊕ Toei Shinjuku line to Shinjuku-sanchōme (exits C5 & C8)
Arty Farty is another stalwart of the queer scene, and has good all-you-can-drink specials. There's a reason it has been around for so long and it's a tried-and-true (although often incredibly crowded) place to start your evening and get the lowdown on what else is happening in the neighbourhood.

▼ BAR PLASTIC MODEL
バープラスチックモデル
Bar
☎ 5273 8441; www.plastic-model.net in Japanese; 1-1-10 Kabukichō, Shinjuku-ku; cover ¥700; 🕓 8pm-5am Mon-Sat, 8pm-2am Sun; Ⓜ Marunouchi line to Shinjuku-sanchōme (exit B5)
This is one of the new incarnations of Golden Gai bars, run by the next generation of bar owners. Decorated with tchotchkes c 1980, there's sometimes a DJ here spinning beats.

▼ BON'S ボンズ *Bar*
☎ 3209 6334; 1-1-10 Kabukichō, Shinjuku-ku; cover ¥900; 🕓 7pm-5am; Ⓜ Marunouchi line to Shinjuku-sanchōme (exit B5)
Drinks start at ¥700 at this sure-fire spot in the Golden Gai. Look for its corner location with 'Old Fashioned American Style Pub' painted across its exterior wall.

▼ KINSWOMYN
キンズウミン
Gay & lesbian bar
☎ 3354 8720; 3F, Daiichi Tenka Bldg, 2-15-10 Shinjuku, Shinjuku-ku; cocktails ¥750; 🕓 7pm-4am Wed-Mon; Ⓜ Toei Shinjuku line to Shinjuku-sanchōme (exit C8)
Counterbalancing some of the more male-dominated gay bars in the neighbourhood, Kinswomyn is a popular and welcoming lesbian bar run by well-known activist Tara. It's perfect for visitors as English is spoken, and it's a comfortable environment for Japanese and foreign women alike.

▼ LA JETÉE ラジェッテイ
Bar
☎ 3208 9645; 1-1-8 Kabukichō, Shinjuku-ku; cover ¥700; 🕓 7pm till late Mon-Sat; Ⓜ Marunouchi line to Shinjuku-sanchōme (exit B5)
A favourite in the Golden Gai, Le Jetée is run by a French-speaking cinema buff and was given the named of a classic film. It's a good introduction to the singular culture of these alleys.

▼ NEW YORK BAR
ニューヨークバー *Bar*
☎ 5323 3458; www.parkhyatttokyo.com; 3-7-1-2 Nishi-Shinjuku, Shinjuku-ku; cover after 8pm ¥2000; 🕓 5pm-midnight Sun-Wed, 5pm-1am Thu-Sat; Ⓜ Toei Ōedo line to Tochōmae (exit A4)
Located in the stratosphere, both physically and socially, the New York Bar towers over the city on the 52nd floor of the Park Hyatt Tokyo in west Shinjuku. With magnificent views, strong drinks and live jazz, this is a swank lounge for that special date.

⭐ PLAY

⭐ FINLANDO SAUNA フィンランドサウナ
Public bath

☎ 3209 9196; B1F, Humax Pavilion, 1-20-1 Kabukichō, Shinjuku-ku; admission noon-5pm ¥1900, 5pm-midnight ¥2100, midnight-noon ¥2600; 🕐 24hr; 🚇 JR Yamanote line to Shinjuku (east exit)

This is a huge 24-hour complex of baths and steam rooms right in the middle of Kabukichō sleaze. This is a good place – for men only – to escape the madness of the streets outside, or to spend the night if you've missed your train.

MANGA KISSA

Kissaten (coffee shops) have long been mainstays for socialising away from home, but the next-generation versions are serious escape hatches. *Manga kissa* (comic-book cafés) are a great place to get inexpensive internet access in a comfy private cubicle. You can also browse their manga library, get a bite to eat, watch DVDs or catch some Z's. *Manga kissa* are open 24 hours per day, and you can prepay for as little as 30 minutes or, if you get caught out after midnight when the trains stop running, overnight. Rates are typically around ¥2500 for eight hours. See p198 for listings.

⭐ GREEN PLAZA LADIES SAUNA グリーンプラザレ ディズサウナ *Public bath*

3207 5411; 9F, 1-29-2 Kabuki-chō, Shinjuku-ku; admission 6am-10pm ¥2700, 10pm-6am ¥3300; 🕐 24hr;
🚇 JR Yamanote line to Shinjuku (east exit)

Women also have a place to wash and crash in Kabukichō. This central, 24-hour *sentō* (public bath) and spa for women is a calming refuge, where you can get a massage after you bathe, have a tasty bite to eat, and then blissfully snooze away until the morning trains begin running. Best of all, there's also a rooftop *rotemburo* (outdoor bath).

⭐ LOFT ロフト *Live music*

☎ 5272 0382; www.loft-prj.co.jp/LOFT /index.html; B2F, Tatehana Bldg, 1-12-9 Kabukichō, Shinjuku-ku; from ¥1000; 🕐 5pm-late; 🚇 JR Yamanote line to Shinjuku (east exit)

This loud and smoky Shinjuku institution is a blast on a good night. Although it's a typically small venue, it draws both local and international acts ranging from punk to emo.

NEIGHBOURHOODS

SHINJUKU

SENTŌ PRIMER

First you'll pay the *sentō* (public bath) fee to an attendant at the front desk, then head into the men's or women's changing room. In the changing room, place your clothes in one of the lockers and your toiletries in a *senmenki* (wash basin), and head into the bath area.

Before stepping into the bath, you'll need to wash at the banks of low showers and water spigots that line the walls. Grab a low stool and scrub thoroughly, making sure you remove all traces of soap so as not to cloud the water. Circulate between the hot tubs, cold pool, sauna and electric bath (which supposedly simulates the sensation of swimming with electric eels). If you soak everything just right, you'll float out in the desired state of *yude-dako* ('boiled octopus').

⭐ NATIONAL NŌ THEATRE
国立能楽堂 *Theatre*

☎ 3423 1331; 4-18-1 Sendagaya, Shibuya-ku; tickets ¥2800-5600; ⏱ reservations 10am-6pm; 🚇 Chūō & Sōbu lines to Sendagaya (west exit)

The National Nō Theatre stages its own *nō* (classical Japanese musical dramas) performances on weekends only, for which it provides printed English synopses, but it also hosts privately-sponsored performances. Exit Sendagaya Station in the direction of Shinjuku on the left and follow the road that hugs the railway tracks; the theatre will be on the left.

⭐ SHINJUKU PIT INN
新宿ピットイン *Live music*

☎ 3354 2024; www.pit-inn.com/index _e.html; B1F, Accord Bldg, 2-12-14 Shinjuku, Shinjuku-ku; cover ¥1300-4000; ⏱ performances 2.30pm & 8pm; 🚇 Toei Shinjuku line to Shinjuku-sanchōme (exits C5 & C8)

Shinjuku Pit Inn is one of the more well-established jazz clubs in Tokyo, showcasing the talents of both foreign and local jazz musicians. The jazz could be generally categorised as classically mainstream. Phone ahead for reservations. The cover includes one drink.

>HARAJUKU & AOYAMA

Travelling from Harajuku to Aoyama takes you from pop culture consumption to upscale, grown-up refinement. From the Harajuku JR station, take the Takeshita exit to Takeshita-dōri, a treasure trove of teenybopper accessories and hair salons that can kink strait-laced hair into dreads and 'fros. Or exit to Omote-sandō, the boulevard lined with branches of Chanel, Prada and Tokyo's favourite: Louis Vuitton. You'll also come across the slanted walkways of the neighbourhood's newest shopping centre, Omotesandō Hills.

On either side of Omote-sandō, Ura-Hara (a nickname for the back alleys of Harajuku) hides tiny European-style cafés, innovative art galleries, restaurants and boutiques catering both to youth and moneyed sophisticates. The further southeast you travel down Omote-sandō, the closer you'll get to Aoyama, a fashionable neighbourhood where several home-grown designers have chosen to base their flagships. And if your credit card has rolled over and is playing dead, you can at least window-shop and watch the live fashion walking the streets.

HARAJUKU & AOYAMA

👁 SEE
Jingū-gaien	1	G2
Laforet Museum Harajuku	(see 19)	
Meiji-jingū	2	C2
Ōta Memorial Art Museum	3	D4
Prada Aoyama	4	F5
Spiral Building	5	E5
Tōgō-jinja	6	D3
Watari Museum of Contemporary Art	7	F3
Yoyogi-kōen	8	B4

🏠 SHOP
Atelier Magic Theater	9	E4
Bapexclusive	10	F5
Book Off	(see 19)	
Commes des Garçons	11	F5
Condomania	12	D4
Daiso	13	D3

Fuji-Torii	(see 18)	
Hanae Mori Building	14	E5
Hysteric Glamour	15	C5
Issey Miyake	16	F5
Kasūkōbō	17	D4
Kiddyland	18	D4
Laforet	19	D4
On Sundays	(see 6)	
Oriental Bazaar	20	E4
Tsumori Chisato	21	F6
Undercover	22	F6
Yohji Yamanoto	23	F6

🍴 EAT
Fonda de la Madrugada	24	E3
Fujimamas	25	D4
Hiroba	26	E5
Kinokuniya (Interim Store)	27	F5
Las Chicas	28	E5

Le Bretagne	29	E4
Maisen	30	E4
Mominoki House	31	E3
Natural Harmony Angolo	32	F3
Ume-no-hana	33	F4

🍸 DRINK
Den Aquaroom	34	F6
Tokyo Apartment Café	(see 19)	

⭐ PLAY
Crocodile	35	C5
Jingū Stadium	36	G2
National Stadium	37	F1
Tokyo Metropolitan Gymnasium	38	F1

Please see over for map

🔘 SEE

🔘 JINGŪ-GAIEN

☎ 3401 0312; Kasumigaokamachi, Shibuya-ku; ⏰ 24 hr; 🚇 Chūō line to Shinanomachi, 🚇 Ginza line to Gaien-mae (exit 1)

The grounds of Jingū-gaien, the Meiji-jingū Outer Gardens, house both the Jingū Baseball Stadium and the National Stadium. But the grounds themselves make a great place for a run or walk in autumn, when the gingko trees lining the main promenade Icho-Namiki-dōri turn bright yellow.

🔘 LAFORET MUSEUM HARAJUKU ラフォーレミュージアム原宿

☎ 3475 3127; www.lapnet.jp/index .html in Japanese; 6F, Laforet Bldg, 1-11-6 Jingūmae, Shibuya-ku; admission varies; ⏰ 11am-8pm; 🚇 JR Yamanote line to Harajuku (Omote-sandō exit), 🚇 Chiyoda line to Meiji-jingūmae (exit 5); ♿

This museum, on the 6th floor of the teenybopper fashionista Mecca that is Laforet department store, is gallery or performance space depending on the event. Small film festivals, art installations and launch parties are held here regularly – after browsing the art-as-streetwear on the floors below, check out art-as-art upstairs.

🔘 MEIJI-JINGŪ 明治神宮

☎ 3379 5511; www.meijijingu.or.jp; 1-1 Yoyogi Kamizonochō, Shibuya-ku; admission free; ⏰ dawn-dusk; 🚇 JR Yamanote line to Harajuku (Omote-sandō exit)

In the grounds of Meiji-jingū, **Meiji-jingū-gyoen** (admission ¥500/200; ⏰ 9am-4.30pm), is a beautiful garden created by Emperor Meiji as a gift to the Empress Shōken. There's also a **Treasure Museum** (admission ¥300; ⏰ 9am-4pm Sat, Sun & public holidays) on the grounds, displaying some imperial artefacts, such as ceremonial clothing worn by the emperor and empress.

🔘 ŌTA MEMORIAL ART MUSEUM 太田記念美術館

☎ 3403 0880; www.ukiyoe-ota-muse.jp /english.html; 1-10-10 Jingūmae, Shibuya-ku; admission ¥1000/700 ⏰ 10.30am-5.30pm Tue-Sun, closed from 27th to end of each month; 🚇 JR Yamanote line to Harajuku (Omote-sandō exit), 🚇 Chiyoda line to Meiji-jingūmae (exit 5)

Leave your shoes in the foyer and pad in slippers through this museum to view its stellar collection of *ukiyo-e* (wood-block prints), which includes works by masters including Hiroshige and Hokusai. There's an extra charge for special exhibits. The museum is up the hill on a narrow road behind Laforet; there's a clear map on the museum's website.

Grid references

A1 — (compass rose) LP

0 200 m
0 0.1 miles

B1 — Shuto Expwy No 4 首都高速道路4号

North Gate

Meiji-jingū Treasure Museum

C1 —

D1 —

A2 —

B2 — 2

Meiji-jingū Kaikan

Kita-sandō

C2 —

D2 —

A3 —

Meiji-jingū Gyōen

Minami-sandō

13

Tōgō-jinja 6

Takeshita-dōri

A4 — South Pond

Yoyogi-kōen M

Shibuya-ku 渋谷区

Harajuku

Harajuku

3

Yoyogi-kōen 代々木公園 8

Meiji-jingūmae M

19

17

Fire-dōri

12

25

18

Yoyogi National Stadium

Meiji-dōri 明治通り

A5 — Inokashira-dōri 井の頭通り

Jinnan 神南

NHK Hall

Kōen-dōri

NHK Studio Plaza Building

15

Kamiyamachō

Jingū-dōri-Kōen 神宮通り公園

Kita-Aoyama

A6 — Kanze Nō-gakudō

Shōtō 松涛

Udagawachō

Jingū-dōri

Miyashita-kōen

Mitake-kōen

Tokyo Metropolitan Children's Hall

Shibuya 渋谷

Shibuya Post Office

Sakae-dōri

Dōgenzaka 道玄坂

Bunkamura-dōri

Shibuya

E   Sendagaya   F   Kokuritsu-   G   H

Sendagaya

Shuto Expwy   No 4

Shinanomachi

1

Tokyo
Metropolitan
Gymnasium

38

37

National
Stadium

Meiji-kōen

Jingū-gaien

1

2

Gaien-higashi-dōri

36

Jingū Stadium

Ichō-Namiki

24

31

Prince Chichibu
Memorial
Rugby Stadium

Aoyama-itchōme   M

3

32

7

Kita-dōri

Bell
Commons
Building
33

Aoyama-dōri

Gaienmae   M

Jingūmae
神宮前

30

Gaien-nishi-dōri

4

29

Omotesandō
Hills

Omote-sandō
表参道

24

27

Aoyama Rei-en
(Aoyama Cemetery)

14

26   Omote-sandō   M   16

28

5

10

11

Minami-
Aoyama

5

Aoyama-
kōen

National
Children's
Castle

4

23

21

Aoyama-dōri

Kottō-dōri

34

6

◎ PRADA AOYAMA
プラダ青山

☎ 6418 0400; 5-2-6 Minami-Aoyama, Minato-ku; ⏰ 11am-8pm; ◉ Chiyoda, Ginza & Hanzōmon lines to Omote-sandō (exits A4 & A5)

Of course you could shop here, but you can also ogle the gorgeous, convex glass bubbles of the exterior. Designed by Herzog & de Meuron, this is one of Aoyama's sexier organic-looking structures.

◎ SPIRAL BUILDING
スパイラルビル

☎ 3498 1171; 5-6-23 Minami-Aoyama, Minato-ku; admission free; ⏰ 11am-8pm; ◉ Chiyoda, Ginza & Hanzōmon lines to Omote-sandō (exit B1); ♿

Its asymmetrical, geometric shape may not look very sinuous on the outside, but the Spiral Building's name will make more sense upon entry. The 1st-floor gallery features changing exhibits, shows, dining and live music. Check out the shop on the 2nd floor for art books, jewellery, *washi* and stylishly designed loot.

◎ TŌGŌ-JINJA 東郷神社

☎ 3403 3591; 1-5-3 Jingūmae, Shibuya-ku; admission free; ⏰ 6am-8pm; ◉ JR Yamanote line to Harajuku (Takeshita exit)

This small shrine was built as a memorial to Admiral Tōgō Heihachiro, who led a pivotal battle against the Russians in 1905.

Peer through the Prada Aoyama building glass for an eyeful of the hottest fashion

DESIGN FESTA

Nowadays the biannual Design Festa happens in May and December at the Tokyo International Exhibition Centre, more fondly known as Tokyo Big Sight (p157). Hundreds of young, undiscovered artists and designers, including budding fashion designers, performance artists, filmmakers and musicians, rent spaces in the massive West Hall to reveal the fruits of their creative genius. Design Festa is *the* place to get a good idea of what Tokyo's working artists are doing, and to get your paws on a one-off T-shirt or piece of jewellery. If you're not in town for Design Festa, check out the insanely-embellished **Design Festa Gallery** (☎ 3479 1442; www.designfesta.com; 3-20-18 Jingūmae, Shibuya-ku; admission free; 11am-8pm), which is open year-round except during Design Festa.

These days, the shrine grounds are the venue for a flea market on the 1st, 4th and 5th Sunday of each month. Wares on sale include vintage kimono, antiques and curios. The market usually winds down around 3pm.

ⓒ WATARI MUSEUM OF CONTEMPORARY ART
ワタリウム美術館

☎ 3402 3001; www.watarium.co.jp in Japanese; 3-7-6 Jingūmae, Shibuya-ku; ¥1000/800; 11am-7pm Tue-Sun
Ⓖ Ginza line to Gaienmae (exit 3)
Known as the Watarium, this place showcases lots of brilliant conceptual and performance art, with visiting Scandinavians choreographing ballets involving vacuum-cleaners, and resident Japanese embalming themselves with glue. Ergo, lots of cutting-edge contemporary art can be found here, especially mixed-media art installations.

ⓒ YOYOGI-KŌEN
代々木公園

☎ 3469 6081; 2-1 Yoyogi Kamizonochō, Shibuya-ku; admission free;
24hr; JR Yamanote line to Harajuku (Omote-sandō exit), Chiyoda line to Yoyogi-kōen (exit 4);
The 54 hectares of Yoyogi Park (p28) were originally developed as part of the 1964 Olympic Village and was established as a city park in 1967. From the Harajuku JR

FREE CYCLING

You don't have to brave Tokyo road traffic (nor even bring your own bicycle) to take a leisurely ride on some fair-weather weekend. On Sundays 500 rental bicycles are available for free on a first-come, first-served basis both at the **Imperial Palace East Garden** (p48; 9am-3pm) and the approximately 2.5km path at **Jingū-gaien** (p103; 9am-4pm), when the roads are closed to motorised vehicles.

station, exit right and turn right again, then follow the road along the edge of park until you reach an entry on your right. Across the road, look for the dramatic swooping lines of the National Yoyogi Gymnasium.

🏠 SHOP

🏠 ATELIER MAGIC THEATER
Jewellery & accessories
☎ 3478 5534; www.magic-theater.org; 3-20-21 Meiji-jingūmae, Shibuya-ku; ⏰ noon-8pm; 🚉 JR Yamanote line to Harajuku (Takeshita exit), Ⓜ Chiyoda line to Meiji-jingūmae (exits 2 & 3)
Run by three friends who craft jewellery in their studio, this shop sells bohemian-style work reflecting themes and patterns in nature. The jewellery lines range from plain-silver designs to sculptural work incorporating stones, wood and gold. Custom orders can also be arranged.

🏠 BAPEXCLUSIVE
ベイプエクスクルーシヴ
Fashion
☎ 3407 2145; 5-5-8 Minami-Aoyama, Minato-ku; ⏰ 11am-7pm; Ⓜ Chiyoda, Ginza, Hanzōmon lines to Omote-sando (exit A5)
BAPE (A Bathing Ape) is no longer the madly exclusive brand that made it so desirable – this shop is

testament to how underground designer Nigo's brand *isn't*, but how wildly successful it's become. BAPE has a dozen or so 'secret', hard-to-find shops around Harajuku and Aoyama; this one's a good starting point for brand fans and architecture buffs.

🏠 BOOK OFF ブックオフ
Books
☎ 5775 6818; 1-8-8 Jingūmae, Shibuya-ku; ⏰ 10am-9pm; Ⓜ Chiyoda line to Meiji-jingūmae (exit 5)
Find a huge selection of new and gently-used, barely-bruised manga here. Budget collectors should head for the shelves of ¥105 (!) manga. This branch is on Meiji-dōri, north of Laforet, but Book Off shops are scattered all over Tokyo.

🏠 COMME DES GARÇONS
コムデギャルソン *Fashion*
☎ 3406 3951; 5-2-1 Minami-Aoyama, Minato-ku; ⏰ 11am-8pm; Ⓜ Chiyoda, Ginza & Hanzōmon lines to Omote-sando (exit A4)
When Rei Kawakubo hit international recognition status in the early '80s, it was with her revolutionary, minimalist, matte-black designs. Her lines have evolved from that simple chic, but even with asymmetrical cuts, illusions of torn fabric and sleeves gone

It's hip to be square amid the sleek designs and simple chic of Comme des Garçons

missing, her style is consistently a departure from the norm. This Aoyama architectural wonder is her flagship store.

🏠 CONDOMANIA
コンドマニア
Homewares & novelties
☎ 3797 6131; 6-30-1 Jingūmae, Shibuya-ku; ⏰ 10.30am-11pm; 🚇 JR Yamanote line to Harajuku (Omote-sandō exit), Ⓜ Chiyoda line to Meiji-jingūmae (exit 4)
Inside this tiny shop you'll find more condoms than you can poke a… stick at. For your love-hotel expeditions or footloose friends

back home, pick up enigmatic prophylactics such as the 'Masturbator's Condom' or the more conservative glow-in-the-dark variety.

🏠 DAISO ダイソー
Homewares & novelties
☎ 5775 9641; Village 107 Bldg, 1-19-24 Jingūmae, Shibuya-ku; ⏰ 10am-9pm; 🚇 JR Yamanote line to Harajuku (Takeshita exit)
When Japan's economy crashed, *hyakkin* (100-yen shops) began raking in the cash…and haven't stopped. Among the hundreds in Tokyo, Daiso is easily accessible

and stocked with four floors full of merchandise costing ¥100. It's a great souvenir stop, where you can find rice bowls painted with cute animals, vampiric nail polish and random, silly kitsch.

🎴 FUJI-TORII 富士鳥居
Art & antiques

☎ 3400 2777; www.fuji-torii.com; 6-1-10 Jingūmae, Shibuya-ku; ⏰ 11am-6pm Wed-Mon, closed every 3rd Mon; Ⓜ Chiyoda line to Meiji-jingūmae (exit 4)

This reliable antique dealer has been in the business since 1948 and stocks everything from exquisite *kutani* (regional ceramics featuring striking enamel designs) to inexpensive modern wood-block prints. It has an especially good selection of beautiful *byōbu* (antique folding screens).

🎴 HANAE MORI BUILDING
ハナエモリビル
Art & antiques

B1F, 3-6-1 Kita-Aoyama, Minato-ku; ⏰ 11am-7pm; Ⓜ Chiyoda, Ginza, Hanzōmon lines to Omote-sandō (exit A1)

In Harajuku, the basement of the Hanae Mori building has more than 30 antique shops hawking everything from over-the-hill kewpie dolls to cloisonné bracelets and antique obi ornaments.

👚 HYSTERIC GLAMOUR
ヒステリックグラモー
Fashion

☎ 3409 7227; www.hystericglamour.jp in Japanese; 6-23-2 Jingūmae, Shibuya-ku; ⏰ 11am-8pm; 🚉 JR Yamanote line to Harajuku (Omote-sandō exit), Ⓜ Chiyoda line to Meiji-jingūmae (exit 4)

It's more attitudinal tongue-in-cheek than hysterical or glamorous, but whatever you want to call it, it's fun stuff spiked generously with that Tokyo flavour. There's even a toddler line, the ultimate in designer punk for your little rocker. Design junkies will want to check out the curvy, futuristic branch at Roppongi Hills (p143).

👚 ISSEY MIYAKE 三宅一生
Fashion

☎ 3423 1407; 3-18-11 Minami-Aoyama, Minato-ku; ⏰ 10am-8pm; Ⓜ Chiyoda, Ginza & Hanzōmon lines to Omote-sandō (exit A4)

Anarchic but wearable conceptual fashion continues to flow from Issey Miyake. At the cluster of Aoyama shops along the south end of Omote-sandō, eye his famous pleated designs, or the A-POC garments – each made from a single piece of fabric. The gallerylike window displays are worth a look, after checking out the many-faceted Prada spaceship down the street.

🖼 KASŪKŌBŌ かすう工房
Jewellery & accessories
☎ 3479 3150; 4-28-14 Meiji-jingūmae, Shibuya-ku; ⏰ noon-8pm; 🚃 JR Yamanote line to Harajuku (Takeshita exit); 🚇 Chiyoda line to Meiji-jingūmae (exit 5)
This open-air jewellery shop on a raised platform has an old-fashioned feel even while the tattooed dude kneeling behind the display cases exudes the casual air of the modern Ura-Hara denizen. Mostly sculpted silver jewellery with themes of lotuses, dragons and *koi* (carp), the pieces here are simultaneously fresh and modern.

🖼 KIDDYLAND
キデイランド *Toys*
☎ 3409 3431; www.kiddyland.co.jp; 6-1-9 Jingūmae, Shibuya-ku; ⏰ 10am-8pm, closed 3rd Tue of each month; 🚇 Chiyoda line to Meiji-jingūmae (exit 4)
Eep! Six floors of *kawaii* (cute) paraphernalia for your children – or, let's face it, you – to fall in lust with. Stuffed with stuffed animals, a candy store selection of hair baubles, 200-yen toy vending machines, an abundance of Hello Kitty products, plastic action figures and noisy games, this store can be dangerously tempting (and *very* crowded on weekends).

🖼 LAFORET ラフォーレ
Fashion
☎ 3475 0411; 1-11-6 Jingūmae, Shibuya-ku; ⏰ 11am-8pm; 🚃 JR Yamanote line to Harajuku (Omote-sandō exit)
Expressing identity and individuality is a function of fashion, and Tokyo youth are famous for taking this concept to the next level. Sample this in action at Laforet; surveying the shoppers is equal to the window shopping, and once you've gotten the hang of the half-floor concept, you can count your way up to the 6th-floor museum (p103).

🖼 ON SUNDAYS *Books*
☎ 3470 1424; www.watarium.co.jp in Japanese; 3-7-6 Jingūmae, Shibuya-ku; ⏰ 11am-8pm Tue-Sun; 🚇 Ginza line to Gaienmae (exit 3)
Connected to Watari Museum of Contemporary Art (p107), On Sundays carries an eclectic collection of avant-garde art for sale. It has a humongous selection of funky to classic postcards, and a marvellous array of functional arthouse objects, such as purses in the shapes of origami balloons and Scandinavian-style office accoutrements. In the basement is a wonderful café/bookshop.

NEIGHBOURHOODS

HARAJUKU & AOYAMA

🏠 ORIENTAL BAZAAR
オリエンタルバザール
Handicrafts
☎ 3400 3933; 5-9-13 Jingūmae,
Shibuya-ku; ⏰ 10am-7pm Fri-Wed;
🚇 Chiyoda line to Meiji-jingūmae
(exit 4)
Carrying a wide-ranging selection
of antiques and souvenirs at very
reasonable prices, Oriental Bazaar
is a great spot for last-minute,
one-stop gift shopping. Among
the wares are fans, folding screens,
pottery, porcelain and *yukata*
(cotton kimono). The branch at
Narita Airport opens at 7.30am
if you need to offload some yen
predeparture.

🏠 TSUMORI CHISATO
ツモリチサト *Fashion*
☎ 3423 5170; 4-21-25 Minami-Aoyama,
Minato-ku; ⏰ 11am-8pm; 🚇 Chiyoda,
Ginza & Hanzōmon lines to Omote-sandō
(exit A4)
After working under Issey
Miyake, designer Tsumori Chisato
launched her own line in 1990
with the blessing of her mentor.
Now she designs fun and well-
tailored clothing that falls grace-
fully along the lines of the body,
while retaining a whimsical
aesthetic, using beading,
embroidery and eye-catching
appliqué.

🏠 UNDERCOVER *Fashion*
☎ 3407 1232; 5-3-18 Minami-Aoyama,
Minato-ku; ⏰ 11am-8pm; 🚇 Chiyoda,
Ginza & Hanzōmon lines to Omote-sandō
(exit A5)
Former punk band frontman Jun
Takahashi's take on youth-minded
streetwear is still pretty crazy after
all this time. His Undercover Lab,
designed by architect Astrid Klein,
is just up and across the street
from Tsumori Chisato.

🏠 YOHJI YAMAMOTO
耀司山本 *Fashion*
☎ 3409 6006; 5-3-6 Minami-Aoyama,
Minato-ku; ⏰ 11am-8pm; 🚇 Chiyoda,
Ginza & Hanzōmon lines to Omote-sandō
(exit A4)
Yohji Yamamoto has maintained
some mystery of himself and his
aesthetic, flouting convention decade after decade in a mischievous
way that keeps his style fresh – a
feat when your colour of choice is
black. He is one of the locals who
has set up house here in Aoyama.

🍴 EAT

🍴 FUJIMAMAS フジママス
Asian fusion ¥¥
☎ 5485 2283; www.fujimamas.com;
6-3-2 Jingūmae, Shibuya-ku;
⏰ 11am-11pm; 🚇 Chiyoda line to
Meiji-Jingūmae (exit 4), 🚃 JR Yamanote
line to Harajuku (Omote-sandō exit);
♿ V 👶

Fujimamas is hugely popular for its Asian fusion cuisine – such as pan-seared salmon with wasabi cream – and its quality Californian wines. Upstairs are airy rooms in what was once a tatamimaker's workshop. Fujimamas also offers a great children's menu. The restaurant is in the first alley south of the Omote-sandō and Meiji-jingū intersection. Reservations are recommended.

🍴 FONDA DE LA MADRUGADA フォンダデラマドゥルガーダ *Mexican* ¥¥¥

☎ 5410 6288; B1F, Villa Blanca, 2-33-12 Jingūmae, Shibuya-ku; ⏰ 5.30pm-2am Sun-Thu, 5.30pm-5am Fri & Sat; 🚇 JR Yamanote line to Harajuku (Takeshita exit); ♿

Fonda de la Madrugada makes the best Mexican food in Tokyo and is a favourite with expats. Complete with open courtyards and mariachi musicians, everything from the roof tiles to the chefs has been imported from Mexico. It's not cheap, but the enchiladas are worth it.

🍴 HIROBA 広場 *Organic vegetarian* ¥

☎ 3406 6409; B1F, Crayon House Bldg, 3-8-15 Kita-Aoyama, Minato-ku; ⏰ 11am-10pm; 🚇 Chiyoda, Ginza & Hanzōmon lines to Omote-sandō (exits B2 & B4); ♿ Ⓥ ♿

Hiroba is a veritable vegetarian oasis, particularly if you go for the lunch buffet (¥1260). The organic Japanese buffet includes both vegetarian and meat options; descriptions are only in Japanese but signs for each dish include cute, helpful drawings of fish or pigs to explain if animal ingredients were used. The building is off Omote-sandō, a block behind the Hanae Mori building.

🍴 KINOKUNIYA (INTERIM STORE) 紀ノ国屋 *International groceries*

☎ 3409 1231; www.e-kinokuniya.com /cont/tp/info-e.html; 3-11-13 Minami-Aoyama, Minato-ku; ⏰ 9.30am-8pm; 🚇 Chiyoda, Ginza & Hanzōmon lines to Omote-sandō (exits A3 & A4)

Kinokuniya carries expat lifesavers such as Marmite and peanut butter, Belgian chocolate and herbal tea. Foreign imports including cheese, salami and Finnish bread generally fetch high prices, much like the flawless fruit in the produce section. If this interim branch has closed, cross Omote-sandō to get to the **original store** (☎ 3409 1236; 3-11-7 Kita-Aoyama, Minato-ku).

🍴 MAISEN まい泉 *Japanese* ¥

☎ 3470-0071; 4-8-5 Jingūmae, Shibuya-ku; ⏰ 11am-10pm; 🚇 Chiyoda, Ginza, Hanzōmon lines to Omote-sandō (exit A2)

Maisen is famous for its crispy and tender *tonkatsu* (deep-fried pork

MOMINOKI HOUSE

Eiichiro Yamada
Chef & owner of Mominoki House (opposite)

Why organic and macrobiotic? When I opened my restaurant in 1976, even among so many restaurants in Tokyo, I couldn't find any that served healthy, safe and delicious food. And I believe that macrobiotic and organic food guarantees the health and happiness of people's lives. **What's the world's most perfect food?** Japanese traditional food, especially *genmai* (brown rice), I think. **Your favourite restaurant in Tokyo?** Café-Restaurant Selan (p116) in Meiji Kinenkan, which has a cosy open-air balcony overlooking a beautiful garden. I hate fast food restaurants – their food is cooked by machines, not chefs. **Most interesting customer?** Stevie Wonder – he came here in 1982. After enjoying dinner here he surprised me with a spontaneous performance, playing the piano and singing for us for an hour. I was so moved and wondered if I was dreaming.

Interview by Mariko Matsumura

cutlets) that draws a continuous crowd. Thankfully, the place occupies a converted bathhouse, so there's plenty of room for the many hungry souls craving Kagoshima *kurobuta* (black pig). If you're on the run, pick up a *bentō* (boxed meal) at the takeaway window.

🍴 LAS CHICAS ラスチカス
Cafe ¥

☎ 3407 6865; 5-47-6 Jingūmae, Shibuya-ku; ⏰ 11am-11pm; ⓂChiyoda, Ginza & Hanzōmon lines to Omote-sandō (exit B2); ♿ Ⓥ ⬧

Chill out on one of the coolest terraces in Tokyo – at Las Chicas, popular with expats and a hip, arty Aoyama crowd. Along with espresso drinks and fine wines, the menu is composed of casual classics such as the Caligula salad (Caesar with a twist). At the time of writing, they were undergoing renovations but set to reopen in February 2008.

🍴 LE BRETAGNE
ルブルターニュ *French* ¥¥

☎ 3478 7855; 4-9-8 Jingūmae, Shibuya-ku; ⏰ 11.30am-11pm Mon-Sat, 11.30am-10pm Sun; ⓂChiyoda, Ginza & Hanzōmon lines to Omote-sandō (exit A2); ♿ Ⓥ ⬧

Le Bretagne's wonderful set menus, with their buckwheat galettes as the centrepieces, are authentic

and filling. The sweet or savoury Breton-style crêpes can also be ordered à la carte for mere pocket change – money well-spent on these fresh and tasty creations.

🍴 MOMINOKI HOUSE
モミノキハウス
Organic vegetarian ¥¥

☎ 3405 9144; www2.odn.ne.jp /mominoki_house; 1F, YOU Bldg, 2-18-5 Jingūmae, Shibuya-ku; ⏰ 11am-11pm; ⓂJR Yamanote line to Harajuku, Takeshita exit); Ⓥ ⬧

For herbivorous relief, stop into Mominoki House, where the largely macrobiotic menu covers the vegan to the vegetarian. There's also free-range organic chicken for the carnivorously inclined. The rambling space is cosily welcoming, as is the friendly chef-owner.

🍴 NATURAL HARMONY ANGOLO ナチュラルハーモニーアンゴロ
Organic vegetarian ¥¥

☎ 3405 8393; 1F, Puzzle Aoyama Bldg, 3-28-12 Jingūmae, Shibuya-ku; ⏰ 11.30am-2.30pm & 5.30-9.30pm ⓂGinza line to Gaienmae (exit 2); Ⓥ ⬧

Refreshingly smoke-free and dishing up live foods and excellent vegetarian fare, Natural Harmony is Tokyo's best-known natural food spot. Tall salads, creamy risottos and organic beer and sake entice those who trek to this veggie haven; the menu is largely vegetarian, but fish and meat dishes augment the menu.

Ⅲ SELAN RESTAURANT
Italian ¥¥

☎ 3478 2200; 2-1-19 Kita-Aoyama, Minato-ku; ⏱ 11.30am-10.30pm Mon-Fri, 10am-10.30pm Sat & Sun; ◎ Ginza, Hanzōmon & Toei Ōedo lines to Aoyama-itchōme (exit 1)

Come here for the lovely atmosphere rather than the Japanese-style Italian food, especially during the fall foliage season, when the surrounding gingko trees blaze, bright yellow.

Ⅲ UME-NO-HANA 梅の花
Traditional Japanese ¥¥¥

☎ 3475 8077; 6F, Aoyama Bell Commons, 2-14-6 Kita-aoyama, Minato-ku; ⏱ 11.30am-3pm & 5-9pm; ◎ Ginza & Hanzōmon lines (exit 2)

This traditional, elegant restaurant is rightfully well-known for their *kaiseki* (elegant, multi-course Japanese meals) meals that showcase tofu and *yuba* (tofu 'skin') in beautifully presented small courses. Both *niku-nashi* (vegetarian) and meat-inclusive sets are available, but ordering will be problematic unless you have a Japanese speaker make the reservation for you and help you decide the best set for you and your party.

🍸 DRINK

🍸 DEN AQUAROOM
デンアクアルーム *Lounge*

☎ 5778 2090; B1F, 5-13-3 Minami-Aoyama, Minato-ku; cover ¥500-1000; ◎ Chiyoda, Ginza, Hanzōmon lines to Omote-sandō (exit B1)

Darting fish within the walls of backlit, blue aquariums make a visual counterpoint to the bop of jazz basslines. Even prettier than the dark décor is the chic clientele floating around in here.

🍸 TOKYO APARTMENT CAFÉ
東京アパートメントカフェ *Lounge*

☎ 3401 4101; 1-11-11 Jingūmae, Shibuya-ku; ⏱ 11am-4am; ◎ Chiyoda line to Meiji-jingūmae (exit 5); 🚇 JR Yamanote line to Harajuku (Omote-sandō exit)

The Apartment Café is a good afternoon refuge for snacks like pasta or spring rolls, but in the evenings it transforms into more of a cocktail lounge where you can spend a low-key evening among locals.

⭐ PLAY

⭐ CROCODILE
クロコダイル *Live music*

☎ 3499 5205; B1F, New Sekiguchi Bldg, 6-18-8 Jingūmae, Shibuya-ku; cover from ¥2000; ⏱ 6pm-2am; ◎ Chiyoda line to Meiji-jingūmae (exit 4)

In Harajuku along Meiji-dōri, Crocodile has live music seven nights a week. It's a spacious place with lots of room for dancing if the music moves you. Tunes cover the gamut from jazz to reggae or rock-and-roll. The cover charge includes one drink.

☆ JINGŪ STADIUM 神宮球場
Spectator sports
☎ 3404 8999; 13 Kasumigaoka, Shinjuku-ku; tickets from ¥1500; ⊖ Ginza line to Gaienmae (north exit)
Jingū Baseball Stadium was originally built to host the 1964 Olympics and is where the Yakult Swallows are based. Baseball season runs from April through to the end of October; check the *Japan Times* to see who's playing.

☆ NATIONAL STADIUM
国立競技場 *Spectator sports*
☎ 3403 1151; Kasumigaokamachi, Shinjuku-ku; tickets from ¥2000; ⊖ Toei Ōedo line to Kokuritsu Kyōgijō (exit A2); ⊞ Chūō line to Sendagaya (east exit)

J-League soccer is booming in Japan, though naysayers had predicted its rapid decline with the departure of the 2002 World Cup (awarded to Japan, jointly with Korea). The increased interest in the game has remained, and the Japanese have embraced it almost as enthusiastically as baseball.

☆ TOKYO METROPOLITAN GYMNASIUM 東京体育館
Sports & recreation
☎ 5474 2111; www.tef.or.jp/tmg/index.php; 1-17-1 Sendagaya, Shibuya-ku; pool/gym for 2 hrs ¥600/450; ⏰ 9am-11pm Mon-Fri, 9am-10pm Sat, 9am-9pm Sun; ⊞ Chūō & Sōbu lines to Sendagaya (main exit), ⊖ Toei Ōedo line to Kokuritsu Kyōgijō (exits A4 & A5)
Easily accessed and with comprehensive facilities that include two swimming pools, this spaceship-like structure is just across the street from Sendagaya Station.

>SHIBUYA

Urban anthropologists will find much of interest in the field here in Shibuya, ground zero for Tokyo youth culture. You've probably seen Shibuya Crossing before, with the flood of humanity that the green light unleashes every few minutes, beneath the moving screens on buildings towering overhead. Shibuya department stores cater to the turnover of trends consumed by the subcultures cruising the street in packs. The more head-turning tribes include (but are certainly not limited to) *mamba*, the girls with the deep, fake tans, white eye makeup and bleached-blonde hair, who are usually decked out in microminis and tall boots. The *mamba* make up only a subset of *gyaru* (gal) culture, which is driven by consumerism, fashion and Shibuya-kei (Shibuya type) music. *Gyaru* culture splits into other variations, much like the alleys snaking off Shibuya Crossing – and these alleys form their natural habitat. You'll find them in its all-you-can-eat dessert cafés, specialised record shops, *izakaya* (pubs-eateries) and clubs, discount shops selling accessories and a million boutiques selling the look of the moment.

SHIBUYA

🔵 SEE

🏠 SHOP

🍴 EAT

🍸 DRINK

⭐ PLAY

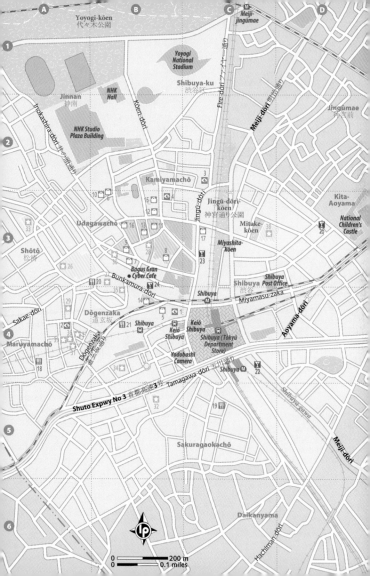

NEIGHBOURHOODS

SHIBUYA

👁 SEE
👁 HACHIKŌ STATUE
ハチ公像

Outside the Hachikō exit of the Shibuya JR station is that exit's namesake and most famous meeting spot: the Hachikō statue (below). While the story behind it is poignant, its function as a meeting place is logical.

👁 LOVE HOTEL HILL

Around the top of Dōgenzaka is the highest concentration of love hotels in Tokyo. While ostensibly a place for amorous couples, keep it in mind as a good place to crash if you're out late clubbing in the

A DOG'S LIFE

In the 1920s a professor who taught at what is now Tokyo University kept a small Akita dog named Hachikō. Hachikō accompanied the professor to Shibuya Station every morning, then returned in the afternoons to await the professor's arrival. One spring day in 1925, the professor died of a stroke while at the university and never came home. Hachikō continued to turn up at the station daily to wait for his master, until Hachikō's own death 10 years later. The dog's faithfulness touched the locals, who built a statue to honour his memory in the place where he died. Nowadays, Hachikō's statue is a favourite meeting spot, so fittingly, he's usually surrounded by people waiting for their someones.

WORTH THE TRIP

The **Hara Museum of Contemporary Art** (☎ 3445 0651; www.haramuseum .or.jp/generalTop.html; 4-7-25 Kita-Shinagawa, Shinagawa-ku, admission ¥700; 🕐 11am-5pm Tue-Thu, Sat & Sun, 11am-8pm Wed; 🚊 JR Yaman-ote line to Shinagawa, Takanawa exit) is an excellent, adventurous museum that showcases contemporary art by local and international avant-garde artists. As well as exhibiting works by the likes of Gilbert & George (UK) and Cindy Sherman (US), the museum sponsors excellent workshops and presentations by those visiting artists. It's a 15-minute walk from Shinagawa Station; there's a good map on the website.

area; rates are pretty reasonable for overnight stays (see opposite).

👁 PARCO MUSEUM
パルコミュージアム

☎ 3477 5873; www.parco-art.com/web /museum; 7F, Parco Part 3, 15-1 Udagawachō, Shibuya-ku; admission from ¥300; 🕐 10am-9pm; 🚊 JR Yamanote line to Shibuya (Hachikō exit); ♿
This progressive gallery exhibits works by leading international artists and high-profile locals. Photography, installation and graphic design figure prominently, and if the current exhibition does nothing for you, you can check out the edgier Wall Gallery on the same floor.

LOVE HOTELS

These days, Japan's famous love hotels are more politely referred to as 'boutique' or 'fashion' hotels. There's a love hotel for everyone, from miniature Gothic castles to Middle-Eastern temples…and these are just the buildings – some room themes can be even more outrageous. Some hotels are now catering more to Japanese women's tastes (think pink and cute). Although they're most highly concentrated on Love Hotel Hill (opposite), there are love hotels in most districts. Peek into a few of the entrances to check out the screen with illuminated pictures of available rooms; some lobbies even have vending machines selling sex toys. You can stay for a 'rest' of several hours, but if you want to stay overnight, check-in is usually after 9pm or 10pm and the rates are fairly inexpensive (around ¥8000). Same-sex couples might have trouble checking in, but insisting that you're *tomodachi* (friends) may get you in.

☎ TEPCO ELECTRIC ENERGY MUSEUM 電力館

☎ 3477 1191; 1-12-10 Jinnan, Shibuya-ku; admission free; ☷ 10am-6pm Thu-Tue; ⧗ JR Yamanote line to Shibuya (Hachikō exit); ♿ ♨

This is one of Tokyo's better science museums, offering seven floors of dynamic exhibitions on every conceivable aspect of electricity and its production. There are innumerable hands-on displays and an excellent, free English hand-out that explains everything.

☎ TOBACCO & SALT MUSEUM たばこと塩の博物館

☎ 3476 2041; 1-16-8 Jinnan, Shibuya-ku; admission ¥100/50; ☷ 10am-6pm Tue-Sun; ⧗ JR Yamanote line to Shibuya (Hachikō exit)

This unusual little museum has detailed exhibits on the labour-intensive methods of salt production practised in premodern Japan. On the tobacco topic, find vintage lighters, cigarette packs and advertisements illustrating the history of tobacco. While there's little English signage, much of the material is self-explanatory.

☐ SHOP

There must be a hundred record shops in Udagawachō alone, many focusing on one genre of music. Their stacks usually include rare vinyl, releases available in Japan only and the standard fare you would expect to find in that reggae/Motown/fill-in-the-blank specialist.

☐ BIC CAMERA
Cameras & electronics

☎ 3477 0002; 2-5-9- Dōgenzaka, Shibuya-ku; ☷ 10am-9pm; ⧗ JR Yamanote line to Shibuya (Hachikō exit)

This cheap camera store also has branches in Ikebukuro (p85) and Shinjuku (p92).

NEIGHBOURHOODS

SHIBUYA

🏠 CISCO RECORDS シスコレコード *Music*

☎ 3462 0366; www.cisco-records.co.jp in Japanese; 2F, 11-1 Udagachō, Shibuya-ku; ◷ noon-10pm Mon-Sat, 11am-9pm Sun; 🚇 JR Yamanote line to Shibuya (Hachikō exit)

Cisco has several small shops scattered around this area, each specialising in a different genre. This one is where you'll find mostly hip-hop and R&B, but others in the neighbourhood carry electronica, trance and dub.

🏠 DISK UNION ディスクユニオン *Music*

☎ 3476 2627; http://diskunion.net in Japanese; Antenna 21 Bldg, 30-7 Udagachō, Shibuya-ku; 🚇 JR Yamanote line to Shibuya (Hachikō exit)

The Disk Union chain sells used and new records here at its location on Center-gai. Each floor specialises in a different genre, including punk and jazz. There's another large branch in Shinjuku (p93) and smaller outposts elsewhere in Tokyo.

🏠 LOFT ロフト *Homewares & novelties*

☎ 3462 3807; 21-1 Udagachō, Shibuya-ku; ◷ 10am-9pm; 🚇 JR Yamanote line to Shibuya (Hachikō exit)

Insert expendable income here. Loft offers an enormous range of useful goodies, such as silk washcloths, sleek furniture and brightly coloured kitchenware, but the best merchandise is the goofier stuff, such as shoe fresheners shaped like smiley-faced hedgehogs, mobile phone charms and other seductive silliness. It has another branch in Ikebukuro (p86).

🏠 MANDARAKE まんだらけ *Books*

☎ 3477 0777; www.mandarake.co.jp; B2 fl, Shibuya Beam Bldg, 31-2 Udagachō, Shibuya-ku; 🚇 JR Yamanote line to Shibuya (Hachikō exit)

The Shibuya branch of Mandarake stocks a range of new manga and also boasts performances by real, live *cosplay* (costume-play) kids in full-on *anime* character drag. Avid fans should also make the trek to Mandarake's huge flagship store in Nakano, with three floors packed with all manner of new and used manga, *anime*, games and character-related collectibles.

🏠 MANHATTAN RECORDS マンハッタンレコード *Music*

☎ 3477 7737; 1F, 10-1 Udagachō, Shibuya-ku; ◷ noon-9pm; 🚇 JR Yamanote line to Shibuya (Hachikō exit)

Rifle through the records in Manhattan for hip-hop and a look at the flyers for local club schedules. There's also a cluster of record shops down the alleys on either side of the Manhattan building, so shop around a bit.

THE OTAKU ONUS

Much in the way that the innocuous French word *avec* (literally meaning 'with') has been co-opted by the Japanese to mean 'together as a couple', the word *otaku* has in recent years become lingo for 'nerd' or 'geek' outside of Japan, mostly in reference to and used among the manga or gamer ilk.

In Japan, though *otaku* can colloquially mean 'geek', the many layers of its meaning make it a loaded word to be used very selectively. The original translation of the word is an obscure honorific for 'your house', which developed into code for 'you' among, well, nerds with a common obsessive interest in manga and a degree of social discomfort. Eventually the word *otaku* became associated in popular culture with socially maladapted shut-ins and those many related negative connotations.

Unless you're pretty certain you're among peers, use with discretion.

🏠 PARCO 1, 2 & 3
パルコパート1, 2&3
Department store
☎ 3464 5111; 15-1 Udagawachō, Shibuya-ku; ⏰ 10am-8.30pm; 🚉 JR Yamanote line to Shibuya (Hachikō exit)
If you see it strutting across Shibuya Crossing, you'll find some version of it at Parco parts 1, 2 and 3. These interconnected department stores are mostly targeted toward fans of Vivienne Westwood and other designers to those favouring the schoolgirl look. They also have art galleries that feature multimedia installations, avant-garde painting and fashion-oriented exhibitions.

🏠 RECOFAN レコファン
Music
☎ 5454 0161; www.recofan.co.jp; 4F, Shibuya Beam Bldg, 31-2 Udagawachō, Shibuya-ku; ⏰ 11.30am-9pm; 🚉 JR Yamanote line to Shibuya (Hachikō exit)

With several branches around town, this arm of Recofan stocks a wide variety of music, including folk, soul, J-pop and reggae. Between this store and the Mandarake (opposite) shop in the basement, you could lose several hours in here.

🏠 SHIBUYA 109 渋谷
Department store
☎ 3477 5111; 2-29-1 Dōgenzaka, Shibuya-ku; ⏰ 10am-9pm Mon-Fri, 11am-10.30pm Sat & Sun; 🚉 JR Yamanote line to Shibuya (Hachikō exit)
Shibuya 109 is the department store selling the trends *du jour* of Shibuya's youth culture, whether it's the minidresses in blindingly saturated colours for the *gyaru* set or the bunched-up ankle socks the schoolgirls are so fond of pairing with their tiny skirts.

NEIGHBOURHOODS

SHIBUYA

🏠 THREE MINUTES HAPPINESS
Homewares & novelties
☎ 5459 1851; 3-5 Udagawachō, Shibuya-ku; ⏰ 11am-9pm; 🚉 JR Yamanote line to Shibuya (Hachikō exit)
Three minutes' worth is guaranteed, but your mileage may vary. This discount shop sells clothes out of decommissioned grocery-store freezers, and makes the shopping experience fun as well as cheap. Downstairs are clothes, shoes and accessories, while lurking upstairs are inexpensive homewares and kitchen knick-knacks.

🏠 TŌKYŪ HANDS
東急ハンズ
Homewares & novelties
☎ 5489 5111; 12-18 Udagawachō, Shibuya-ku; ⏰ 10am-8.30pm; 🚉 JR Yamanote line to Shibuya (Hachikō exit)
Although this branch is a little more cramped than the one at Takashimaya Times Square, this detracts not at all from the appeal of the wonderful wares. Other stores can be found in Shinjuku (p94) and Ikebukuro (p86).

🏠 TOWER RECORDS
タワーレコード *Music*
☎ 3496 3661; 7F, Tower Records Bldg, 1-22-14 Jinnan, Shibuya-ku; ⏰ 10am-11pm; 🚉 JR Yamanote line to Shibuya (Hachikō exit)
Yep, it's a chain, but this Tower is Tokyo's largest music store. Despite its size, this place gets packed.

Shop for shark suits and novelties at Tōkyū Hands

Tower also carries a large selection of English-language books and an extensive array of magazines and newspapers from around the world. Magazines here are considerably cheaper than elsewhere around town.

🍴 EAT
🍴 DEN ROKUEN-TEI
デンロクエンテイ
Asian fusion   ¥¥
☎ 6415 5489; 8F, Parco Part 1, 15-1 Udagawacho, Shibuya-ku; ⏰ 11am-midnight; 🚉 JR Yamanote line to Shibuya (Hachikō exit)
Modern twists on seasonally changing Japanese *izakaya* dishes are matched with an array of wine,

beer and sake cocktails. Private tatami (woven floor matting) rooms are available, but at this relaxed, stylish perch on the top of Parco 1, the lovely open-air terrace is the prime property.

🍴 KAIKAYA 開花屋
Izakaya   ¥¥

☎ 3770 0878; www.kaikaya.com; 23-7 Maruyamachō, Shibuya-ku; ⏱ 5-11.30pm Sun, 11.30am-2pm & 5-11.30pm Mon-Thu, 5pm-4am Fri & Sat; ⓔ Keiō Inokashira line to Shinsen (main exit) 🚊 JR Yamanote line to Shibuya (Hachikō exit)

This friendly *izakaya* is a little tricky to find, but once you're there you'll be rewarded by its friendly atmosphere and excellent, seasonal fish dishes that use fusion elements without losing too much of the food's essential Japanese strengths. Also, happily, this place has an English menu. Walking along Dōgenzaka away from Shibuya station, turn right at the police box and ask for directions.

🍴 KANTIPUR カンティプール
Nepalese   ¥¥

☎ 3770 5358; B1F, 16-6 Sakuragaokachō, Shibuya-ku; ⏱ 11.30am-3pm & 5-11pm; 🚊 JR Yamanote line to Shibuya (south exit); Ⓥ

Happily for vegetarians, this Nepalese restaurant has a broad range of acceptable edibles, and the portions of curries and tandoori

dishes are large. Kantipur is in the basement of its building, whose entrance is marked by the brightly coloured signs on the street.

🍴 SAKANA-TEI 酒菜亭
Izakaya   ¥¥

☎ 3780 1313; 4th fl, Koike Bldg, 2-23-15 Dōgenzaka, Shibuya-ku; ⏱ 5.30-11pm Mon-Sat; 🚊 JR Yamanote line to Shibuya (Hachikō exit)

This unpretentious but slightly posh *izakaya* is a sake specialist much sought after by connoisseurs, and is good value for the quality. Though there's no English menu, you can point to dishes displayed on the counter, and start with a sampler set of sake. Call ahead for reservations, but turn off your mobile phone once you're in – house rules.

🍴 SONOMA ソノマ
American   ¥¥

☎ 3462 7766; www.sonomatokyo.com; 2-25-17 Dōgenzaka, Shibuya-ku; ⏱ 5.30-11.30pm Sun-Thu, 5.30pm-4am Fri & Sat; 🚊 JR Yamanote line to Shibuya (Hachikō exit); ♿ Ⓥ

Sonoma's well-balanced menu of California cuisine is further enhanced by a warm, well-lit space. Mains on offer include pork chops with apples, brown sugar and sage, and pan-seared salmon with herb risotto. Dinner here gains free entry to the Ruby Room (p128) upstairs, a fitting place for all-night drinking.

🍴 TORIYOSHI DINING
鳥よしダイニング
Yakitori ¥¥

☎ 5784 3373; B1F Sekaido Bldg, 2-10-10 Dōgenzaka, Shibuya-ku; ⏰ 5pm-4am; 🚇 JR Yamanote line to Shibuya (Hachikō exit)

Toriyoshi does *yakitori* (skewers of grilled chicken) stepped up a notch in sophistication, pairing it with wine and cocktails without sacrificing its earthy, charcoal-grilled appeal. Set dinners are a good way to try a variety of *yakitori* and tofu.

🍸 DRINK
🍸 BELGO ベルゴ *Bar*

☎ 3409 4442; B1F, Shibuya; chigo-kan Bldg, 3-18-7 Shibuya, Shibuya-ku; ⏰ 5.30pm-2am Mon-Sat; 🚇 JR Yamanote line to Shibuya (south exit)

If you're into Belgian beer, have we got a bar for you. This sweet well of ale has over 100 kinds of beer to drink, with an emphasis on all shades of Belgian goodness. There's Guinness and Chimay on draught, and you can round out the liquid fare with fish and chips.

🍸 DOMA DOMA 土間土間
Izakaya

☎ 5728 1099; B1F, Minagawa Bldg, 1-22-10 Jinnan, Shibuya-ku; ⏰ 5pm-5am; 🚇 JR Yamanote line to Shibuya (Hachikō exit)

This is an easy-to-find *izakaya* along Jingū-dōri, serving a younger crowd than the salarymen boozing it up at its Shinjuku counterparts. Order a pitcher of *nama biiru* (draught beer) and a few Japanese dishes off the picture menu, but beware of the more fusion-style offerings that are less hit and more miss.

🍸 INSOMNIA LOUNGE
インソムニアラウンジ
Lounge

☎ 3476 2735; B1F; Kushin Bldg, 26-5 Udagawachō, Shibuya-ku; ⏰ 6pm-5am; 🚇 JR Yamanote line to Shibuya (Hachikō exit)

Red is the colour of Insomnia. Mirrored by reflective surfaces all around you, your red-eye will blend right into the ruby interior of this laid-back lounge. It doesn't promise any miracle cures for insomniacs but will keep the sleepless going 'til dawn with a good mix of music, cocktails and decent food.

🍸 PINK COW ピンクカウ
Bar

☎ 3406 5597; www.thepinkcow.com; B1F, Villa Moderna, 1-3-18 Shibuya, Shibuya-ku; ⏰ 5pm-late Tue-Sun; 🚇 JR Yamanote line to Shibuya (Hachikō exit)

The Pink Cow is a funky, sociable place where something's always going on – local artwork adorns the walls, live music happens, and the place hosts gatherings of venture-capital seekers to stitch-and-bitchers (knitting groups) alike. There's often a cover charge for a special event. Come for the terrific all-you-can-eat buffet (¥2625) every Friday and Saturday evening, and mingle with an international crowd.

⭐ PLAY

⭐ BUNKAMURA THEATRE COCOON
文化村シアターコクーン *Theatre*
☎ 3477 9111; www.bunkamura.co.jp /english; 2-24-1 Dōgenzaka, Shibuya-ku; tickets from ¥4000; 🕙 10am-7pm Sun-Thu, 10am-9pm Fri & Sat; 🚇 JR Yamanote line to Shibuya (Hachikō exit); ♿

Bunkamura, a behemoth of an arts centre, houses a cinema, theatre, concert hall and art gallery. Theatre Cocoon provides an intimate space for musical and theatrical performances from a variety of backgrounds, from the innovative to the offbeat traditional. Check the website for info on current productions.

⭐ CINE AMUSE EAST & WEST
シネアミューズ *Cinema*
☎ 3496 2888; 2-23-12 Dōgenzaka, Shibuya-ku; tickets ¥1800/1000, ¥1000 on 1st day of month (except Jan); 🕙 10am-11pm; 🚇 JR Yamanote line to Shibuya (Hachikō exit)

Equipped with two screens and an excellent sound system, Cine Amuse has regular screenings

of Japanese movies subtitled in English, as well as international releases. It's a small but comfy space, and well-placed for post-cinema amusement in Shibuya.

⭐ CINEMA RISE
シネマライズ *Cinema*
☎ 3464 0051; 13-17 Udagawachō; tickets ¥1800/1000, ¥1000 on 1st day of month (except Jan); 🕙 10am-11pm; 🚇 JR Yamanote line to Shibuya (Hachikō exit)

Quality independent films are what you'll catch at Cinema Rise, another cinema in the heart of Shibuya.

⭐ CLUB ASIA
クラブアジア *Club*
☎ 5458 2551; www.clubasia.co.jp in Japanese; 1-8 Maruyamachō, Shibuya-ku; cover around ¥2500; 🕙 5pm-5am; 🚇 JR Yamanote line to Shibuya (Hachikō exit)

This massive techno/soul club is worth a visit if you're on the younger end of twenty-something. Events here are usually jam-packed every night. If you need some fuel to burn on the dance floor, they have a restaurant serving Southeast Asian food until 10pm.

⭐ CLUB QUATTRO
クラブクアトロ *Live music*
☎ 3477 8750; www.club-quattro.com /schedule_shib.php in Japanese; 4F & 5F, Parco Quattro Bldg, 32-13 Udagawachō, Shibuya-ku; cover varies; 🕙 6pm-late; 🚇 JR Yamanote line to Shibuya (Hachikō exit)

NEIGHBOURHOODS

SHIBUYA

Club Quattro is an established showcase venue for local and international rockers. It's actually in one of the Parco department store buildings (Parco Quattro), which makes for a slightly odd entry. Be sure to buy tickets in advance.

⭐ HARLEM *Club*
☎ 3461 8806; www.harlem.co.jp; 2F & 3F, Dr Jeekahn's Bldg, 2-4 Maruyamachō, Shibuya-ku; cover ¥2000-3000; ⏰ 10pm-5am Tue-Sat; 🚇 JR Yamanote line to Shibuya (Hachikō exit)

Wanna see where some of those Japanese boys with Afros and corn rows are heading? On the 2nd and 3rd floor of the Dr Jeekahn's Building, this club is where Tokyo B-boys and B-girls come for soul and hip-hop spun by international DJs. The cover includes one drink.

⭐ JZ BRAT *Live music*
☎ 5728 0168; www.jzbrat.com in Japanese; 2F, Cerulean Tower Tōkyū Hotel, 26-1 Sakuragaokachō, Shibuya-ku; cover varies; ⏰ from 6pm Mon-Sat; 🚇 JR Yamanote line to Shibuya (south exit)

This sleek jazz club is an intimate venue with a sophisticated vibe, hosting performances not limited solely to jazz, though even the jazz ranges from solo vocalists to improvisational trios. Touring performers of folk and electronica also pass through; check local listings to find out what's on.

⭐ KANZE NŌ-GAKUDŌ
観世能楽堂 *Theatre*
☎ 3469 6241; 1-16-4 Shōtō, Shibuya-ku; tickets from ¥3000; ⏰ times vary; 🚇 JR Yamanote line to Shibuya (Hachikō exit)

This theatre is associated with one of the oldest and most highly respected schools of *nō* (classical Japanese musical drama) in Tokyo. By far the most exciting performances are the occasional outdoor night ones of Takigi Nō, where the masked actors are illuminated by huge burning torches. It's a transporting experience, only a 15-minute walk from Shibuya station.

⭐ LA.MAMA ラママ
Live music
☎ 3464 0801; www.lamama.net in Japanese; B1F, Primera Dogenzaka Bldg, 1-15-3 Dōgenzaka, Shibuya-ku; cover from ¥2000; ⏰ 6pm-late; 🚇 JR Yamanote line to Shibuya (Hachikō exit)

For a dose of current local-centric music, La.mama is a good bet for catching live, mainstream Japanese acts. The room is fairly spacious, but even when the place gets crowded you'll be close enough to get be-sweated by the next rising star out of Tokyo.

⭐ RUBY ROOM ルビルーム
Lounge
☎ 3780 3022; www.rubyroomtokyo.com; 2F, Kasumi Bldg, 2-25-17 Dōgenzaka, Shibuya-ku; cover ¥2000; ⏰ 9pm-late; 🚇 JR Yamanote line to Shibuya (Hachikō exit)

This cool, sparkly gem of a cocktail lounge is on the hill behind the 109 Building. With both DJed and live music, the Ruby Room is an appealing spot for older kids hanging in Shibuya. The cover includes one drink, but if you dine downstairs at Sonoma, admission is free. There's a simple map with directions on their website.

☆ SHIBUYA O-EAST
渋谷オーイースト
Live music
☎ 5458 4681; www.shibuya-o.com; 2-14-8 Dōgenzaka, Shibuya-ku; cover from ¥2500; 🕑 7pm-late; 🚇 JR Yamanote line to Shibuya (Hachikō exit)
O-East (formerly known as On-Air East) is a long-running club where you can catch electronica-style live acts with all sorts of wacky extras, such as bubbles, shadow puppets and video embellishments. You'll need to book ahead, as this is a popular place that tends to sell out.

☆ SHIBUYA O-WEST
渋谷オーウエスト
Live music
☎ 5784 7088; www.shibuya-o.com; 2-3 Maruyamachō, Shibuya-ku; cover from ¥2500; 🕑 7pm-late; 🚇 JR Yamanote line to Shibuya (Hachikō exit)
Another outpost in the 'O' empire of Shibuya TV, O-West is just across the street from its eastern

counterpart and tends more towards punk rock and J-pop. As with its sister club, reserve your tickets in advance.

☆ TOKYO METROPOLITAN CHILDREN'S HALL
東京都児童会館
Amusement park
☎ 3409 6361; www.fukushihoken .metro.tokyo.jp/jidou/English/index.html; 1-18-24 Shibuya, Shibuya-ku; admission free; 🕑 9am-5pm; 🚇 JR Yamanote line to Shibuya (Hachikō exit)
This place has six floors of fun activities for children, and best of all, it's free! On weekends, the rooftop playground is open for romping around. But every day, there are age-appropriate art projects, storytelling and music-making, and lots of creative indoor play areas.

☆ WOMB ウーム *Club*
☎ 5459 0039; www.womb.co.jp in Japanese; 2-16 Maruyama-chō, Shibuya-ku; cover ¥1500-4000; 🕑 8pm-late; 🚇 JR Yamanote line to Shibuya (Hachikō exit)
'Oomu' (as pronounced by the Japanese) is all house, techno and drum 'n' bass. The four floors of this place get jammed on weekends. Check Shibuya record shops to pick up a flyer beforehand, or print one from the website, and they'll knock ¥500 to ¥1000 off the cover. Photo ID required at the door.

>EBISU & DAIKANYAMA

Ebisu and Daikanyama don't offer much in the way of spectacular sights, but for a relaxed walk in a hip, low-key area, they exude an effortlessly stylish air. At the southern terminus of the Ebisu Skywalk (a moving walkway) is Yebisu Garden Place, an ersatz Euro-style shopping and entertainment complex surrounding a large courtyard. Apart from the usual restaurants and boutiques, there's also a beer museum and a marvellous photography museum.

To the north of Ebisu station, Daikanyama is one of Tokyo's upscale neighbourhoods with an artsy leaning, where the streets have a more European feel. Fashion here is aimed towards a young yet upscale demographic that has lost none of its edge while pumping up the sophistication. Shops in the Daikanyama alleys offer styles from established international designers to independent locals, while outdoor café culture thrives here. Design fiends will feel right at home here.

EBISU & DAIKANYAMA

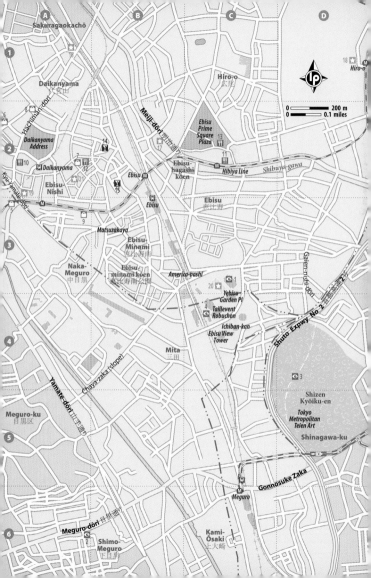

A
1 Sakuragaokachō
桜丘町

Daikanyama
代官山

8 Hachinan-dōri
6

2 Daikanyama
Address

10 Daikanyama

**Ebisu-
Nishi**
恵比寿西

19
5

B
14

7 **32**
21
15

Meiji-dōri 明治通り

Ebisu M

Matsuzakaya

9

**Ebisu-
Minami**
恵比寿南

**Naka-
Meguro**
中目黒

**Ebisu-
minami kōen**
恵比寿南公園

Chaya-zaka (slope)

Yamate-dōri 山手通り

Meguro-ku
目黒区

C
Hiro-o
広尾

**Ebisu
Prime
Square
Plaza**

13
11

Hibiya Line

**Ebisu-
hagashi
kōen**

Ebisu
恵比寿

America-bashi

20
1

**Yehisu-
Garden Pl**

4
**Taillevent
Robuchon**

**Ichiban-kan
Ebisu View
Tower**

Mita
三田

3

**Shizen
Kyōiku-en**

**Tokyo
Metropolitan
Teien Art**

Shinagawa-ku

D
18
Hiro-o

Shibuya-gawa

Garien-nishi-dōri

Shuto Expwy No 2 首都高速2号線

0 ——— 200 m
0 ——— 0.1 miles

Meguro

Gonnosuke Zaka

Meguro-dōri 目黒通り

8
2
**Shimo-
Meguro**
下目黒

**Kami-
Ōsaki**
上大崎

1 **2** **3** **4** **5** **6**

NEIGHBOURHOODS

EBISU & DAIKANYAMA

◉ SEE

◉ BEER MUSEUM YEBISU
恵比寿麦酒記念館

☎ 5423 7255; www.sapporobeer.jp
/english/guide/yebisu; 4-20-1 Ebisu,
Shibuya-ku; admission free; ⏱ 10am-6pm
Tue-Sun; 🚈 JR Yamanote line to Ebisu
(east exit to Skywalk)

Run by Sapporo Breweries, this
museum has lots of good exhibits
on the brewing process, but the
real pull is the Tasting Lounge,
where you can sample Sapporo's
various limited-edition brews.
Sorry, no freebies here – it's ¥200
per glass or ¥400 for a sampler of
four – but that's still quite a deal.

◉ MEGURO
PARASITOLOGICAL MUSEUM
目黒寄生虫館

☎ 3716 1264; http://kiseichu.org
/english.aspx; 4-1-1 Shimo-Meguro,
Meguro-ku; admission free; ⏱ 10am-5pm
Tue-Sun; 🚈 JR Yamanote line to Meguro
(west exit); ♿

Those inclined to stifling shrieks
upon encountering a spider will
not find this museum to their
liking, but for others, it's grue-
somely fascinating. One of the
more impressive exhibits is a nearly 9m-long tapeworm extracted
from an unfortunate host. Kids
will get a kick out of this place,
and the gift shop teems with cute
(creepy?) keepsakes.

◉ NATIONAL INSTITUTE FOR
NATURE STUDY
国立自然教育園

☎ 3441 7176; www.ins.kahaku.go.jp
/english/english.html; 5-21-5
Shirokanedai, Minato-ku; admission
¥300/free; ⏱ 9am-4.30pm Tue-Sun
Sep-May, 9am-5pm Tue-Sun Jun-Aug;
🚈 JR Yamanote line to Meguro (east exit),
🚇 Namboku line to Shirokanedai (exit 1);
♿

Prosaic in name but perfect in
nature, this garden (known as Shizen Kyōiku-en in Japanese) is one
of Tokyo's least known and most
appealing getaways. It preserves
the city's original flora in undisci-
plined profusion. Take a walk on
Tokyo's wild side through woods
and swamps, in this haven for
bird-watchers, botanists and those
overdosing on urban rhythms.

◉ TOKYO METROPOLITAN
MUSEUM OF PHOTOGRAPHY
東京都写真美術館

☎ 3280 0099; www.syabi.com/top/top
_eng.html; 1-13-3 Mita, Meguro-ku;
admission varies; ⏱ 10am-6pm Tue,
Wed, Sat & Sun, 10am-8pm Thu & Fri;
🚈 JR Yamanote line to Ebisu (east exit
to Skywalk)

Japan's first large-scale museum
devoted entirely to photography,
this wonderfully curated space is
comprised of several galleries. The
emphasis is on Japanese photography, but international work is

Shop in Euro-style amid the charming green spaces of Yebisu Garden Place

also well represented. As you enter Yebisu Garden Place, the museum is at the very back, towards the right.

🛍 SHOP
🛍 EVISU TAILOR
エビスヤテーラー *Fashion*
☎ 3710 1999; www.evisu.com; 1-1-5 Kami-Meguro, Meguro-ku; ⏱ 11am-8pm; 🚇 Hibiya line to Naka-meguro

In the early '90s the detail-obsessed founder of Evisu began producing jeans the old-fashioned way, using rescued looms and weaving methods, helping to spawn the Japanese selvedge denim craze. At Evisu Tailor you can choose the pair you want and have the Evisu logo custom-painted on, or discreet denim-wearers can opt to go logoless.

🛍 FRAPBOIS *Fashion*
☎ 5459 2625; www.frapbois.jp in Japanese; 19-5 Sarugakuchō, Shibuya-ku; ⏱ 11am-8pm; 🚉 JR Yamanote line to Ebisu (west exit) or Tōkyū Tōyoko line to Daikanyama (main exit)

Frapbois is all the rage among young Japanese fashionistas. Frapbois designs have a free-flowing hippie aesthetic and are worth a look to gauge which way the trend is blowing.

📕 HACKNET
ハックネット *Books*
☎ 5728 6611; www.hacknet.tv in Japanese; 1-30-10 Ebisu, Shibuya-ku; ⏰ 11am-8pm; 🚉 JR Yamanote line to Ebisu (west exit)

Hacknet, a tiny shop with tall shelves, is a haven for art and design junkies, full of absorbing design porn (we mean it metaphorically) in Ebisu's Q-Flagship Building.

📕 KAMAWANU かまわぬ
Handicrafts
☎ 3780 0182; www.kamawanu.co.jp in Japanese; 23-1 Sarugakuchō, Shibuya-ku; ⏰ 11am-7pm; 🚉 JR Yamanote line to Ebisu (west exit) or Tōkyū Tōyoko line to Daikanyama (main exit)

This little shop in Daikanyama specialises in beautifully-dyed *tenugui,* those ubiquitous Japanese hand towels that you can fold on your head at the *sentō* (public baths), use to genteelly pat the sweat off the back of your neck on the JR platform, or wrap your *bentō* (boxed meal) in to take with you for lunch. Colourful designs incorporate traditional abstract patterns and representations of natural elements.

📕 RESTORE *Fashion*
☎ 5768 9877; 3-2-2 Ebisu-Minami, Shibuya-ku; ⏰ noon-8pm; 🚉 JR Yamanote line to Ebisu (west exit), 🚇 Hibiya line to Ebisu (exit 5)

This small but selective second-hand shop along Komazawa-dōri is stocked with middleweight vintage as well as last-year's look. APC and Yohji Yamamoto rub shoulders on the hangers here, and they carry both men's and women's garb. Recycle and refresh your wardrobe.

🍴 EAT

🍴 CAFÉ ARTIFAGOSE
カフェアルトファゴス
Cafe ¥
☎ 5489 1133; 20-23 Daikanyama, Shibuya-ku; ⏰ 11am-8pm; 🚉 JR Yamanote line to Ebisu (west exit) or Tōkyū Tōyoko line to Daikanyama (main exit); ♿ 🅥 👶

Up Daikanyama way, Café Artifagose is easy to spot by its appealing alfresco seating and the heavenly, yeasty scent of fresh bread and flaky pastry. Reasons for stopping awhile include superb breads, crispy pizza, European cheeses and a wide selection of tea, coffee, and imported beer and wine.

🍴 IPPŪDŌ 一風堂
Rāmen ¥
☎ 5420 2225; 1-3-13 Hiroo, Shibuya-ku; ⏰ 11am-4pm; 🚉 JR Yamanote line to Ebisu (east exit), 🚇 Hibiya line to Ebisu (exits 1 & 2); 👶

Nationally famous, this *rāmen* shop specialises in *tonkotsu* (pork broth) noodles. While the *akamaru rāmen* (rich pork broth with red seasoning oil) is tailored towards the Tokyo palate, the *shiromaru* (milder, 'white' pork broth) is pure Kyūshū (grate fresh garlic over it for authenticity). You'll have to queue at peak periods and, as a courtesy, should take no more than 20 minutes to eat, but it's well worth it.

🍴 KM FILS カーエムフィス
French ¥¥
☎ 5457 1435; 1-30-14 Ebisu, Shibuya-ku; ⏰ noon-3pm & 6-11pm Mon & Wed-Fri, 11.30am-2pm & 6-9pm Sat & Sun; 🚇 JR Yamanote line to Ebisu (west exit), ⓗ Hibiya line to Ebisu (exit 4)

The menu at this sophisticated, Mediterranean-leaning little bistro is designed by Kiyoshi Miyashiro, the initials behind the name. Complementing the Gallic cuisine is the jazz in the background and the knowledge that you're enjoying a sweet deal – all of which compensates for the sometimes snooty service.

🍴 SHUNSENBŌ 旬泉坊
Shabu-shabu & kaiseki ¥¥
☎ 5469 9761; 1F, Ebisu Prime Square Tower, 1-1-40 Hiroo, Shibuya-ku; ⏰ 11am-3pm & 5.30-10pm; 🚇 JR Yamanote line to Ebisu (east exit) ⓗ Hibiya line to Ebisu (exits 1 & 2); ♿ Ⓥ 🚼

Specialising in *tōfu kaiseki* and *shabu-shabu*, courses here are a real bargain considering the quality of the food and the elegant surroundings. Shunsenbō's smooth, silky tofu is prepared in-house, and they have an English menu.

🍸 DRINK
🍸 ENJOY! HOUSE
エンジョイハウス *Lounge*
☎ 5489 1591; 2F, Kokuto Bldg, 2-9-9 Ebisu-Nishi, Shibuya-ku; ⏰ 1pm-2am Sun & Tue-Thu, 1pm-4am Fri & Sat, closed 1st Sun of each month; 🚇 JR Yamanote line to Ebisu (west exit)

This retro lounge is run by a free-spirited owner who will elevate your mood. The mix here runs from '80s pop to reggae, and the vibe is relaxed. Best of all, there's no cover charge. Enjoy!

🍸 WHAT THE DICKENS
ワットザディケンズ *Pub*
☎ 3780 2099; www.whatthedickens.jp; 4F, Roob 6 Bldg, 1-13-3 Ebisu-Nishi, Shibuya-ku; ⏰ 5pm-late Tue-Sat, 5pm-midnight Sun; 🚇 JR Yamanote line to Ebisu (west exit), ⓗ Hibiya line to Ebisu (exit 2)

One of Tokyo's better British-style pubs, this one has a pleasant, spacious feel, and there's usually a live band in the corner playing good, mellow music. Good tunes, hearty

pub food and Guinness on tap –
what more could you want?

⭐ PLAY

⭐ AIR エアー *Club*
☎ 5784 3386; www.air-tokyo.com; B1F
& B2F, Hikawa Bldg, 2-11 Sagurakuchō,
Shibuya-ku; 🚇 Tōkyū Tōyoko line to
Daikanyama (main exit) or JR Yamanote
line to Shibuya (south exit)
DJs spin mostly house here, and
the crowd tends to be happy
and friendly – though not huge
on dancing. Air is in an alley
northwest of Hachiman-dōri,
south of Shibuya station; there's a
decent map on their website. The
entrance to the basement is inside
the Frames restaurant. Remember
to bring your ID.

⭐ LIQUID ROOM
リキッドルーム *Live music*
☎ 5464 0800; www.liquidroom.net;
3-16-6 Higashi, Shibuya-ku; cover from
¥3000; ⏱ 7pm-late; 🚇 JR Yamanote
line to Ebisu (east exit)
Some of the world's greatest
performers have graced the
stage of the Liquid Room, from
the Flaming Lips to Linton
Kwesi Johnson. This spacious
place in Ebisu is an excellent
place to see an old favourite or
find a new one.

⭐ MILK ミルク *Live music*
☎ 5458 2826; www.milk-tokyo.com;
B1F, Roob 6 Bldg, 1-13-3 Ebisu-Nishi,
Shibuya-ku; cover ¥1000-3000;
⏱ 8pm-4am; 🚇 JR Yamanote line to
Ebisu (west exit) 🚇 Hibiya line to Ebisu
(exit 2)
One of Tokyo's best small live
clubs, Milk features international
and local punk, rock and underground. This is a cool space, with
three underground levels and a
crowd of weirdly wonderful local
characters. Check out the out-
of-commission kitchen – a great
place to chat and sip a vodka tonic
between sets.

⭐ SMASH HITS
スマシヒッツ *Karaoke*
☎ 3444 0432; www.smashhits.jp;
B1F, M2 Hiro-o Bldg, 5-2-26 Hiro-o,
Shibuya-ku; admission ¥3000;
⏱ 7pm-3am Mon-Sat; 🚇 Hibiya line to
Hiro-o (exit B2)
Watch your friends wince as you
deafen them with the Sid Vicious
version of 'My Way'. Smash Hits
provides excruciating fun of
the highest order, with 12,000
English-language songs to choose
from for your 15 minutes of fame.
There's no time limit, and the
cover includes two drinks.

☆ UNIT ユニット *Club*
☎ 5459 8630; www.unit-tokyo.com; B1F-B3F, Za House Bldg, 1-34-17 Ebisu-Nishi, Shibuya-ku; cover from ¥3000; 🕑 varies; 🚇 Tōkyū Tōyoko line to Daikanyama, 🚇 Hibiya line to Naka-Meguro

This subterranean space contains a restaurant, club and bar on each descending floor. Shows are mostly big-name Japanese DJ events, but live bands also play here. Be sure to bring ID to get in.

☆ YEBISU GARDEN CINEMA 恵比寿ガーデンシネマ *Cinema*
☎ 5420 6161; Yebisu Garden Place, 4-20-2 Ebisu, Shibuya-ku; tickets ¥1800/1000, on 1st day of month ¥1000; 🕑 10am-11pm; 🚇 JR Yamanote line to Ebisu (east exit to Skywalk)

At Yebisu Garden Place, where you can have a bite beforehand and a cocktail afterwards, this cinema is a good place to catch a variety of films. Patrons are called into the theatre in groups according to ticket numbers (first come, first served), bypassing the usual mad rush for the best seats.

☆ YOGAJAYA ヨガジャヤ *Sports & recreation*
☎ 5784 3622; www.yogajaya.com; 2F, 1-25-11 Ebisu-Nishi, Shibuya-ku; trial class/mat rental ¥1500/300; 🕑 7am-9.30pm Mon-Fri, 11am-7.30pm Sat & Sun

Mainly Hatha, Ashtanga and Sivananda practices; classes in Japanese and English.

>AKASAKA & ROPPONGI

In a very general sense Akasaka and Roppongi can be compartmental-ised into two distinct districts: business and pleasure. In Akasaka and nearby Nagatachō, business folk and government suits toil away in service to big machines and political matters. But just down the road in Roppongi, the business has historically been leisure. For more than half a century Roppongi has been the place to cut loose and has not always had such a savoury reputation. Nowadays, it's the least Japanese part of Japan – but that doesn't mean it's no fun. Nightlife is concentrated here so intensely that on Saturday nights you may just choke on the phero-mone cloud hanging above Roppongi Crossing.

And since Roppongi Hills made its debut in 2003, the nature of the neighbourhood has evolved again into a daytime destination as well as the place to pull an all-nighter, rising a notch in class and respectability.

AKASAKA & ROPPONGI

Please see over for map

SEE

COMPLEX
コンプレックス

☎ 5411 7510; 6-8-14 Roppongi, Minato-ku; 🕙 11am-7pm Tue-Sat; 🚇 Hibiya & Toei Ōedo lines to Roppongi (exits 1c & 3)
In the shadow of Roppongi Hills, this aptly named building will give a brief glimpse into the Tokyo art scene. Several of the best commercial galleries in town inhabit the five-storey structure, with a mix of graphic and painterly contemporary styles in firmly established galleries as well as newer standouts.

HIE-JINJA 日枝神社

☎ 3581 2471; www.hiejinja.net/jinja/english/index.html; 2-10-5 Nagatachō, Chiyoda-ku; admission free; 🕙 dawn-dusk; 🚇 Ginza & Namboku lines to Tameike-sannō (exits 5 & 7)

One of the casualties of WWII bombing was Hie-jinja, which dates back to 1659 in its present location. Although the shrine itself isn't a major attraction, the highlight is the walk up, through a 'tunnel' of red *torii* (shrine gate). It's also the backdrop for one of Japan's most spectacular *matsuri* (festivals). Look for the concrete plaza-style entrance on Sotobori-dōri.

MORI ART MUSEUM
森美術館

☎ 5777 8600; www.mori.art.museum; 53F, Mori Tower, Roppongi Hills, 6-10-1 Roppongi, Minato-ku; admission ¥1500; 🕙 10am-10pm Wed-Mon, 10am-5pm Tue, closed btwn exhibitions; 🚇 Hibiya & Toei Ōedo lines to Roppongi (exits 1c & 3)
Past exhibitions at this consistently well-curated contemporary

Contemplate the cutting-edge exhibits at Mori Art Museum, Roppongi Hills

To National
Azabu Supermarket (400m)

arts museum have ranged from a comprehensive exhibition of contemporary African art to a huge, walk-through installation by Kusama Yayoi. Museum admission also gets you into the spectacular 360-degree city views of Tokyo City View (and vice versa).

NATIONAL DIET BUILDING
☎ 3581 3111; www.sangiin.go.jp; 1-7-1 Nagatachō, Chiyoda-ku; ⏰ 8am-5pm Mon-Fri; ◉ Hanzōmon, Namboku & Yūrakuchō lines to Nagatachō (exit 1) or Marunouchi & Chiyoda lines to Kokkai-gijidōmae (exit 1)

When the Diet is not in session, you can take free 60-minute tours (☎ 5521 7445) of this government hall, completed in 1936. Its

structure was meant to combine the modern styles of both Asian and European architecture.

NEW OTANI JAPANESE GARDEN ホテルニューオータニ日本庭園
www.newotani.co.jp/en/group/garden/index.html; admission free; ⏰ 6am-10pm; ◉ Ginza & Marunouchi lines to Akasaka-mitsuke (Belle Vie exit) or Hanzōmon & Yūrakuchō lines to Nagatachō (exit 7)

This stunning 400-year-old Japanese garden in the grounds of the New Otani Hotel is worth a stop if traditional landscapes are your thing. Although the garden is open to the public, the hotel doesn't go out of its way to make

For a taste of government life take a tour of the National Diet Building

it accessible. The easiest way to find it is via the first floor of the hotel's Garden Court shopping complex.

ⓒ ŌKURA SHŪKOKAN
大倉集古館

☎ 3583 0781; 2-10-3 Toranomon, Minato-ku; admission ¥800/500/300; ⏰ 10am-4.30pm Tue-Sun; ⓜ Hibiya line to Kamiyachō (exit 4b) or Ginza & Namboku lines to Tameike-sannō (exit 13)
Surrounded by a small but well-populated sculpture garden, this museum has an impressive collection of lacquer writing boxes, scrolls, ancient sculptures and several national treasures. The two-storey museum – with a collection that's rotated seasonally – is definitely worth a look if you're on this side of town.

ⓒ ROPPONGI HILLS
六本木ヒルズ

☎ 6406 6000; www.roppongihills.com/en; Roppongi 6-chōme, Minato-ku; tours ¥1500/1000/500; ⏰ 9am-6pm; ⓜ Hibiya & Toei Ōedo lines to Roppongi (exits 1c & 3); ♿
This city within a city has it all, including public gardens and spectacular architecture. Shops and restaurants are topped off with the excellent high-rise Mori Art Museum (see p139) and the luxurious Virgin Toho Cinemas (p153).

RENDEZVOUS SPOTS EVERYONE KNOWS…
> *Hachikō* statue (p120); Shibuya
> Studio Alta building (p88); Shinjuku
> Mitsukoshi lion (p56); Ginza
> *The Spider* (Maman sculpture; left); Roppongi
> *Takamori Saigō* statue (p69); Ueno

ⓒ SŌGETSU KAIKAN
草月会館

☎ 3408 1126; www.sogetsu.or.jp/english/index.html; Sōgetsu Kaikan Bldg, 7-2-21 Akasaka, Minato-ku; ⏰ 10am-5pm Mon-Thu & Sat, 10am-8pm Fri; ⓜ Ginza, Hanzōmon & Toei Ōedo lines to Aoyama-itchōme (exit 4)
The avant-garde Sōgetsu School of Ikebana, whose philosophy is that ikebana (Japanese flower arrangement) can go beyond its traditional roots, offers ikebana classes in English. Stop by the Sōgetsu Kaikan building for a look at current ikebana exhibits or to enquire about classes.

ⓒ TOKYO TOWER
東京タワー

☎ 3433 5111; www.tokyotower.co.jp/333/foreign/eng/index.html; 4-2-8 Shiba-kōen, Minato-ku; main observation deck ¥310-820, special observation deck extra ¥350-600; ⏰ 9am-10pm; ⓜ Hibiya line to Kamiyachō (exits 1 & 2); ♿
Although it might play second fiddle to Roppongi Hills'

Watch the city fade away at Tokyo Tower

52nd-floor Tokyo City View, Tokyo Tower still affords a great 360-degree view of the city, best appreciated at night. It retains a sort of oldster charm next to the architectural wonders that have succeeded it. A Wednesday night attraction is live music on the main observatory.

🛍 SHOP

Roppongi Hills lit up the neighbourhood when it opened as the biggest, baddest and brightest beacon Roppongi has ever seen. On arrival you'll want to pick up an English-language guide to help you navigate this minimetropolis that brims with high-end shops in sparkly digs. But remember that equally worthy (but perhaps not as eye-catching) are the shops that continue to prosper in Roppongi and Akasaka.

📖 AOYAMA BOOK CENTER
青山ブックセンター
Art & antiques
☎ 3479 0479; 6-1-20 Roppongi, Minato-ku; ⏰ 10am-5am Mon-Sat, 10am-10pm Sun, closed 2nd & 3rd Tue each month; 🚇 Hibiya & Toei Ōedo lines to Roppongi (exit 3)
The beautifully remodelled Roppongi-dōri branch of Aoyama Book Center is a prime spot for night owls, with a great international selection of reads and a carefully chosen collection of foreign art books. There's another branch nearby in the Roppongi Hills West Walk.

📖 AXIS BUILDING
アクシスビル
Homewares & novelties
☎ 3587 2781; 5-17-1 Roppongi, Minato-ku; ⏰ 11am-7pm Mon-Sat; 🚇 Hibiya & Toei Ōedo lines to Roppongi (exit 3)
Salivate over some of Japan's most innovative interior design at this Roppongi design complex. Of the 20 or so galleries and retail shops selling fabrics, furniture and art

books, one highlight is ceramics specialist Kisso (p147) associated with the *kaiseki* (multicourse Japanese meals) restaurant of the same name.

🏠 JAPAN SWORD 日本刀剣
Art & antiques
☎ 3434 4321; www.japansword.co.jp; 3-8-1 Toranomon, Minato-ku; 🕐 9.30am-6pm Mon-Fri, 9.30am-5pm Sat; 🚇 Ginza line to Toranomon (exit 2)
If *Kill Bill* revived a long-dormant childhood attraction to swords, this highly respected dealer has a beautiful showroom and lots of experience helping foreigners choose the right *katana* (sword) for their taste and budget. Priciest are the macabre *tameshi-giri* blades that have been 'used on humans'.

🏠 KUROFUNE 黒船
Art & antiques
☎ 3479 1552; www.kurofuneantiques .com; 7-7-4 Roppongi, Minato-ku; 🕐 10am-6pm Mon-Sat; 🚇 Toei Ōedo line to Roppongi (exit 7)
Kurofune, run for the past quarter century by a friendly American collector, carries an awesome treasure trove of Japanese antiques. Correspondingly awesome amounts of cash are necessary for acquiring some of these items, such as painstakingly constructed

Edo-period *tansu* (Japanese chests of drawers), but serious antique connoisseurs are well advised to have a look.

🏠 TOLMAN COLLECTION
Art & antiques
☎ 3434 1300; www.tolmantokyo.com; 2-2-18 Shiba-Daimon, Minato-ku; 🕐 11am-7pm Wed-Mon; 🚇 Toei Asakusa & Toei Ōedo lines to Daimon (exits A3 & A6)
For collectors keen on picking up some contemporary art, this well-established, estimable gallery represents a strong stable of printmakers both Japanese and foreign. Although the artists exhibit a fairly broad range of styles ranging from abstract to representative, all of the work has a distinctly Japanese feel.

🍴 EAT

This being a historically *gaijin* (foreigner) heavy neighbourhood – and now with the addition of Roppongi Hills – there's a cornucopia of international cuisine as well as some of Tokyo's best Japanese restaurants. Consequently, dining out tends to be more expensive than in other areas of the city, but the venues also put forth the extra effort to give all five senses a memorable experience of Tokyo.

🍴 ASTERIX アステリックス
French ¥¥
☎ 5561 0980; B1F, 6-3-16 Akasaka, Minato-ku; ⏱ 11.30am-2pm & 6-10pm Mon-Sat; Ⓜ Chiyoda line to Akasaka (exits 6 & 7); ♿
A French lunch here is a smashing deal, but dinner has its own merits (ie not so rushed, allowing you to linger over your wine). Portions are large but the dining room is tiny, so reservations are advised. The menu is in French, but servers can translate into English if needed.

🍴 ERAWAN エラワン
Thai ¥¥
☎ 3404 5741; 13F, Roi Bldg, 5-5-1 Roppongi, Minato-ku; ⏱ 5.30-11.30pm Mon-Fri & 5-11.30pm Sat & Sun; Ⓜ Hibiya & Toei Ōedo lines to Roppongi (exit 3)
Not a new kid on the block; Erawan serves spicy curries and green papaya salad, in a setting reminiscent of an outdoor Thai café on some southern shore. Except here, you get a glittering urban view from this top-floor dining venue.

🍴 FUKUZUSHI 福寿司
Sushi & sashimi ¥¥¥
☎ 3402 4116; 5-7-8 Roppongi, Minato-ku; ⏱ 11.30am-1.30pm & 5.30-10pm Mon-Sat; Ⓜ Hibiya & Toei Ōedo lines to Roppongi (exit 3); Ⓥ
Although the atmosphere here is upscale, Fukuzushi is decidedly more relaxed than some places in Ginza and Tsukiji. The sushi is some of the best in town, the portions are large, and there's even a full cocktail bar. It's in the alley beyond the Hard Rock Café.

🍴 GONPACHI 権八
Izakaya ¥¥
☎ 5771 0170; 1-13-11 Nishi-Azabu, Minato-ku; ⏱ 11.30am-5am; Ⓜ Hibiya, Toei Ōedo lines to Roppongi (exit 2); ♿
The Edo-village décor and festive buzz in the air makes Gonpachi a great place for celebratory dinners, but do you really need a reason to thrill your palate with half a dozen exotic and untried Japanese morsels? Upstairs, you can order everything on the menu, plus sushi. Book ahead.

🍴 HAVANA CAFE ハバナカフェ
Cafe ¥
☎ 3423 3500; 4-12-2 Roppongi, Minato-ku; ⏱ 11.30am-5am; Ⓜ Hibiya & Toei Ōedo lines to Roppongi (exits 3 & 6); Ⓥ
Fuel up or chill out at this casual spot that's open late for dance-floor burnouts. Respectably hefty burritos and very good burgers go for less than ¥1000, and Havana offers great happy-hour drink specials. The streetside seating and large-windowed dining room open onto a quiet backstreet, a quick escape from crowds.

🍴 INAKAYA 田舎屋
Robatayaki   ¥¥¥¥

☎ 3408 5040; 5-3-4 Roppongi, Minato-ku; ⏰ 5-11pm; Ⓜ Hibiya & Toei Ōedo lines to Roppongi (exit 3)

Inakaya has gained fame as a top-end *robatayaki* (grilled-to-order seafood and meat). It does raucous, bustling, don't-stand-on-ceremony *robatayaki* with gusto. Point at what you'd like to eat and they'll grill it for you and serve it with a boisterous flourish. You'll pay for the privilege and have a rocking good time doing so.

🍴 KISSO 吉左右 *Kaiseki*   ¥¥¥

☎ 3582 4191; B1F, Axis Bldg, 5-17-1 Roppongi, Minato-ku; ⏰ 11am-2pm & 5.30-10pm Mon-Sat; Ⓜ Hibiya & Toei Ōedo lines to Roppongi (exit 3); ♿ 🚻

KAISEKI

Kaiseki (elegant, multicourse Japanese meals) grew as a complement to the traditions of the tea ceremony, with a similar ceremonial emphasis on attention to all of the senses during the dining experience. Each course is not only painstakingly prepared to bring out the flavours of the seasonally changing dishes, but also the colours, textures, and smells, which must be carefully presented to be aesthetically pleasing in every way. It's the height of Japanese cuisine and a singular experience. One of the most accessible places in Tokyo to sample *kaiseki* dining is at Kisso (above) in Roppongi.

Set in a contemporary, urban-style setting, Kisso is doubtless the most accessible place in Tokyo to sample Japan's traditional *haute cuisine – kaiseki ryōri –* presented in gorgeous lacquer and ceramic ware. It's best to order *omakase* (chef's choice) and put your dining fate into the hands of the chef. Lunch is a great deal, but dinner will feel more serene.

🍴 L'ATELIER DE JOËL ROBUCHON ラトリエドゥ ジョエルロブション
French   ¥¥¥

☎ 5772 7500; 2F Hillside, Roppongi Hills, 6-10-1 Roppongi, Minato-ku; ⏰ 11.30am-2pm, 2.30-4pm & 6-11pm; Ⓜ Hibiya & Toei Ōedo lines to Roppongi (exits 1c & 3)

Wonder chef Jöel Robuchon styled this upscale French diner in the fashion of the sushi bar counter. While the fantastic dishes are not overly fussy, everything is made on order, which can mean long waits in the queue and over your meal – leaving plenty of time for conversation and anticipation.

🍴 MOTI モティ *Indian*   ¥¥

☎ 3584 6640; 3F, Kinpa Bldg, 2-14-31 Akasaka, Minato-ku; ⏰ 11.30am-10pm; Ⓜ Chiyoda line to Akasaka (exit 2); Ⓥ 🚻

You'll get the red-carpet treatment at Moti, where some of

Tokyo's best Indian food is served up by attentive and friendly staff, in elegant surrounding. The lunch sets are a terrific deal, and this branch serves *dosa* (rice pancakes) and other South Indian specialities. Moti has another branch in Akasaka, one in Roppongi, and several others beyond.

🍴 NATIONAL AZABU SUPERMARKET ナショナル麻布スーパーマーケット
International groceries
☎ 3442 3181; 4-5-2 Minami-Azabu, Minato-ku; ⏰ 9.30am-7pm; Ⓜ Hibiya line to Hiro-o (exits 1 & 2)
Posher than posh can be, National Azabu is where the ambassadorial lackeys are sent to stock up on pâté de foie gras and truffles or their Japanese equivalents, *uni* (sea urchins) and *matsutake* (mushrooms). It's also got an awesome selection of imported wines and natural foods, and, importantly, has a pharmacy staffed with English speakers.

🍴 SERYNA 瀬里奈
Sukiyaki & shabu-shabu　　¥¥¥
☎ 3402 1051; 3-12-2 Roppongi, Minato-ku; ⏰ noon-11pm; Ⓜ Hibiya & Toei Ōedo lines to Roppongi (exits 3 & 5); ♿
Although it feels a bit aged, like the high-quality Kōbe beef that

draws expats and visiting guests here, Seryna provides a dignified backdrop for *shabu-shabu*, sukiyaki and *teppanyaki* (table-top grilling). The restaurant surrounds an attractive rock garden.

🍴 SUSHI-SEI 寿司清
Sushi & sashimi　　¥¥
☎ 3582 9503; 3-11-14 Akasaka, Minato-ku; ⏰ 11.30am-2pm & 5-11.30pm; Ⓜ Ginza & Marunouchi lines to Akasaka-mitsuke (Belle Vie exit)
Taste top-notch sushi at Sushi-sei, which traces its ancestry back to Tsukiji. Like Akasaka itself, Sushi-sei conducts serious business. Try to hit it during off-peak hours, or expect to queue with hungry government officials and financial movers and shakers. The low-profile shop is set back slightly from the street.

🍴 UMAYA うまや
Traditional Japanese　　¥¥
☎ 6229 1661; 4-2-24 Akasaka, Minato-ku; ⏰ 11am-1.30pm & 5pm-1am Mon-Sat; Ⓜ Ginza & Marunouchi lines to Akasaka-mitsuke (Belle Vie exit); Ⓥ
This atmospheric, traditionally styled restaurant serves a variety of Japanese dishes, incorporating free-range chicken, house-made tōfu and a surprising number of vegetarian dishes (though not so many at lunch). To find it from

Hitotsugi-dōri, head for Akasaka-fudōson-jinja but turn left just inside the shrine gate.

DRINK

If, at the end of a long day, you need to unwind in a quiet corner nursing a single-malt whiskey, the lobbies and high-rise bars of Akasaka hotels will serve nicely. But gearing up for a big night out means starting in Roppongi, where you can drink up for cheap in a dive bar, or begin your evening with a stylish cocktail.

☗ AGAVE アガベ Bar
☎ 3497 0229; B1F, Clover Bldg, 7-15-10 Roppongi, Minato-ku; ⏰ 6.30pm-2am Tue-Thu, 6.30pm-4am Fri & Sat; ⊕ Hibiya & Toei Ōedo lines to Roppongi (exit 2)
This amiable spot is for those more interested in savouring the subtleties of its 400-plus varieties of tequila than tossing back shots of Cuervo. Sip an *añejo* (aged tequila) or try one of their margaritas.

☗ BERND'S BAR バーンズバー Bar
☎ 5563 9232; www.berndsbar.com; 2F, Pure Roppongi Bldg, 5-18-1 Roppongi, Minato-ku; ⏰ 5pm-late Mon-Sat; ⊕ Hibiya & Toei Ōedo lines to Roppongi (exit 3)

More a German *izakaya* (pub/eatery) than a bar, the very friendly Bernd's is slightly removed from the mad parade of Roppongi Crossing. Hearty, authentic German food goes with the German draught *bier*. Menus are in German, Japanese and English – languages that the owner speaks with aplomb.

☗ CASTILLO カスティロ Bar
☎ 3470 3624; www.castillo-tokyo.com; 3F & 4F, Win Roppongi Bldg, 3-15-24 Roppongi, Minato-ku; ⏰ 7pm-late Mon-Sat; ⊕ Hibiya & Toei Ōedo lines to Roppongi (exit 3)
Good happy-hour specials continue at this long-standing Roppongi bar, now in one of the rowdier Roppongi alleys. Castillo has '80s tunes on rotation and is a good place to have a few drinks before setting out (and shelling out) for the clubs.

☗ GERONIMO ジェロニモ Bar
☎ 3478 7449; www.geronimoshotbar.com; 2F, Yamamuro Bldg, 7-14-10 Roppongi, Minato-ku; ⏰ 5pm-late; ⊕ Hibiya & Toei Ōedo lines to Roppongi (exits 3 & 4)
Geronimo is poised over Roppongi Crossing, making it a logical place to start out a bar crawl through the neighbourhood. The place has

a friendly vibe, and if you're feeling superfriendly you can bang on the drum that signals your intention to buy a round for everyone in the bar.

▼ MADO LOUNGE
マドラウンジ *Lounge*
☎ 3470 0052; www.ma-do.jp; 52F, Mori Tower, 6-10-1 Roppongi Hills, Roppongi, Minato-ku; cover Sun-Wed ¥1000, Thu-Sat ¥2000; ⏰ 7pm-1am; ⓜ Hibiya & Toei Ōedo lines to Roppongi (exits 1c & 3)

On the 52nd floor of Mori Tower, the views are indeed stunning from this very cool window lounge. To get in, you'll have to first pay admission to the Mori Museum (p139) and/or Tokyo City View (p143), so it's only worth the additional cover if you're here anyway.

▼ MADURO マヅロ *Lounge*
☎ 4333 8888; 4F, Grand Hyatt Tokyo, 6-10-3 Roppongi, Minato-ku; cover around ¥1500; ⏰ 6pm-2am; ⓜ Hibiya & Toei Ōedo lines to Roppongi (exits 1c & 3)

Make a dramatic entrance into Maduro from the 6th floor over the bridge and pond inside the labyrinthine Grand Hyatt Tokyo. Swanky and sleek, this is a chic spot to start your evening. There's live music nightly, but get here before 9pm to avoid the cover charge.

⭐ PLAY

⭐ ABBEY ROAD
アビーロード *Live music*
☎ 3402 0017; www.abbeyroad.ne.jp; B1F, Roppongi Annex Bldg, 4-11-5 Roppongi, Minato-ku; cover ¥1600-2100; ⏰ 6pm-midnight Mon-Thu, 6pm-1am Fri & Sat; ⓜ Hibiya & Toei Ōedo lines to Roppongi (exits 4a & 7)

Abbey Road is one of the two Roppongi clubs with uncannily good live Beatles tribute bands. Pull up a chair and prepare to be flabbergasted by the house Beatles cover bands – all Japanese, all seriousness, and appearances aside, pretty dang impressive. Aside from the cover, there's a two-drink minimum. Book ahead if you can, especially on weekends.

⭐ AZABU-JŪBAN ONSEN
麻布十番温泉 *Hot spring*
☎ 3404 2610; 3F, 1-5-22 Azabu-jūban, Minato-ku; cover ¥1260; ⏰ 11am-9pm Wed-Mon; ⓜ Namboku & Toei Ōedo lines to Azabu-jūban (exit 4)

Helpful English signage hints that this *onsen* (hot spring) has experience with foreigners – a great thing, as the dark, tea-coloured water is scalding hot, and there's a lovely *rotemburo* (outdoor bath) it would be shame to miss out on. Downstairs there's a less expensive, more bare-bones *sentō* (public bath). The nondescript building is on the corner of Kurayami-zaka and Azabu-Jūban-dōri.

⭐ **BLUE NOTE** ブルーノート
Live music
☎ 5485 0088; www.bluenote.co.jp;
Raika Bldg, 6-3-16 Minami-Aoyama,
Minato-ku; cover ¥6000-10,000;
🕐 5.30pm-1.30am Mon-Sat;
🚇 Chiyoda, Ginza, & Hanzōmon lines to
Omote-sandō (exit B3)
Serious cognoscenti roll up at
Tokyo's prime jazz spot, where you
can get up close and personal with
greats such as Maceo Parker and
Chick Corea. Walk down Kotto-dōri
towards Nishi-Azabu, and hang a
left when you see Papas Café.

⭐ **BUL-LET'S** ブレッツ *Club*
☎ 3401 4844; www.bul-lets.com; B1F,
Kasumi Bldg, 1-7-11 Nishi-Azabu, Minato-
ku; cover from ¥1500; 🚇 Hibiya & Toei
Ōedo lines to Roppongi (exits 2 & 3)
This mellow basement space plays
worldwide trance and ambient
sounds for barefoot patrons. Beds
and sofas await for those who
need a soft spot. But don't get the
wrong idea – it's not all tranquillity
and lazing away. Get your groove
on to live electronica and experimental rhythms.

⭐ **CAPSULE HOTEL FONTAINE
AKASAKA** *Public bath*
☎ 3583 6554; 4-3-5 Akasaka, Minato-
ku; sentō around ¥1000; 🚇 Ginza &
Marunouchi lines to Akasaka-mitsuke
(Belle Vie exit)

Along Hitotsugi-dōri, this is one
of the few capsule hotels in Tokyo
that admit and cater to women –
but only on weekends, and
only on one floor, which usually
resembles a grown-up slumber
party. The selling point, however,
is that the clean, well-maintained
men's and women's saunas here
are open daily if you need to pop
in and freshen up.

⭐ **CAVERN CLUB**
キャヴァンクラブ
Live music
☎ 3405 5207; www.cavernclub.jp; 1F,
Saito Bldg, 5-3-2 Roppongi, Minato-ku;
cover men/women ¥1890/1595;
🕐 6pm-2.30am; 🚇 Hibiya & Toei Ōedo
lines to Roppongi (exit 3)
Eerily flawless renditions of Beatles
covers have to be heard to be
believed, sung by four Japanese
mop-heads calling themselves the
Silverbeats. This club is named for
the place where the Beatles first
appeared in Liverpool. Reserve a
table ahead of time.

⭐ **CLUB 328** 三二八 *Club*
☎ 3401 4968; www.3-2-8.jp; B1F, Kotsu
Anzen Center Bldg, 3-24-20 Nishi-Azabu,
Minato-ku; cover ¥2000-2500;
🕐 8pm-5am; 🚇 Hibiya & Toei Ōedo
lines to Roppongi (exits 1c & 3)
DJs at San-ni-pa (aka San-ni-
hachi) spin a quality mix, from
funk to reggae to R&B. With its

refreshing un-Roppongi feel and a cool crowd of Japanese and *gaijin*, 328 is a good place to boogie 'til the break of dawn. Two drinks are included with the cover.

⭐ LEXINGTON QUEEN
レキシントンクィーン *Club*
☎ 3401 1661; www.lexingtonqueen .com; B1F, Gotō Bldg, 3-13-14 Roppongi, Minato-ku; cover from ¥2000; ☽ 8pm-5am; Ⓜ Hibiya & Toei Ōedo lines to Roppongi (exit 3)
The Lex was one of Roppongi's first discos and is still one of those plac- es where visiting celebrities turn up. The cover here starts around ¥2000 unless you've had your visage on the cover of *Vogue* or *Rolling Stone*. But, even noncelebrities get a free drink with admission.

⭐ MUSE ミューズ *Club*
☎ 5467 1188; www.muse-web.com; 4-1-1 Nishi-Azabu, Minato-ku; cover ¥1000-2000; ☽ 7pm-4am Sun-Thu, 7pm-5am Fri & Sat; Ⓜ Hibiya & Toei Ōedo lines to Roppongi (exits 1b & 3)
With a friendly, international crowd, multilevel Muse has some- thing for everyone – packed dance floor, several bar areas, cosy al- coves big enough for two, as well as pool tables, darts and karaoke. Women usually don't pay a cover, which includes a drink or two.

⭐ SALSA SUDADA
サルサスダーダ *Club*
☎ 5474 8806; 3F, La Palette Bldg, 7-13-8 Roppongi, Minato-ku; cover ¥1500; ☽ 6pm-6am; Ⓜ Hibiya & Toei Ōedo lines to Roppongi (exits 3 & 4a)
Salsa and Latin dance have swept Tokyo off its feet, and Salsa Sudada is a popular haunt for local salsa and merengue dancers. Beginners can take lessons here early every evening, and then practise their new moves with the dancers from all over the world who frequent this place.

⭐ SPACE LAB YELLOW
スペースラボイエロー *Club*
☎ 3479 0690; www.club-yellow.com; B1F & B2F, Cesaurus Bldg, 1-10-11 Nishi-Azabu, Minato-ku; cover ¥2000-3500; ☽ 10pm-late; Ⓜ Hibiya & Toei Ōedo lines to Roppongi (exits 2 & 3)
Located by Nishi-Azabu crossing, this is one of the most progres- sive and hippest places in town. Everything from house to acid jazz, Brazil jazz, techno and foreign DJ nights are featured at Yellow. Look for the entrance to this inky basement space next to a parking lot, and bring your ID.

⭐ STB 139 *Live music*
☎ 5474 1395; http://stb139.co.jp; 6-7-11 Roppongi, Minato-ku; cover ¥3000-7000; ☽ 6-11pm Mon-Sat; Ⓜ Hibiya & Toei Ōedo lines to Roppongi (exit 3)

SHIATSU SESSIONS

Has Tokyo chewed you up and spat you out? Spring back to life with a Shiatsu massage. One stop from Shinjuku station, Kimura-sensei at the **Kimura Shiatsu Institute** (Map p89; ☎ 3485 4515; shiatsusk@yahoo.co.jp; 1-48-19 Sasazuka, Shibuya-ku; shiatsu from ¥5000; ☼ 10am-8pm; ☒ Keiō line to Sasazuka station) not only practises but teaches Shiatsu, and he speaks English. Or make an appointment with **Azabu-Roppongi Studio** (☎ 3586 8909; Rm 301, Roppongi Five Bldg, 5-18-20 Roppongi, Minato-ku; shiatsu from ¥4000; ☼ 9.30am-10pm; ◉ Hibiya or Toei Ōedo lines to Roppongi, exit 3). They offer Western-style, Shiatsu massage and acupuncture, in studio or on house calls.

A two-minute walk south of Roppongi station, this is a large, lovely space that draws similarly big-name acts. Performances are predominantly jazz, covering the spectrum from acid to big band. Even if the act is unknown to you, the ambience will be wonderful and the standards high. Call for reservations between 11am and 8pm.

⭐ VANILLA ヴァニラ Club
☎ 3401 6200; www.clubvanilla.com; TSK Bldg, 7-14-30 Roppongi, Minato-ku; cover ¥2000; ☼ 9pm-late; ◉ Hibiya & Toei Ōedo lines to Roppongi (exits 3 & 4)
Attracting a largely Japanese clientele, Vanilla tends to have fewer drunken kooks than other nearby clubs. Three floors of dance space are filled with different beats and crowds of peeps. It's at the end of the small alley off Roppongi-dōri, west of Roppongi crossing.

VIRGIN TOHO CINEMAS ROPPONGI HILLS ヴァージンシネマズ六本木ヒルズ
Cinema
☎ 5775 6090; 6-10-2 Roppongi, Minato-ku; adult ¥1800-3000, concession ¥1000, 1st day of month ¥1000, women on Wed ¥1000; ☼ 10am-midnight Sun-Wed, 10am-5am Thu-Sat; ◉ Hibiya & Toei Ōedo lines to Roppongi (exits 1c & 3)
Virgin's nine-screen multiplex has the biggest screen in Japan, as well as luxurious reclining seats and internet booking for reserved seats up to two days in advance. This state-of-the-art theatre also holds all-night screenings Thursday through Saturday, and on nights before holidays.

>ODAIBA

Odaiba, an artificial island built on landfill in Tokyo Bay, is a great way to escape from Tokyo without leaving the city. Most people will arrive here via the driverless monorail from Shimbashi station, and will be treated with superb views of Tokyo and the bay. But this isn't all. Odaiba is an entertainment district, a setting for unconventional architecture and a showcase for futuristic innovations, displayed in museums and show-rooms around town. Kids couldn't get bored here, between the Tokyo Joypolis (an indoor, high-tech amusement park), the world's biggest Ferris wheel and excellent museums whose exhibits include remote-controlled boats. Lovers of kitsch will be equally delighted to come across the replica of the Statue of Liberty and the theme parks made in the images of old Edo, Hong Kong and even 17th-century Italy (a bathhouse, restaurant row and shopping mall, respectively). If there's a comprehensive theme to the architecture of Odaiba, you could call it 'experimental', but mostly it stands as a record of the 'bubble era' and the futuristic aesthetics and intentions of that period.

ODAIBA

👁 SEE

🛍 SHOP

🍴 EAT

🍸 DRINK

⭐ PLAY

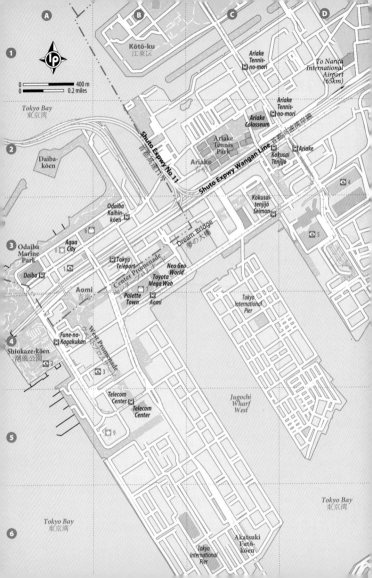

A

B
Kōtō-ku
江東区

C
Ariake
Tennis-
no-mori

Ariake
Tennis-
no-mori

Ariake
Colosseum

Ariake
Tennis
Park

Ariake
有明

Kokusai
Tenjijō ● Ariake

D
To Narita
International
Airport
(65km)

Shuto Expwy Wangan Line 首都高速湾岸線

Kokusai-
tenjijō
Seimon

● 4

● 5

1
Tokyo Bay
東京湾

Daiba-
kōen

2
Shuto Expwy No 11 首都高速11号

3
Odaiba
Marine
Park

Daiba ▣

Aqua
City

6 ▣

Odaiba
Kaihin-
kōen ▣

8 ▣

1 ▢

▣ Tokyo
Teleport

Center Promenade

Dream Bridge
夢の大橋

Neo Geo
World
Toyota
Mega Web

Palette
Town

Aomi
青海

Aomi ▢

Tokyo
International
Pier

4
Shiokaze-kōen
潮風公園

Fune-no-
Kagakukan

West Promenade

● 2

● 3

Jugochi
Wharf
West

5
Telecom
Center ▣

Telecom
Center

▣ 9

Tokyo
International
Pier

6
Tokyo Bay
東京湾

Tokyo Bay
東京湾

Akatsuki
Futō-
kōen

0   400 m
0   0.2 miles

👁 SEE

Because Odaiba doesn't have the typical glut of traffic that mainland Tokyo has, the island is quite pleasant to traverse on foot. But if you're covering a lot of ground between museums and malls and *onsen* (hot springs), you might opt to take the free shuttle bus that makes a circuit around Odaiba between 11am and 8pm. The red buses come around every 15 minutes or so and stop at a dozen locations on the island, including Aqua City and Fuji TV. Bus stops are not signposted in English but have red markers with bus symbols on them.

👁 FUJI TV フジテレビ

☎ 5500 8888; 2-4-8 Daiba, Minato-ku; observation deck ¥500/300; 🕙 10am-8pm Tue-Sun; 🚈 Rinkai line to Tokyo Teleport or Yurikamome line to Odaiba Kaihin-kōen

Designed by the late, great Kenzō Tange, the Fuji TV headquarters building is recognisable by the 90-degree angles of its scaffold-inglike structure, topped with a 1200-tonne ball. You can actually go into the ball, which is a terrific observation deck. Pick up an English guide at the dog bone (err, desk?) out front, for information on a self-guided tour.

👁 MUSEUM OF MARITIME SCIENCE 船の科学館

☎ 5500 1111; www.funenokagakukan .or.jp; 3-1 Higashi-Yashio, Shinagawa-ku; admission ¥1000/600; 🕙 10am-5pm Mon-Fri, 10am-6pm Sat & Sun; 🚈 Yurikamome line to Fune-no-Kagakukan; ♿ 🚼

This is one of Tokyo's better museums, containing four floors of excellent displays with loads of detailed models, lots of hands-on exhibits that kids will love, and a pool on the roof where, for ¥100, they can wreak havoc with radio-controlled boats and submarines.

👁 NATIONAL MUSEUM OF EMERGING SCIENCE AND INNOVATION (MIRAIKAN) 日本科学未来館

☎ 3570 9151; www.miraikan.jst.go.jp; 2-41 Aomi, Kōtō-ku; admission ¥500/200, free on Sat; 🕙 10am-5pm Wed-Mon; 🚈 Yurikamome line to Fune-no-Kagakukan or Telecom Center

Kids will love the engaging exhibits at this science museum, where most displays have excellent explanations in English and English-speaking guides fill in the blanks. There's the spectacular planetarium (buy tickets for a show as soon as you arrive), demonstrations of robots and opportunities to interact with them, and tons of exhibits about space, medicine and the environment.

☉ TOKYO BIG SIGHT
東京ビッグサイト
☎ 5530 1111; www.bigsight.jp/english; 3-21-1 Ariake, Kōtō-ku; Ⓜ Rinkai line to Kokusai-Tenjijō or Yurikamome line to Kokusai-Tenjijō-Seimon
Odaiba is full of oddball architecture and Tokyo Big Sight (officially known as Tokyo International Exhibition Hall) is no exception – appropriate, since it's the semi-annual venue for Tokyo's coolest design festival, Design Festa (p107). Look for the upside-down pyramids of the conference tower rising above the exhibition complex.

🛍 SHOP

☐ DECKS TOKYO BEACH
デックス東京ビーチ
Department store
☎ 3599 6500; www.odaiba-decks.com; 1-6-1 Daiba, Minato-ku; ⏰ 11am-9pm; 🚉 Yurikamome line to Odaiba Kaihin-kōen; ♿ 👶
Fashioned after a beachside boardwalk, Decks Tokyo Beach is split into two sides: the Seaside Mall and Island Mall. Both house shopping and dining, and this is also the place you'll find the indoor amusement park, Tokyo Joypolis (p159).

☐ VENUS FORT
ヴィーナスフォート
Department store
☎ 3599 0700; www.venusfort.co.jp /index.html; Palette Town, Aomi 1-chôme, Kōtō-ku; ⏰ 11am-9pm Sun-Fri, 11am-10pm Sat, restaurants 11am-11pm; 🚉 Yurikamome line to Aomi or Rinkai line to Tokyo Teleport; ♿
Venus Fort embodies a Japanese vision of a young woman's shopping paradise, in a building that mimics 17th-century Rome where the ceilings simulate the sky turning from day to night. With around 170 boutiques and restaurants all aimed at young women, this kitschy shopping centre also boasts the distinction of having Japan's biggest lavatory (64 stalls).

Open skies inside the Romanesque Venus Fort

🍴 EAT

🍴 BARBACOA STEAKHOUSE
バルバッコアステーキハ
ウス *Brazilian*   ¥¥
☎ 3599 4071; 5F, Mediage, Aqua City,
1-7-1 Daiba, Minato-ku; ⏲ 11am-3pm &
5-11pm; 🚉 Yurikamome line to Daiba;
♿ Ⓥ ♿
True, the speciality at this Brazil-
ian-style steakhouse is the slab of
steak, but Barbacoa also makes
a kind concession to herbivores
with its all-you-can-eat salad bar.
This place also gets a great view of
the bay and bridge.

🍴 DAIBA LITTLE HONG KONG
Food-themed park   ¥¥
☎ 3599 6500; 6F & 7F, Decks Tokyo
Beach, 1-6-1 Daiba, Minato-ku;
⏲ 11am-10pm; 🚉 Yurikamome line to
Ōdaiba Kaihin-Kōen; ♿ ♿
Among the quirky attractions of
Odaiba is this kooky replica of
Hong Kong's streets, complete
with a recorded soundtrack of
simulated street noise, neon signs,
souvenir shops and restaurants
slinging *gyōza* (dumplings) and
yum cha.

🍴 KHAZANA カザーナ
Indian   ¥
☎ 5500 5082; 5F, Decks Tokyo Beach,
1-6-1 Daiba, Minato-ku; ⏲ 11am-10pm;
🚉 Yurikamome line to Ōdaiba
Kaihin-Kōen; ♿ Ⓥ ♿

Come early to snag one of the
coveted tables out on the deck for
maximum sensory pleasure. This
Indian restaurant serves a good
all-you-can-eat buffet lunch and
has a fair amount of vegetarian
options on the menu.

🍴 TSUKIJI TAMA SUSHI
築地玉寿司
Sushi & sashimi   ¥¥
☎ 3599 6556; 5F, Decks Tokyo Beach,
1-6-1 Daiba, Minato-ku; ⏲ 11am-11pm;
🚉 Yurikamome line to Odaiba
Kaihin-kōen
Seat yourself near the windows
and sip from a huge cup of
green tea while you wait for your
sushi – it will come immaculately
presented and perfectly fresh.
The menu also includes set meals
and *udon*.

🍸 DRINK

HANASHIBE はなしべ
Izakaya
☎ 3599 5575; 3F, Aqua City, 1-7-1
Daiba, Minato-ku; ⏲ 11am-11pm;
🚉 Yurikamome line to Daiba; ♿ ♿
For Kyoto specialities and house-
brewed sake, check out Hanashibe
in the Mediage entertainment
complex in Aqua City. You can try
three types of sake in a tasting set
(¥700), which you can match with
small dishes typical of an *izakaya*
(pub eatery).

� SUNSET BEACH BREWING COMPANY サンセットビーチブルーイングカンパニー *Brewery*

☎ 3599 6655; 5F, Decks Tokyo Beach, 1-6-1 Daiba, Minato-ku; ⏱ 11am-11pm; 🚃 Yurikamome line to Ōdaiba Kaihin-Kōen; ♿

After roaming around Odaiba put your feet up and enjoy expansive views with an island-brewed beer. There are reasonably priced lunch and dinner buffets, but the house Italian food isn't worth the trip.

★ PLAY

CINEMA MEDIAGE シネマメディアージュ *Cinema*

☎ 5531 7878; 1F & 2F, Mediage, Aqua City, 1-7-1 Daiba, Minato-ku; tickets ¥1800/1500/1000, women ¥1000 on Wed; ⏱ ticket sales 11am-11pm; 🚃 Yurikamome line to Daiba; ♿

This enormous 3000-seat multiplex shows Japanese and foreign films, many of which are subtitled and some of which are dubbed into Japanese. Check the *Japan Times* or *Metropolis* for current listings. Mediage is located inside the Aqua City shopping centre.

☐ ŌEDO ONSEN MONOGATARI 大江戸温泉物語 *Hot spring*

☎ 5500 1126; www.ooedoonsen.jp; 2-57 Aomi, Kōtō-ku; admission ¥2827/1575; ⏱ 11am-9pm, last entry at 7am; 🚃 Yurikamome line to Telecom Center

This *onsen* is set up like an Edo-era town and pipes in natural mineral water from 1400m beneath Tokyo Bay. Although the setup might seem cheesy, the *onsen* is attractively designed, with old-fashioned restaurants and souvenir shops for a post-bath bite and browse. Admission fees cover the rental of *yukata* (cotton kimonos) and towels. Fees vary between morning and night, so check the website for full details.

☐ TOKYO JOYPOLIS 東京ジョイポリス *Amusement park*

☎ 5500 1801; 3F-5F, Decks Tokyo Beach, 1-6-1 Daiba, Minato-ku; passport ¥3300/3100, after 5pm ¥2300/2100; ⏱ 10am-11pm; 🚃 Yurikamome line to Odaiba Kaihin-Kōen; ♿

Joypolis is Sega's high-tech playland for overstimulating your kids, or yourself. Your visit here will be full of nonstop action, with crazy indoor roller coasters, video games and virtual-reality rides.

>SNAPSHOTS

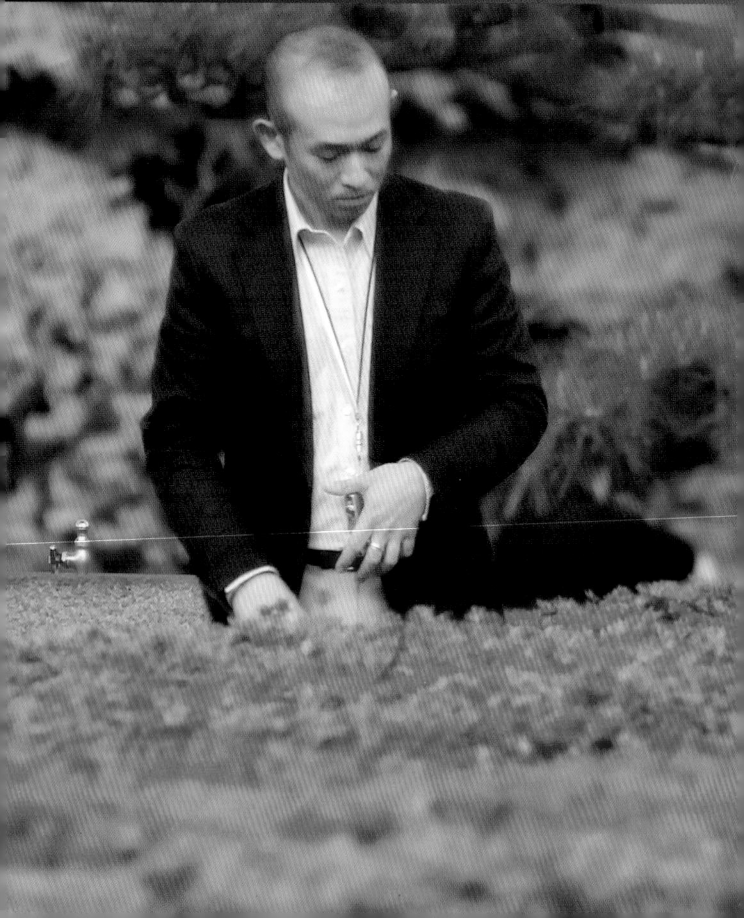

Tokyoites rise early and work late; they're always on the move and connected to their *keitai* (mobile phones). Since most live in cramped quarters, entertaining and socialising happens outside the home. Subsequently, Tokyo's mix of social and cultural activities, galleries and eateries provide the perfect backdrop for a varied and rich experience.

A kaleidoscope of colours bloom in the Imperial Palace East Garden (p48)

SNAPSHOTS

ACCOMMODATION

Staying anywhere along the Yamanote loop (p194) gives you easy access to nearly every corner of the city. If it's not on the loop, some subway line will quickly connect you. Central Tokyo hotels put you in strolling distance of Ginza shopping and myriad dining options, while Shinjuku has a slew of solid hotels catering to business travellers. Ebisu doesn't have many places to stay, but is a quieter, stylish part of the city that's also connected to the Yamanote loop. For those who want nothing to do with quiet nights in, staying around Roppongi means being able to stumble to bed at any hour without worrying about the trains shutting down at midnight. Additionally, despite its reputation as an exorbitantly expensive city to visit, Tokyo does have pleasant budget options, including capsule hotels, generic but reasonably-priced 'business hotels' and some excellent ryokan (Japanese-style inns).

Ryokan in Tokyo don't fit the traditional definition in the strictest sense – in this city, they typically won't include meals, and on the budget end you may even have to bring (or buy) your own towel. Most have tatami (woven floor matting) floors; you should always remove your shoes or slippers before entering a tatami room. At a typical Japanese ryokan, a futon is usually laid out and made up in the evenings, then folded up and put away in the mornings; however, in budget ryokan you'll do this yourself or simply leave the futon out all day. Be sure to also take advantage of at least one soak in the *sentō* (public baths; see p176) available here, an experience most modern hotels don't offer. You'll find most of Tokyo's ryokan in Asakusa and Ueno.

lonely planet Hotels & Hostels

Need a place to stay? Find and book it at lonelyplanet.com. Over 60 properties are featured for Tokyo – each personally visited, thoroughly reviewed and happily recommended by a Lonely Planet author. From hostels to high-end hotels, we've hunted out the places that will bring you unique and special experiences. Read independent reviews by authors and other travellers, and get practical information including amenities, maps and photos. Then reserve your room simply and securely via Hotels & Hostels – our online booking service. It's all at lonelyplanet.com/hotels.

Seekers of Japanese kitsch will want to stay in one of the famed love hotels (p121). These days they're more politely referred to as 'boutique' or 'fashion' hotels, and there's one for every taste, from miniature Gothic castles to Middle-Eastern temples – and these are just the buildings. Some rooms even have bath grottoes or ceiling swings. Love hotels are most highly concentrated on Love Hotel Hill (p120).

Solo travellers could also check into that uniquely Japanese invention: the capsule hotel. Making the most of limited space, these individual capsules are not as cheap as you might imagine (around ¥4000), but they are tall enough for lounging and come outfitted with personal TVs. Personal storage space is limited to lockers, so don't bring a ton of baggage; personal space is obviously at a premium, so do bring earplugs.

To search for and book Tokyo accommodations, check out www.jpinn.com for ryokan, and www.japanhotelfinder.com or Lonely Planet's own online booking service (see boxed text opposite).

BEST RYOKAN

> Ginza Yoshimizu (www.yoshimizu
  .com/en/ginza/index.html)
> Kimi Ryokan (www.kimi-ryokan.jp)
> Ryokan Shigetsu (www.shigetsu
  .com)
> Sawanoya Ryokan (www.sawanoya
  .com)
> Sukeroku no Yado Sadachiyo (www
  .sadachiyo.co.jp)

BEST LUXURY HOTELS

> Conrad (www.conradtokyo.co.jp)
> Four Seasons Chinzan-sō (www.four
  seasons.com/tokyo)
> Grand Hyatt (www.grandhyatttokyo
  .com)
> Hotel Marunouchi (www.marunouchi
  -hotel.co.jp)
> Park Hyatt (http://tokyo.park.hyatt
  .com)

BEST BUSINESS BETS

> Hotel Century Southern Tower (www
  .southerntower.co.jp)
> Mercure, Ginza (www.mercure-asia
  .com/5701/detail/default.aspx)
> Mitsui Garden Hotel (www.garden
  hotels.co.jp/eng/ginza.html)
> Park Hotel Tokyo (www.parkhotel
  tokyo.com)
> Tōkyū Cerulean Tower Hotel (www
  .ceruleantower-hotel.com/en)
> Westin Hotel Tokyo (www.westin
  -tokyo.co.jp)

BEST BOUTIQUE HOTELS

> Granbell Hotel (www.granbell
  hotel.jp)
> Hotel Claska (www.claska.com)
> Hotel Seiyō Ginza (www.seiyo-ginza
  .com)

ANIME & MANGA

Akihabara is *the* manga Mecca for Tokyoites and visitors alike, and is even becoming an attraction for those seeking a glimpse of the distinctly Japanese *otaku* (geek) subculture. It's the best place to start a quest for manga. The burly Mandarake chain, whose exhaustive flagship is located in Nakano, has a large outpost here, filled with all manner of manga from the kid-friendly *Doraemon* (a blue robotic cat from the future) to *dōjinshi* (self-published, fan-drawn spin-offs and parodies) to *hentai* (perverse) manga, DVDs, games and figurines.

One of the richest treasure troves in the city is the chain bookshop Book Off, which buys and sells used manga and has an entire section of paperbacks for only ¥100 apiece. You could easily collect an entire series for what amounts to lunch money. There's also a burgeoning female *otaku* culture (see boxed text p85) and its own geek haven in Ikebukuro, a hotbed of the 'boys' love' manga genre.

BEST PLACES TO PERUSE
> Book Off (p108)
> Mandarake (p122)
> Tora no Ana (p57)

BEST MUSEUMS TO VISIT
> Ghibli Museum (p91)
> Yayoi & Yumeji Takehisa Museums (p71)

BEST OTAKU HANGOUTS
> Akihabara (p44)
> Otome Rd (p85)

ARCHITECTURE

After WWII incendiary bombing flattened much of Tokyo, the city collected itself and began the long decades of reconstruction. Tokyo hit a boom period in the '50s, during which the subway system started to take shape. And when the city won the privilege of hosting the 1964 summer Olympics, buildings seemed to sprout like mushrooms after a long rain. One of the structures built for the Olympics was the National Yoyogi Stadium, a structure of curves sloping down from a suspension roof. The building was designed by Kenzō Tange, an Osaka-born architect who taught at Tokyo University and died in 2005. During his long career he influenced the reshaping of the cityscape, and his designs stand out all over Tokyo.

But diversity reigns in the vibrant architectural face of the city. Although not the most sustainable strategy, aging buildings are demolished to make way for bigger, newer and ever more innovative structures that astound and inspire. Because real estate is at a premium in this denser-than-dense megalopolis, the only way to go is up.

BEST STRUCTURAL STATEMENTS
> National Diet Building (p142)
> Roppongi Hills (p143)
> Tokyo International Forum (p51)
> Tokyo Metropolitan Government Offices (p91)

BEST COPYCATS
> Statue of Liberty (p154; pictured right)
> Tokyo Tower (p143)

MOST FASHIONABLE & FUNCTIONAL
> BAPExclusive (p108)
> Comme les Garcons (p108)
> Hanae Mori Building (p110)
> Prada Aoyama (p106)

FOOD

Epicureans will find no shortage of new tastes to sample in the city, where renowned chefs from around the world set up shop, balancing out Tokyo's wasabi and soy sauce with balsamic vinegar and olive oil. A taste of the traditional can be sampled in venues as humble as the local *rāmen* shop or in the refined, minimalist tatami room of a *kaiseki* (elegant, multicourse Japanese meals) restaurant, while there's also an incredible diversity of international cuisine, representing culinary traditions from Sweden to Senegal. And of course comfort foods like burgers or pasta – while sometimes Japanese renditions of those dishes – are easily found across the city.

Japanese food runs the gamut between the raw fish of your sushi or sashimi platter and the deep-fried *panko* (Japanese bread crumb) crust of a crispy, tender pork cutlet *(tonkatsu)* on a bed of shredded cabbage. In addition to *tonkatsu*, there's tempura and *kushi katsu* (deep-fried skewers of meat and vegetables), both of which are often served in small courses, as they are cooked so that everything comes to the table piping hot. If on an oppressively humid day the last thing you want to eat is fried food, do as the Tokyoites do and have an *unagi* (barbecued eel) lunch to keep up your stamina. *Unagi* is especially tasty when it's grilled perfectly in its sweet soy marinade and served in a *bentō* (boxed meal) over rice. An even cooler (temperature-wise) option is cold *soba* (buckwheat noodles) that you dip in cold broth and slurp noisily. *Soba* can also be served hot, as are *udon* (thick wheat noodles) and *rāmen*.

Cook-it-yourself affairs such as sukiyaki or *shabu-shabu* are the most fun with a few people, where the morsels of simmered meat and vegetables are meant to be shared and the communal pot is tended by all. You can do the DIY experience alone, cooking up *okonomiyaki* or *monjayaki* – egg-batter pancakes full of cabbage, vegetables, seafood and meat – at your own table.

Adventurous eaters can also have a festive meal of *fugu* (puffer fish), that famously poisonous fish that is safely prepared by trained experts. *Fugu* restaurants usually offer multicourse dinners featuring *fugu* sashimi, *shabu-shabu*, and *fugu* cooked a dozen ways. While the taste and texture of *fugu* may not wow you like the transcendent tuna of your sushi lunch, eating tuna doesn't come with the same satisfaction of having cheated death at the dinner table.

In general, most restaurants, whatever the type, often serve tasty *teishoku* (lunch sets) that are more reasonably priced than their dinner courses; keep this in mind if you wish to dine somewhere at the higher end of the spectrum, as lunch will often fit into your budget even if supper won't. Lunch sets at department store *resutoran-gai* ('restaurant towns') are very economical and tend to be of good quality. Browse the plastic food models and choose the shops specialising in one thing: *unagi*, tempura, *kushi-katsu*, sushi or *soba*. And if you just need something to tide you over for the next museum stop, convenience-store *onigiri* (rice ball; around ¥125) and iced tea is always just around the corner.

BEST UPMARKET JAPANESE
> Inakaya (p147)
> Kisso (p147)
> Kyūbei (p60)
> Ten-Ichi (p61)
> Ume-no-Hana (p116)

BEST FUSION
> Daidaiya (p95)
> Den Rokuen-tei (p124)
> Fujimamas (p112)
> Vin Chou (p80)

BEST BITES ON A BUDGET
> Hiroba (p113)
> Ippūdo (p134)
> Kantipur (p125)
> Sakata (p61)

BEST SHITAMACHI ATMOSPHERE
> Hantei (p72)
> Kanda Yabu Soba (p60)
> Komagata Dozeu (p79)

Opposite Feast your eyes on a delicate arrangement of sushi

GALLERIES

You can't really turn anywhere in Tokyo without seeing evidence of its thriving, dynamic visual arts scene. No self-respecting commercial district in Tokyo goes without its major department stores, and no department store worth its grand façade would dream of not installing an art gallery on one of its upper floors. Ginza is good place to start a gallery-hop. Between its department store *grande dames* and its well-established art galleries, there's a hefty concentration of classy exhibition spaces. For more experimental fare, you might also venture into Ura-Hara (p102), the back alleys off of Omote-sandō, and then still further west into Aoyama.

Japanese art has historically blurred the lines between art and craft, high and low, and this is reflected in many of the works you'll find in Tokyo's galleries. Graphic-style art is ubiquitous, but installation, sculpture, electronic media, painting and photography are well-represented – sometimes all in one bright package.

BEST ONE-STOP VARIETY
> Complex (p139)
> Design Festa Gallery (p107; pictured right)
> Kiyosumi art galleries (p51)

BEST NEIGHBOURHOODS FOR GALLERY CRAWLS
> Aoyama (p103)
> Ginza (p52)
> Marunouchi (p45)

TOP GINZA STALWARTS
> Ginza Graphic Gallery (p45)
> Leica Ginza Salon (p50)
> Shiseido Gallery (p50)

BEST DEPARTMENT-STORE MUSEUMS
> Laforet Museum (p103)
> Parco Museum (p120)

GAY & LESBIAN

Tokyo is more tolerant than most of its Asian counterparts in regards to homosexuality and alternative lifestyles, as long as public displays of affection are kept on the down-low. The active international scene encompasses a healthy club and bar life, newsletters and support groups. Intriguing cultural phenomena include the relatively mainstream theatre of the all-women Takarazuka Gekijō (p65), which attracts all manner of housewives and young women with crushes on the drag-king actors. Meanwhile, the defining feature of *otome* (p85) – the female version of *otaku* (p123) – is a shared obsession with 'boys' love' manga that depicts the romantic relationships between gay males. While on the ground level, Tokyo society does not actively acknowledge the non-heterosexual population, its existence is normalised in a rich array of art forms and as a fact of fantasy life dissociated from quotidian concerns. So while the societal sanctions may be don't-ask, don't-tell, the social scene is alive and kicking.

For more information on the GLBT scene in Tokyo, check out www .fridae.com/cityguides/tokyo/tk-intro.php and www.utopia-asia.com /japntoky.htm. Also look for the current issue of *Tokyo Journal* (p196), online and in print, for local listings on gay events and venues.

BEST BARS
> Advocates Bar (p97)
> Arch (p98)
> Arty Farty (p98)
> Kinswomyn (p99)

TOP EVENTS
> Gay & Lesbian Pride Parade
  (p33; pictured right)
> Tokyo International Lesbian & Gay
  Film Festival (p32)

KIDS

Tokyo is a child-friendly, attention-deficit paradise, and foreign kids will find distractions aplenty in the cute toys, electronic gadgetry, weird candy, high-tech toilets and noisy *pachinko* games. All those novel things you'll pass on the streets will catch their interest, like *fugu* (poisonous puffer fish) jetting around the tanks in front of restaurants, or the flashing neon in Shinjuku and Shibuya. On weekends the parks are full of weird and wonderful culture that both adults and kids will get kick out of – the rockabilly dancers of Yoyogi Park (p28) and the *cosplay-zoku* of Meiji-jingūbashi (p12), for starters. But for specifically child-centric entertainments, Tokyo has many pleasure districts. Amusement parks, fun museums and tantalising toy stores abound in this, the world capital of *kawaii* (cute). The Ghibli Museum (p91) is a must, but be absolutely sure to book your appointment well in advance.

Restaurants often provide children's menus or special set meals, and even picky eaters who might turn their noses up at sashimi will love tender, crunchy *tonkatsu* (deep-fried pork cutlets) or *yakitori* (grilled chicken on a stick) and noodles. And if you're desperate, convenience stores and fast-food chains exist everywhere for the little ones who subsist solely on burgers and pizza.

BEST PLACE TO WIND 'EM UP & RUN 'EM DOWN
> Kōrakuen Amusement Park (p63)
> Namco Namjatown (p87)
> Paddle-boating (p92)
> Tokyo Disneyland (p52)
> Tokyo Joypolis (p159)
> Tokyo Metropolitan Children's Hall (p129)

BEST SPOTS FOR YOUR KIDS TO EMPTY YOUR POCKETS
> Hakuhinkan Toy Park (p54)
> Kiddyland (p111)
> Loft (p122)
> Tōkyū Hands (p94)

BEST KID-FRIENDLY INTERACTIVE MUSEUMS
> Museum of Maritime Science (p156)
> National Museum of Emerging Science and Innovation (p156)
> National Science Museum (p68)
> Shitamachi History Museum (p68)
> Taikokan (p77)

BEST PLACES TO OGLE ANIMALS (LIVING AND DEAD)
> Meguro Parasitological Museum (p132)
> Sunshine International Aquarium (p84)
> Tsukiji Market (p51)
> Ueno Zoo (p71)

LIVE MUSIC

Aficionados of all genres will find kindred souls in Tokyo, whether your aural medication of choice is jazz, electronica, Motown, punk, classical, *reggaetón* or hip-hop. Big international acts like U2 regularly play Tokyo, as do popular home-grown musicians such as J-pop songstress Hikaru Utada and jazz instrumentalists P'ez. Smaller venues often book more underground bands, which you might not see in such intimate environs abroad. Check *Metropolis* (www.metropolis.co.jp) or *Tokyo Journal* (http://tokyo.to) for current listings.

While 'live houses' are scattered all over the city, the best are naturally centred in active, hip neighbourhoods such as Shibuya, Ebisu and Roppongi. Live shows tend to keep school-night hours so that music fans can hop their trains before midnight, and it's best to purchase tickets beforehand from the venue itself, or using **Ticket Pia** (☎ 0570-029 999; http://t.pia.co.jp in Japanese) with the help of a Japanese-speaking friend.

BEST LIVE HOUSES
> Club Quattro (p127)
> Crocodile (p116)
> La.mama (p128)
> Liquid Room (p136)
> Loft (p100)
> Milk (p136)
> Shibuya O-West (p129)

BEST JAZZ JOINTS
> Blue Note (p151)
> JZ Brat (p128)
> Shinjuku Pit Inn (p101)
> STB 139 (p153)

BEST BEATLES ACTS
> Abbey Road (p150)
> Cavern Club (p151)

SNAPSHOTS

MARKETS

Street markets are not such a large part of Tokyo's urban landscape as they are in other cities, as stratospheric real estate costs make open spaces prohibitively expensive. That said, one of Tokyo's highlights happens to be one of the few markets in town. Tsukiji Market, which moves more than 2000 tonnes of seafood every day, is slated to move to new digs sometime around 2012, so catch it here while you can. Blueprints for the new market plan for a larger, more modern space that visitors won't be able to get into as down and dirty as they can now.

The open spaces of some temple grounds become commercial squares on various Sundays. While it's unlikely that you'll find truly rare antiques at these flea markets, there's usually some decent vintage kimono, metalwork, lacquerware and interesting odds and ends to browse. Most markets close down by around 3pm. Also operating out-doors is the unusual Ameyoko Arcade in Ueno, where you can wander among the stalls of dried squid and discount sneakers. And of course, Tokyo's take on the traditional market is the bountiful, beautiful *depachika*.

BEST TEMPLE FLEA MARKETS
> Hanazono-jinja (open all Sun except in May & Nov; p90)
> Tōgō-jinja (open 1st, 4th & 5th Sun; p106)

BEST MARKET HIGHLIGHTS
> Ameyoko Arcade (p71)
> Tsukiji Market (p13)

MUSEUMS

The cup runneth over for museum lovers in this city. Not only are there art museums displaying archaeological artefacts from a couple of thousand years ago and contemporary works in all manner of media, but tiny one-room shacks showcasing only buttons or *byōbu* (folding screens). Some of Tokyo's top museums have only been around for a few years, like the wonderfully multifaceted experience of the Edo-Tokyo Museum (p65) and the sky-high singularity of the Mori Art Museum (p139) at Roppongi Hills.

If you'll be in town for an extended period of time or expect to hit several museums during your visit, consider picking up a Grutt Pass (p71) to save a significant amount on what can add up to be hefty admission fees.

BEST TOKYO MUSEUMS
> Edo-Tokyo Museum (p65)
> National Museum of Modern Art (p50)
> Ōta Memorial Art Museum (p103)
> Tokyo Metropolitan Museum of Photography (p132)
> Tokyo National Museum (p69)

QUIRKIEST SHOWCASES
> Beer Museum Yebisu (p132)
> Criminology Museum of Meiji University (p45)

> Kite Museum (p49)
> Meguro Parasitological Museum (p132)
> Tobacco & Salt Museum (p121)

BEST FOR CONTEMPORARY ART
> Hara Museum of Contemporary Art (p120)
> Mori Art Museum (p139)
> Museum of Contemporary Art Tokyo (p51)
> Watarium (p107)

V

SNAPSHOTS

NIGHTLIFE

Tokyo's thriving nightlife means no shortage of bars, karaoke lounges, dance clubs and *izakaya* (pub/eatery) populating every corner of the city. But some neighbourhoods are better than others. Roppongi has historically been the centre of rowdy all-night ragers, where military goons and newly arrived expats collide with hard-partying locals looking for foreign action. But it's not all downscale pick-up joints, and the diversity of clubs and bars all located in one area make it the obvious destination for a night out. Still, it's not the last word in nightlife – Love Hotel Hill on Shibuya's Dōgenzaka is packed with clubs, large live music venues, and bars and *izakaya*. These clubs attract those in their 20s, and the music tends to be mainstream (ie hip-hop, marquee Japanese pop and flavour-of-the-month). For the slightly older and more indie-inclined, there are the hip clubs and bars of Ebisu and Daikanyama. East Shinjuku is probably the least pretentious of these hotspots.

Clubs typically charge a cover from ¥1500 to ¥3000, usually including a drink or two. Weekend covers tend to be higher than on weeknights, and at some venues men and women are charged differently. Some clubs give discounts if you bring in a flyer (check their websites, or the record stores around Shibuya), and it's often a good idea to bring a photo ID.

BEST TOP-VIEW BARS
> Asahi Sky Room (p80)
> Mado Lounge (p150)
> New York Bar (p99)

BEST UNPRETENTIOUS CLUBS
> Club 328 (p151)
> Muse (p152)
> Space Lab Yellow (p152)
> Unit (p137)
> Vanilla (p153)

BEST BARS FOR LOOKING AND LOUNGING
> Aux Amis des Vins (p62)
> Den Aquaroom (p116)
> Insomnia Lounge (p126)
> Maduro (p150)

BEST SAKE IZAKAYA
> Sakana-tei (p125)
> Sasashū (p87)
> Takara (p62)
> Tonerian (p87)

PARKS & GARDENS

Apartment-dwellers of Tokyo may not have the luxury of gardens, but they have hectares of open space in the city's large parks. All parks in Tokyo are free with the notable exception of Shinjuku-gyoen, and they provide respite and refuge from the rhythms of urban life. On weekdays you're likely to get a laid-back experience at the city's parks and gardens, but weekends see them at their best, when families and couples turn out for strolls and picnics.

During *hanami* (cherry-blossom viewing; p31) season, blue tarps are spread on the grass and the sake flows at *hanami* parties crowding popular parks such as Shinjuku-gyoen and Ueno-kōen. From around mid-October to early November, *kōyō* (autumn foliage season) brings its spectacular palette of golds, yellows, oranges and fiery scarlet hues to parks including Yoyogi-kōen and Koishikawa-Kōrakuen (p49).

The beautifully landscaped gardens of Tokyo make even better escapes. Gardens usually charge a small admission fee, and on weekdays you're likely to have the carp ponds and well-groomed paths practically to yourself.

BEST PARKS
> Shinjuku-gyoen (p91)
> Ueno-kōen (p66)
> Yoyogi-kōen (p107)

MOST GORGEOUS GARDENS
> Dembō-in (p76)
> Hama-rikyū-teien (p48)
> Imperial Palace East Garden (p48; pictured right)
> Meiji-jingū-gyoen (p103)
> National Institute for Nature Study (p132)

BEST PLACES FOR HANAMI
> Hama-rikyū-teien (p48)
> Shinjuku-gyoen (p91)
> Ueno-kōen (p66)

SENTŌ & ONSEN

As much for gossip as for hygiene, *sentō* (public baths) and *onsen* (hot springs) are pulse points for strengthening social bonds in Japan. Although modern dwellings have bath facilities, many Tokyoites bathe regularly at *sentō* and often go with friends or family members. The metropolitan government generously subsidises the city's *sentō* and *onsen*, making them inexpensive (admission around ¥500) and easily accessible to everyone.

In Tokyo, where both institutions do business in modern buildings, the difference between *sentō* and *onsen* may not seem clear. The essential distinction is that *sentō* can heat up their own tap water, but water at an *onsen* must come from a natural hot spring. The concept of a such a bubbling spring existing in this paved-over urban wilderness might sound laughable, but natural sources underneath Tokyo Bay actually do supply the city's *onsen* with mineral-rich, dark water.

Bathing communally in traditional Japanese baths is an excellent balm for the stresses of the streets and a transcendent experience even if the backdrop isn't the rushing waterfall of a mountain resort. In them you'll encounter people of all ages and walks of life, and catch a glimpse of city folk at their most relaxed. For more information see p101.

BEST KITSCHY ONSEN EXPERIENCE
> Ōedo Onsen Monogatari (p159; pictured right)

BEST CITY ONSEN
> Azabu-Jūban Onsen (p150)

BEST OLD-SCHOOL NEIGHBOURHOOD ONSEN
> Jakotsu-yu Onsen (p81)

BEST SENTŌ & SLEEP
> Capsule Hotel Fontaine Akasaka (p151)
> Finlando Sauna (p100)
> Green Plaza Ladies' Sauna (p100)

SHRINES & TEMPLES

Japan's two major religions, Shintōism and Buddhism, have coexisted peacefully and influenced each other for more than a thousand years. Shintō's animistic tradition, which views the environment as one inhabited with *kami* (gods or spirits), is Japan's native religion. Buddhism, and its belief in the cycle of reincarnation, was an import from India by way of China and Korea.

In day-to-day life most Tokyoites do not consider themselves religious, conducting and participating in religious ceremonies only at those defining moments of birth, marriage and death. But while Shintōism may not play an overt role in people's lives, its basic tenets have seeped so deeply into the Japanese culture that they are inseparable from what are considered quotidian matters. For example, the Shintō practice of purification isn't limited to the rinsing of mouths and hands at the entrance of shrines, but also led to the lasting tradition of the thorough, ritualistic cleansing at *sentō*.

Shintō shrines honour *kami*, which also reside in natural features such as waterfalls and mountains. Once a person dies, they too become a *kami*, but upon death Buddhism defines the funereal rituals. Keep this in mind when you notice that Buddhist temples often house cemeteries, while Shintō shrines do not. Shintō shrines range in size from tiny *inari* (fox deity) shrines occupying narrow spaces between buildings to the grand Meiji-jingū (p103), and are scattered far and wide across Tokyo. Long-established Buddhist temples also dot the cityscape in every neighbourhood and make up an integral part of the community.

BEST SHRINES
> Asakusa-jinja (p76)
> Chingodō-ji (p76)
> Hie-jinja (p139)
> Tōshōgū (p69)
> Yasukuni-jinja (p51)

BEST TEMPLES
> Benten-dō (p68)
> Kiyomizu Kannon-dō (p68)
> Meiji-jingū (p103; pictured right)
> Sensō-ji (p77)

SNAPSHOTS

SHOPPING

Shopping is a serious endeavour in this city: it's the number one recreational activity. It's therapy, investment, and a way to socialise and show off status. It's also intertwined with ritual and expectation – on Valentine's Day, women are expected to give *giri* (obligation) chocolate to all the men in their lives, and it ain't for love. Shopping is part of the Tokyo lifestyle, and gift-giving is a tradition that has evolved into an art. It's no wonder, then, that this city is a candy store for the consumer with cash. And you don't need a lot of it for inexpensive treats like delicate *washi* (handmade paper), kitchen tools and stationery at ¥100 shops and small Japanese toys.

Stores are generally open daily but closed on one Monday or Wednesday of each month. Keep in mind that Japan may very well be the only Asian country where bargaining, unless you're at a flea market (p172), is simply not done. While plastic is being accepted at more shops nowadays, it's a good idea to come armed with cold, hard cash. On luxury items like pricey electronics, the 5% VAT can be waived for foreigners, but you'll have to have your passport on you to take advantage of it.

Upscale shopping districts such as Ginza (p52) and Aoyama (p108) are good places to start for luxury items at fashion houses of international repute, including Chanel, Gucci or Mikimoto Pearl. If your stay is particularly short, hit Aoyama first – there's a good mix of international and Japanese heavyweights who've set up shop along Omote-sandō, and some of the architecture itself is as beautifully designed as the wares. Plus, the Harajuku backstreets (p108) adjacent to Aoyama complement the couture with Tokyo's famous street fashion. Takeshita-dōri is the best place to plunge in with an exploration of teenybopper culture. Ginza, on the other hand, has Tokyo's oldest, grand department stores, some of which have rooftop gardens and restaurant cities above and *depachika* (p57) below.

Other shopping districts around Central Tokyo include Jimbōchō, where bookshops trade in antique and rare books, as well as used books and manga. But a bigger scene for manga lies to the east of here in Akihabara, once famed (and still nicknamed for) its discount electronics.

Sprawling shopping malls that could each swallow several Southeast Asian villages whole include the older Sunshine City (p86) in Ikebukuro and the newer Roppongi Hills (p139). More intimate, human-scale shopping experiences can be sought in Daikanyama (p133) or Kichijōji (p92), where the smaller shops have their unique styles and sensibilities.

Even if shopping isn't your bag, any visitor to Tokyo should at least pop into Tōkyū Hands (p94), the 'Creative Life Store', which is sure to offer some captivating bauble to even the most consumption-averse. Shopping is leisure in this city, so come out to play and gain a little insight into the societal psyche in the bargain.

BEST SHOPS FOR OFFBEAT SOUVENIRS
> Don Quijote (p93)
> Kiddyland (p111)
> Kite Museum (p49)
> Meguro Parasitological Museum (p132)
> Tōkyū Hands (p94)

BEST TRADITIONAL HANDICRAFTS
> Bingoya (p95)
> Hashi Ginza Natsuno (p54)
> Japan Traditional Crafts Center (p85)
> Kamawanu (p134)
> Takumi Handicrafts (p57)

BEST PLACES TO FIND WASHI
> Haibara (p52)
> Itōya (p54)
> Sekaido (p94)

Opposite Temptations behind the glass in the shopping Mecca of Harajuku

SPECTATOR SPORTS

SNAPSHOTS

No sport in Japan is more popular than baseball, and the Tokyo area is home to no fewer than six of the country's 12 professional teams. The most popular team in Japan, the Yomiuri Giants, is based out of Tokyo Dome (also known as the 'Big Egg'). Tokyo Dome is probably the best place in town to catch a game, where fan clubs cheerleaders dressed in *happi* (half-coats) lead thousands of fans in synchronised cheers and singing. Beer girls with mini-kegs strapped to their backs run up and down the steep aisles pouring brews to customers while a small dirigible floats around the inside of the dome filming the action. In fair weather, however, it's equally enjoyable to take in a game at the outdoor Jingū Stadium, home of the Yakult Swallows. Baseball season begins at the end of March or the first week of April and runs until October.

Of course, besides the big two of baseball and *sumō* (p11), martial arts events and smaller-scale sports competitions occur year-round. Check *Metropolis* (www.metropolis.co.jp) for extensive listings on current events.

BEST (ONLY) PLACE TO WATCH SUMŌ
> Ryōgoku Kokugikan (p65; pictured above)

BEST STADIUM FOR J-LEAGUE SOCCER
> National Stadium (p117)

BEST BASEBALL STADIUM
> Tokyo Dome (p64)
> Jingū Stadium (p117)

Get on board during rush hour at Ueno Station

BACKGROUND
HISTORY
THE EARLY YEARS
Around the mid-15th century, a poet named Ōta Dōkan constructed Edo's first castle on the site of an old fortress. When Portuguese traders first set eyes on 16th-century Edo, it was little more than an outpost for aristocrats and monks who had fled a civil war in Kyoto. Within three centuries Edo would oust Kyoto as Japan's traditional seat of imperial power – and Tokyo would be born.

TOKUGAWA EDO
The father to this upstart child was the wily, madly ambitious shōgun, Tokugawa Ieyasu. His appointment by the emperor in 1603 was to change the fate of Tokyo (and Japan) forever.

A political survivor, Ieyasu knew he must 'divide and conquer' his political foes. In a masterstroke, he forced all *daimyō* (feudal lords) throughout Japan to spend at least one year of every two in Edo. This policy of dislocation made it difficult for ambitious *daimyō* to usurp the Tokugawas.

Ieyasu systematically created a rigidly hierarchical society, comprising, in descending order: nobility; *daimyō* and their samurai; farmers; and finally artisans and merchants. Class dress, living quarters and even manner of speech were strictly codified. Class advancement was prohibited, though one could always, terrifyingly, descend to the underclasses, to the 'non-human' *hinin* and to *eta,* the untouchable class.

ISOLATION
After Ieyasu's death in 1616, his grandson Tokugawa Iemitsu, fearing Christian power, closed the country's borders in 1638. Japan was effectively removed from the world stage for nearly 300 years.

By the early 17th century, Edo (population over one million) was the largest city on earth. Its castelike society divided Edo into the *daimyō* high city (Yamanote) and a low working-class city (Shitamachi). Destructive fires often swept through its shantytowns. The locals christened these fires 'Edo-no-hana' ('flowers of Edo'). The cocky bravura of the expression sums up the tough Shitamachi spirit, still to be found in the backstreets of Ueno and Asakusa.

TOKYO RISING

When US Commodore Matthew Perry's armada of 'black ships' entered Edo (Tokyo) Bay demanding 'free trade' in 1853, despite spirited resistance from 2000 Tokugawa loyalists at the brief Battle of Ueno, the shōgunate fell apart and power reverted to Tokyo.

The Meiji Restoration refers to this consequent return of power to the emperor; however, Emperor Meiji's rule was more revolution than restoration. A crash course in industrialisation and militarisation began and by 1889 Japan had adopted a Western-style constitution – and Western-style empire building.

Nowhere was revolutionary change more evident than on the streets of the country's new capital city. Job seekers flocked from the country and Tokyo boomed.

CATASTROPHE & WAR

The Great Kantō Earthquake struck the boom town at noon on 1 September 1923. The subsequent fires, lasting some 40 hours, laid waste to the city. Although 142,000 lost their lives, worse was to come.

From the accession of Emperor Hirohito in 1926, nationalist fervour gripped the government. In 1931 the Japanese army invaded Manchuria, then China. By 1940 a pact with Germany and Italy had been signed and 'Greater Asia Co-Prosperity Sphere' was touted as the new order. On 7 December 1941 the Japanese attacked Pearl Harbor.

WWII was catastrophic for Tokyo. Incendiary bombing of the mostly wooden city commenced in March 1944. On the nights of 9 and 10 March 1945, 40% of the city was engulfed in a terrible firestorm and between 70,000 and 80,000 perished. By the time Emperor Hirohito made his famous address to the Japanese people on 15 August 1945, much of Tokyo was a wasteland.

BUBBLE & BUST

Tokyo rose phoenixlike from the ashes of WWII, and the economy flourished as almost no other in history. Ironically, it was sparked by US involvement in the neighbouring Korean War. The 1960s, '70s and early '80s saw unprecedented growth. Japan was suddenly an economic superpower – incredibly wealthy, globally powerful and omnipotent.

And then, suddenly, it wasn't. Japan's `bubble economy' of the '80s floated ever higher on the strength of its technology and automobile exports. Emboldened by the belief that the bullish stock market and climbing property values would continue to rise, investors financed all manner of huge developments and projects. But this growth was unsustainable, and the burst of the bubble threw Japan into a recession from which it is still recovering.

But the cracks ran deeper than the fiscal fault lines. The Kōbe earthquake of January 1995 shook not only that city but the nation's confidence in the government's ability to respond quickly and effectively to such a monumental disaster. In March 1995, when members of the Aum Shinrikyō cult released sarin nerve gas on a crowded Tokyo commuter train, killing 12 and injuring 5000, Japan's self-belief took a severe blow.

TOKYO TODAY

While Japan's population greys and the birth rate declines, Tokyo continues to rev along at a youthful pace. As the age gap between generations keeps widening, so does anxiety about who will support the aging population in the decades to come. But for now, anxiety is not the first word that comes to mind in describing the entrepreneurial spirit, the relative openness to doing things in new ways and the attitudes of a younger generation who never knew life in the 'bubble era'.

LIFE AS A TOKYOITE

The life of the average Japanese citizen is bound by a massive network of obligation and counter-obligation to family, colleagues, the guy next door, ancestors who passed away generations ago – the list is endless. Those individuals who just can't stand it flee to Tokyo. The anonymity of the megalopolis is a magnet for misfits, rebels, artists and all the famous 'nails that stand out' (and duly get bashed down) in mainstream Japanese society. Thus it is, in many senses, the most liberated of Japanese cities. People scarcely know their neighbours, or care to.

With the disintegration of the family and continuing economic lethargy, the times they are a-changing. The generation gap between conventional, self-sacrificing parent and pierced, part-time-employee child has never been greater. Younger people who were born after the bubble era are not hampered so much by the conventions of that time, and are more open to creativity and experimentation. Career adjustments – like bouncing back from losing a job – come more naturally to the younger generation. Old systems and cultural attitudes are slow to change, but the societal flux is probably most apparent and dynamic in Tokyo.

ETIQUETTE

Given Tokyo's distinctly different place in Japanese society, it's difficult to offend. Moreover, Japanese people are highly forgiving of foreign visitors' minor social gaffes. But there are a few rules of etiquette that must always be followed. When entering a house or any tatami (woven-floor matting) room, always take off your shoes. If in doubt, do as everyone else does. It's considered rude (and disgusting) to blow your nose in public – maintain a stoic and noisy sniffle until you find a private place. Except for ice cream, eating while walking down the street is also just not done.

For those in Tokyo on business, *meishi* (business cards) carry a lot of weight in society and are ritually exchanged on first meetings. Politely accept – or offer – a card with both hands and examine it before putting it away, and don't write on a card that someone has given you.

And when invited to someone's home, bring a small gift that's presented attractively – an occasion for requesting the elaborate wrapping available when you make your purchase. As with *meishi,* offer the gift with both hands and a slight bow, and expect it to be politely refused a few times before you insist they accept it.

GOVERNMENT & POLITICS
THE CHRYSANTHEMUM THRONE

In September 2006 Princess Kiko (wife of Prince Akishino, second in line to the throne after Crown Prince Naruhito) gave birth to the first male heir to the Japanese throne in over 40 years. Man-on-the-street TV interviews showed the emotional reactions of Tokyoites to this momentous news. Although Emperor Akihito and Empress Michiko are but figureheads, the Imperial Family is still very much revered and deeply respected in Japan. This outpouring of happiness also coincided with a sudden – though not unexpected – tapering-off of the controversy that marked the years before the new prince was born.

Increasingly intense debate had been growing about changing the Japanese constitution to allow a female heir to ascend the Chrysanthemum Throne. The Crown Prince Naruhito and Crown Princess Masako have only a daughter. And while recent polls showed that 76% of the general population supported the idea of female ascendancy, conservative elements in Japan's governing body, the Diet, opposed it strongly enough to support alternatives as – dare we say – backwards as instituting imperial concubines to produce a male heir. The debate remains open, but for the moment Prince Hisahito's birth has significantly lessened its urgency.

Unfortunately, the pressure to have a son – coupled with the isolated life inside the Imperial Palace – has had a deleterious effect on Crown Princess Masako, once a promising young diplomat. Two years after the birth of her daughter, Princess Aiko, in 2001, she largely withdrew from public life, though of late she has begun making more frequent public appearances. It remains to be seen what the future will hold for young Princess Aiko, as times change and traditional restrictions do not.

THE RULING DIET

The governing body, known as the Diet, is based here in the capital and is made up of two houses. The party controlling the majority of seats in the Diet is the ruling party and has the right to appoint the prime minister. Since its inception in 1955, the conservative Liberal Democratic Party (LDP) has controlled the Diet, barring a few years during the mid-90s.

In theory, Japan is a democratic country, with members of the Diet elected by popular vote. However, in practice, real power is held by powerful political cliques descended from generations of the nation's elite, who are allied with Japan's dominant *keiretsu* (business cartels). Until recently, this seemed to suit Japanese voters just fine, but the recession plus structural reforms by the last prime minister Junichirō Koizumi have stoked more political fire among the populace.

The popular, lion-maned Koizumi stepped down at the end of his last term in September 2006, which saw not only saw the birth of a prince but also ushered in a new PM, Shinzō Abe. Although Koizumi broke with tradition and did not personally appoint him, Abe served as Koizumi's Chief Cabinet Secretary. He was voted in by the LDP and will likely carry on the policies of his predecessor, but will certainly cut a less colourful figure.

ECONOMY

With the world's second-largest GDP, Japan's economy is just behind that of the USA – which doesn't mean it's been easy street for Japan these past two decades. The country is still feeling, though no longer reeling from, the effects of the 'bubble economy' bursting in the early '80s. The Asiawide financial collapse, ineffectual government response and tough competition from the USA were all key contributing factors, and the resulting recession lasted well into the '90s and early 2000s.

WORKING STIFFS

The Japanese love incorporating foreign words into their vocabulary; here are a few examples of local lingo for naming that employee.

> Salarymen – These are the guys in suits of sombre colours, often with a matching dour demeanour. But, after staying late at work to keep up appearances, they're often found red-faced and slap-happy at their favourite *izakaya* (pub/eatery) as they booze with their colleagues.

> OLs – Short for 'office ladies' – they may do the same work as salarymen but receive appallingly less pay. Others might be secretaries biding their time before they can marry a salaryman, quit the office job and take up recreational shopping. OLs often travel in packs, dressed in matching corporate vest-and-skirt combos.

> Freeters – A combination of 'freelance' and *arbeiter* ('worker' in German), these are the young people handing out advert-emblazoned packs of tissues on the streets or working that convenience-store register. They pick up work when they need it, and drop it when they don't.

However, the bright side of those darker financial days is that the economic slump inspired – or forced – businesspeople to reassess the traditional career arc that meant a lifetime allegiance to one's company. The concept of a job for life is no longer taken for granted, nor necessarily desired, by the younger generation. Part-time and casual employment are on the rise, with younger people working merely to make a living, and living more alternatively than their elders. Occasionally 'parasite singles' are blamed for the sluggish economy, with economic experts claiming that they should be buying property instead of living with (and mooching off) their parents. But unemployment has hovered at a respectable 4.1% over the past year or so, according to government numbers.

For visitors, the levelling-off of Japan's economy means a more even playing field for travellers to stretch their yen a little further.

ENVIRONMENT

On a fundamental geographical level, Japan is part of the Pacific 'Ring of Fire', the tectonic activity of which created the majestic conical shape of Mt Fuji and crumbled the city of Kōbe in 1995. Although minor earthquakes occur all the time, there's no telling when the next big one will strike. There's little point in paranoia, but it pays to note where exits are located.

BAG IT

The straightforward request that your purchase not be bagged may be met with some confusion, but environmental awareness is growing in Tokyo. The tradition of wrapping every single solitary purchase is an art bordering on obsession in Japan, where even the humblest of items – a pastry, for example – is wrapped in plastic before being wrapped in paper before then being placed reverentially into a bag with handles (prominently displaying a status-bearing logo, for luxury items).

You can cut down on the plague of bags by saying, *'Fukuro wa iranai desu'* ('I don't need a bag').

On a more human level, Japan's limited land mass plus its dense population equals an environmental quandary. Consequently, Tokyo's garbage collection services are quite strict about adhering to their own stringent regulations, which require the separation of burnable, non-burnable and recyclable refuse. If it's not properly separated before being left out for pickup, it's simply not picked up. There's still too much plastic packaging in use in the first place, but you can do your small part by cutting back on plastic bag consumption (see above).

Vending machines, convenience stores and some train stations usually have recycling receptacles clearly marked, but there's a distinct lack of rubbish receptacles around Tokyo in general.

THE ARTS
FILM

Kurosawa Akira, the most famous director of Japanese cinema's golden era, brought Japanese film into the spotlight when his *Rashōmon* (1950) took top prize at the Venice Film Festival. Illustrious filmmakers who followed include Imamura Shohei, who examines human behaviour with a piercing eye in works such as *The Profound Desire of the Gods* (1968) and Oshima Nagisa's *Ai no Corrida* (In the Realm of the Senses), a tale of an obsessive love that was banned in many countries when it was released in 1976.

More contemporary films include Itami Jūzō's *Tampopo* (1985), a characteristically quirky comedy about sex and food, and the award-winning *Zatoichi* (2003), featuring actor-director Kitano 'Beat' Takeshi as a blind swordsman. Japan's gorgeous anime gems, such as Miyazaki Hayao's *Spirited Away* (2001), continue to issue from Tokyo onto international screens. More recent works include the brilliant but a tad depressing *Dare mo Shira-*

nai (2004) by Koreeda Hirokazu, based on the true story about a wayward mother who abandoned her four children in an apartment in Tokyo.

LITERATURE

Often with a surrealist edge or a dose of magical realism, Japanese contemporary literature – much of which is written by authors who've spent most of their lives in Tokyo – provides a perspective on the more elusive emotional side of life in the city. Nobel Laureate Ōe Kenzaburo 's clear-eyed *A Personal Matter* tells the story of a man faced with a conflict of freedom and responsibility that transcends Japanese social mores. A departure from his more surrealist work, Murakami Haruki's celebrated *Norwegian Wood* chronicles the coming of age of a university student in late 1960s Japan. And for lighter, but surprisingly solid fare, pick up *Kitchen* (1998) by Banana Yoshimoto; seemingly superficial themes of food, pop culture and unconventional sexuality speak to an immediate sort of urban existentialism.

MUSIC

Live gigs rock the 'live houses' every night of the week in Tokyo's basement bars, mostly on the city's west side. You name it, someone makes or hosts it – from Japanese hip-hop and punk rock to acid jazz.

Japan has an enormous domestic record market, and Tokyo is very much a part of the international live-music circuit. Many top performers, from every genre of contemporary and classical music, book shows here. Along with Tokyo's better-known exports, such as composer Sakamoto Ryūichi and food-fetish rockers Shonen Knife, are musical collage artists Buffalo Daughter, and postmodern mixmaster Cornelius, who overlays samples of birdsong with harmonic vocal tracks, guitar and synthesized beats. Veteran DJ Takkyu Ishino packs 'em in, while bands like Dragon Ash and Kreva bring a Japanese flavour to hip-hop and reggae.

Tokyo mainstream consists significantly of *aidoru* (idol singers) and girl- or boy-bands, manufactured J-pop confections sweetened to perfection for mass marketing. Don't overindulge, or you'll get a toothache.

PERFORMANCE ARTS

Kabuki, *nō* (classical Japanese drama), and bunraku (puppet theatre) are well represented throughout the city, with several theatres featuring regular performances. *Taiko* (traditional Japanese drumming) is where music meets martial art and mysticism.

Tokyo is also a centre for Japan's enigmatic, challenging modern dance form, *butō*. Its bizarre movements, weird lighting, and long periods of inaction are not everyone's cup of *o-cha* (green tea), but most certainly memorable. Check with a tourist information centre (p202), or local listings for current performances. Seek out Dairakudakan (www.dairakudakan.com), Sankaijuku (www.sankaijuku.com), or most powerful of all, Taihen (www.ne.jp/asahi/imaju/taihen), whose members are all severely physically disabled.

VISUAL ART

Tokyo's contemporary art scene is thriving. Its galleries possess a lack of pretension that is startlingly refreshing – it's easy to walk into a show and start a conversation with the artists themselves. Progressive spaces all over town give space to exciting work, much of it by the talented young artists of the city's prestigious art colleges.

Bigger museums tend to go for heavy-hitting names: Rodin, Renoir, Da Vinci, Degas. The superstars of Western art are most oft-found at the National Museum of Western Art (p68). But don't be surprised if they pop up, along with their Japanese counterparts, in the department-store galleries dotted around town. The greatest concentration of small galleries – with roughly 400 exhibition spaces – clusters in Ginza (p45).

DIRECTORY
TRANSPORT
ARRIVAL & DEPARTURE
AIR
Narita Airport

Tokyo's main international airport is **Narita International Airport** (Map p154, www.narita-airport.jp/en), 66km from the city. When flying out of Narita, be sure to check which terminal your airline departs from, as the distance between the two is significant enough to warrant separate train stops.

Information
Flight information (☎ 0476-345 000)
General inquiries (☎ 0476-322 802)
Air Canada (☎ 5405 8800; www.aircanada.ca)
Air France (☎ 3570 8577; www.airfrance.com)
American Airlines (☎ 4550 2111; www.aa.com)
ANA (☎ 0120-029 709; www.ana.co.jp/eng)
British Airways (☎ 3570 8657; www.ba.com)
Cathay Pacific Airways (☎ 5159 1700; www.cathaypacific.com)
Japan Airlines (☎ 5460 0511; www.jal.co.jp/e/index.html)
KLM (☎ 3570 8770; www.klm.com)
Korean Air (☎ 0476-327 561; www.koreanair.com)
Lufthansa (☎ 5750 5713; www.lufthansa.com)
Qantas Airways (☎ 3593 7000; www.qantas.com.au)
United Airlines (☎ 3817 4411; www.ual.com)
Virgin Atlantic Airways (☎ 3499 8811; www.virgin-atlantic.com)

Airport Access
Train N'EX (JR Narita Express) runs to Tokyo Station (¥2940, 53 minutes), Shinjuku Station (¥3110, 1½ hours), Ikebukuro Station (¥3110, one hour and 40 minutes) and Yokohama Station (¥4180, 1½ hours). Airport Narita Kaisoku (rapid service) also goes to Tokyo station (¥1280, 1½ hours). Keisei Skyliner goes to Ueno (¥1920, 56 minutes). The private Keisei line also runs a Tokkyū (limited express; ¥1000, one hour and 11 minutes) service.
Bus Limousine Buses (www.limousinebus.co.jp/en/) connect Narita with central Tokyo

---

CLIMATE CHANGE & TRAVEL

Travel – especially air travel – is a significant contributor to global climate change. At Lonely Planet, we believe that all who travel have a responsibility to limit their personal impact. As a result, we have teamed with Rough Guides and other concerned industry partners to support Climate Care, which allows people to offset the greenhouse gases they are responsible for with contributions to energy-saving projects and other climate-friendly initiatives in the developing world. Lonely Planet offsets all staff and author travel.

For more information, turn to the responsible travel pages on www.lonelyplanet.com. For details on offsetting your carbon emissions and a carbon calculator, go to www.climatecare.org.

DIRECTORY

STAY AWHILE

Short city breaks make great getaways, but air travel is a becoming a devastating contributor to global warming. What can you do to lessen the impact? Why not take a longer holiday? If a few days in Tokyo has given you a taste of the city in all its beautifully bizarre and uniquely Japanese glory, consider making your next trip a longer one: take a day-trip out to the lovely mountain resort town of Hakone near Mt Fuji, or to the temples, shrines and Great Buddha statue in Kamakura. Or go even further and travel across Japan using its world-class rail system.

(¥3000, 1½ hours), making stops directly at many major hotels around the city, among them the Cerulean Tower Tōkyū Hotel in Shibuya, Keiō Plaza Hotel in Shinjuku, Marunouchi Hotel in Central Tokyo and ANA Hotel in Akasaka. Pick-up points are along this same circuit. Limousine bus ticket counters are located on the arrival floors of both terminals, and the bus stops are directly outside both terminals.

Taxis From Tokyo to Narita airport will cost about ¥30,000; travel times vary widely depending on traffic.

Haneda Airport

While the vast majority arrive at Narita International Airport, a few international flights operate through Haneda Airport (Map p46-7), near central Tokyo.

Information
General inquiries & flight information

(☎ 5757 8111; www.tokyo-airport-bldg .co.jp)

Airport Access

Train The Tokyo Monorail (www.tokyo-mono rail.co.jp/english/) is a great way to get to and from Haneda. The monorail connects each terminal at Haneda with Hamamatsuchō Station on the JR Yamanote line (¥470, 20 minutes). You can then easily catch a Yamanote line train to your final destination. Purchase tickets at the station vending machines, which have an English option.

Bus Limousine buses (www.limousinebus.co .jp/en/) run between Haneda and various points around Tokyo, including Tokyo Station and Shinjuku Station (¥1200, one hour). Purchase your ticket at the counters on the arrival floor of each terminal; bus stops are directly outside the 2nd floor of each terminal.

Taxis A trip between Haneda and Tokyo station costs around ¥7000.

TRAIN

Japan Railways' (JR) famed *shinkansen* (bullet trains) serve Northern Honshū, Central and Western Japan and Kyūshū. The slower, less expensive *tokkyū* (limited express), *kyūko* (express) and *futsū* (ordinary) are options on every route between cities; however, not many people use them for long-distance travel. One-way, reserved-seat *shinkansen* fares for *nozomi* trains (which make the fewest stops) are ¥13,500 from Kyoto to Tokyo, ¥22,100 from

Fukuoka to Tokyo, and ¥13,800 from Osaka to Tokyo. The main terminals are Tokyo (Map pp46–7, E5) and Ueno (Map p67, C4) stations.

Private lines running from stations on the Yamanote line are the quickest, cheapest bet to Kamakura, Mt Fuji, Hakone and Yokohama. They connect to Shinjuku (Map p89, B4) and Shibuya (Map p119, C4) stations. The Tōbu line for Nikkō runs from Asakusa Station (Map p75, C4).

BUS
Domestic long-distance buses mainly arrive at Tokyo station's Highway Bus Terminal (Map pp46–7, E5) near the Yaesu south exit. Highway buses also depart from the west side of Shinjuku Station (Map p89, B4). Services to both Osaka and Kyoto are operated by JR (☎ 3215 1468); you can buy tickets from a Green Window

office at most larger JR train stations.

VISA
Citizens of 62 countries, including Singapore, Hong Kong, Korea, Canada, USA, Australia, New Zealand, UK, France, Germany, the Netherlands and Sweden, do not require visas to enter Japan for stays of 90 days or fewer. Consult www.mofa.go.jp/j_info/visit/visa/02.html for a complete list of visa-exempt countries.

GETTING AROUND
Short-term visitors and long-term residents alike mainly use the city's excellent subway system and the JR train lines, especially the JR Yamanote line. It rings the inner city, making most everywhere accessible in under an hour. All stations have signposts and maps in English. The Tokyo Metro subway lines are colour coded,

ELUSIVE ADDRESSES
In Tokyo, finding a place by address alone is challenging at best, even for locals. Apart from *dōri* (main roads), very few streets have names – addresses indicate their locations in relation to their larger contexts. So, for example, an address listed as 1-11-2 Ginza, Chūō-ku in this book means that the place is in Tokyo's Chūō ward, in Ginza's 1-*chōme* (an area consisting of several blocks), in block 11, in building 2 of that block.

Chōme, blocks and building numbers aren't necessarily located in a logical order, so it's best to use a map (the bilingual *Tokyo City Atlas*, published by Kodansha, is invaluable if you'll be spending much time in Tokyo). Most establishments print simple maps on their business cards. Another effective way to find your way is to stop at a *kōban* (police box) in the area, where the friendly neighbourhood police spend much of their time giving directions.

and regular English signposting makes the system easy to use. The train and subway services in Tokyo are famed for their punctuality, and trains are frequent. Nearest stations are listed after the 🚉 (for the Yamanote and above-ground lines) and 🚇 (for subway lines) in listings.

TRAVEL PASSES

Short-stay visitors should consider getting the Tokyo Combination Ticket day pass that can be used on all JR, subway and bus lines within the Tokyo metropolitan area. It costs ¥1580 (¥790 for children aged six to 11) and is available from Pass offices, which can be found in most JR and subway stations.

TRAIN

Tokyo is serviced by a combination of JR, private inner-city subway lines and private suburban lines, all of which are *gaijin* (foreigner) friendly. Trains run from around 5am to midnight. Most useful is the JR Yamanote line, which is augmented by the Chūō and Sōbu lines. Fares begin at ¥130, and the green maps above ticket vending machines have fares clearly marked. At stations where the maps do not include English, simply buy the minimum fare and pay the balance at a fare adjustment machine

when you arrive at your destination. For English-language train information, you can call the **JR English Information line** (☎ 3423 0111; 🕙 10am-6pm Mon-Fri).

SUBWAY

The subway system is essential for getting to areas inside the Yamanote loop. There are 13 subway lines, nine of which are TRTA lines (fares start at ¥160) and four of which are TOEI lines (fares start at ¥170). Services on the two systems are essentially the same, and connections are seamless except for the fact that they have separate ticketing systems. You can circumvent the hassle of puzzling over and buying transfer tickets by purchasing a Passnet card, which is sold at ticket vending machines in denominations of ¥1000, ¥3000 and ¥5000. The card can be used on any subway line and will automatically calculate your fare every time you insert it into a subway wicket.

Ticket vending machines that operate in English are available at every station. If you can't work out how much your fare will be, buy the cheapest ticket and pay the difference at a fare adjustment machine at your destination. Services run from around 5.30am, with last trains leaving around midnight.

Recommended Subway Routes

	To Ginza	To Shinjuku	To Shibuya	To Roppongi	To Asakusa
From Ginza	n/a	Marunouchi line (16mins)	Ginza line (15mins)	Hibiya line (10mins)	Ginza line (17mins)
From Shinjuku	Marunouchi line (16mins)	n/a	JR Yamanote line (7mins)	Toei Ōedo line (9mins)	Marunouchi line to Akasaka-mitsuke, transfer to Ginza line (34mins)
From Shibuya	Ginza line (15mins)	JR Yamanote line (7mins)	n/a	Hanzōmon line to Aoyama-itchōme, transfer to Toei Ōedo line (12mins)	Ginza line (32mins)
From Roppongi	Hibiya line (10mins)	Toei Ōedo line (9mins)	Toei Ōedo line to Aoyama-itchōme, transfer to Hanzōmon line (12mins)	n/a	Toei Ōedo line to Daimon, transfer to Toei Asakusa line (28mins)
From Asakusa	Ginza line (17mins)	Ginza line to Akasaka-mitsuke, transfer to Marunouchi line	Ginza line (32mins)	Toei Asakusa line to Daimon, transfer to Toei Ōedo line (28mins)	n/a

TAXI

Rates start at ¥660 per 2km (after 11pm it's 1.5km), then the meter rises by ¥100 every 350m (after 11pm it's every 300m or so). You also rack up about ¥100 every two minutes while you relax in a typical Tokyo traffic jam.

Taxi vacancy is indicated by a red light; a green light means there's a night-time surcharge and a yellow light means that the cab is on call. Watch out for the automatic doors on taxis; they'll magically close

themselves when you get in or out. Taxi drivers can plug a venue's telephone number into their GPS system to find its location.

CAR & MOTORCYCLE

On a short trip to Tokyo you're unlikely to need or want your own wheels, what with Tokyo's outstanding rail system and miserable traffic congestion. However, if you do need to hire a vehicle, be sure to obtain an International Driving Permit before you arrive in

Japan as well as bringing a driver's licence from your own country.

Typical rates for small cars are ¥8000 or ¥9000 for the first day, and ¥5500 to ¥7000 each day thereafter. On top of this there is a ¥1000-per-day insurance fee. Mileage is usually unlimited.

We recommend the following:

Mazda Rent-a-Lease (☎ 5286 0740)
Nippon Rent-a-Car (☎ 3485 7196)
Toyota Rent-a-Lease (☎ 3264 0100)

BOAT

Water buses are a great way to see a different slice of Tokyo, either as a short tour or as a relaxing means of getting around. **Suijo Bus** (Map p75, C4; ☎ 3841 9178; www.suijobus.co.jp/english /index.html; Azumabashi-mae, Asakusa, Taitō-ku; from ¥720; ⏲ 9.55am-7.10pm, hours vary seasonally; Ⓜ Ginza & Toei Asakusa lines to Asakusa, (exits 4 & A5)) lines can shuttle you from Asakusa to Central Tokyo and on again to Odaiba.

PRACTICALITIES

BUSINESS HOURS

Banks 9am-3pm or 5pm Mon-Fri, closed national holidays
Convenience stores 24hr
Museums 9.30am-4.30pm
Offices 9am-5pm Mon-Fri (some open Sat am)
Post offices 9am-5pm Mon-Fri (major post offices 8am-8pm)
Public offices 9am-noon & 1-5pm Mon-Fri
Restaurants 11.30am-2.30pm & 6-10.30pm (family-run restaurants open from 11.30am-11.30pm)
Shops 10am-8pm

CLIMATE & WHEN TO GO

Spring (March to May) and Autumn (September to November) are the most balmy seasons. Typhoons usually occur in September and October. Summers are hot and humid, with temperatures getting into the high 30s. The *tsuyu* (rainy season), in June,

GOOD THINGS TO KNOW

> Electricity – 100V 50Hz AC, two-pronged flat-pin plugs.
> Metric System – Japan uses the international metric system.
> Newspapers & Magazines – *The Japan Times, Daily Yomiuri* and the *Asahi/International Herald Tribune* are English-language newspapers available at newsstands in or near train stations. *Tokyo Journal* is a good events magazine sold in bookstores, and the free *Metropolis* is an excellent, intelligent weekly magazine available every Friday at cafés and bookstores around Tokyo.
> Radio – InterFM on 76.1FM broadcasts news and daily life information mainly in English, and in seven other languages, including Spanish and Chinese.
> Time – Japan is nine hours ahead of Greenwich Mean Time (GMT). Daylight-saving time is not used in Japan.
> TV – NHK is the government-run TV station; its 7pm news is bilingual. CNN and BBC World services are available in all major hotels.

means several weeks of torrential rain can wreak havoc with a tight travel itinerary. In winter the weather is good with mainly clear, sunny skies and the occasional snowfall. Avoid major holidays such as Golden Week (29 April to 5 May) and the mid-August O-bon festival. The city tends to close down over New Year (around 29 December to 6 January).

DISCOUNTS

In general, not many discounts are offered to sights in Tokyo. Most major sights offer discounts for children, and very young children may get in free. An international student card will earn discounts on entry fees to many museums and prices on long-distance train travel. Seniors can get discounts to some major sights, and Japanese domestic airlines (JAS, JAL and ANA) offer senior discounts of about 25% on some flights. However, that's about the extent of it.

Prices are listed in this book in the following order: adult/student/child six to 12/child under six; typically, a listing like $ ¥1000/500 refers to adult/child prices.

One excellent investment, if you'll be in Tokyo for awhile and plan to visit several museums, is the Grutt Pass (p71). The pass grants discounted or free entry to nearly 50 museums and zoos around Tokyo.

EMERGENCIES

Violent crime and theft, though they exist, are rare in Tokyo; that said, you should exercise the same awareness of your surroundings as you would anywhere else. Women should be aware of *chikan* (gropers) working crowded trains. Yelling '*chikan!*' will often shame the offender into stopping, but look before you let loose – sometimes a crowded train is just a crowded train.

Although most emergency operators in Tokyo don't speak English, they will immediately refer you to someone who does. For free English assistance or advice, you can also call the **Japan Helpline** (☎ 0120-461 997; ☽ 24hr), or the **Tokyo English Life Line** (☎ 5774 0992; www .telljp.com; ☽ 9am-11pm).

Other useful numbers:
Ambulance ☎ 119
Fire ☎ 119
Police ☎ 110

HEALTH

All hospitals listed here have English-speaking staff and 24-hour accident and emergency departments. Travel insurance is advisable to cover any medical treatment you may need while in Tokyo. Medical treatment is among the best in the world, but also the most expensive. Note also that you will be expected to pay in full for treatment or provide sufficient proof that your insurance company will cover the payment.

We recommend:

Japanese Red Cross Medical Center (Nihon Sekijūjisha Iryō Sentā; Map pp140-1, B6; ☎ 3400 1311; www.med.jrc.or.jp in Japanese; 4-1-22 Hiro-o, Shibuya-ku; Ⓜ Hibiya line to Hiro-o, exits 1 & 2)

St Luke's International Hospital (Seiroka Byōin; Map pp46-7, F7; ☎ 3541 5151; www.luke.or.jp; 9-1 Akashichō, Chūō-ku; Ⓜ Hibiya line to Tsukiji, exits 3 & 4)

Tokyo Medical & Surgical Clinic (Map pp140-1, G6; ☎ 3436 3028; www.tmsc.jp; 2F, 32 Shiba-kōen Bldg, 3-4-30 Shiba-kōen, Minato-ku; Ⓜ Toei Mita line to Onarimon, exit A1)

PHARMACIES

Pharmacies are easy to find and some have Japanese-English symptom charts. Staff speak English at the listed pharmacies:

American Pharmacy (Map pp46-7, D5; ☎ 5220-7716; B1F, Marunouchi Bldg, 2-4-1 Marunouchi, Chiyoda-ku; 🕑 9am-9pm Mon-Fri, 10am-9pm Sat, 10am-8pm Sun; Ⓜ Marunouchi line to Tokyo, exit 4)

National Azabu Supermarket (Map pp140-1; ☎ 3442 3181; 4-5-2 Minami-Azabu, Minato-ku; 🕑 9.30am-7pm; Ⓜ Hibiya line to Hiro-o, exits 1 & 2).

HOLIDAYS

When a public holiday falls on a Sunday, the following Monday is taken as a holiday. If a business remains open on a holiday, it will usually be closed the following day.

New Year's Day 1 January
Coming-of-Age Day 2nd Monday in January
National Foundation Day 11 February
Spring Equinox Day 21 March
Green Day 29 April
Constitution Day 3 May
Children's Day 5 May
Marine Day 3rd Monday in July
Respect-for-the-Aged Day 3rd Monday in September
Autumn Equinox Day 23 September
Sports Day 2nd Monday in October
Culture Day 3 November
Labour Thanksgiving Day 23 November
Emperor's Birthday 23 December

INFORMATION & ORGANISATIONS

Contact the **Japanese Red Cross Language Service Volunteers** (Map pp140-1, H5; ☎ 3438 1311; http://accessible.jp.org /tokyo/en; 1-1-3 Shiba Daimon, Minato-ku) to get a copy of their indispensable *Accessible Tokyo* guide, or peruse the website for the same detailed, current information on getting around Tokyo.

INTERNET ACCESS

Internet access is rapidly improving. Some bars and cafés offer net access and/or wi-fi for free – check out **Freespot** (www.freespot .com /users/map_e.html) for locations near you. The Apple Store (Map pp46–7) in Ginza and the **Marunouchi Café** (Map pp46-7, D5; ☎ 3212 5025; 3-3-1 Marunouchi, Chiyoda-ku; admission free; 🕑 8am-9pm Mon-Fri, 11am-8pm Sat-Sun; 🚃 JR Yamanote line to Yūrakuchō) near Tokyo Station are good places for a quick stop. Many midrange hotels and most top-end hotels offer in-room LAN access, though you may be charged a usage fee.

Alternatively, you could do as the Tokyoites do and head to one of the *manga kissa* (p100) around town.

We recommend:

Aprecio (Map p89, C2; ☎ 3205 7336; www .aprecio.co.jp in Japanese; B1F, Hygeia Plaza, 2-44-1 Kabukichō, Shinjuku-ku; 1st 30min ¥300, 10min thereafter ¥100; 🕐 24hr; 🚉 JR Yamanote line to Shinjuku, east exit) This clean, comfortable spot in Kabukichō offers all the usuals in smoking and nonsmoking wings, and has massage and beauty services, billiards and darts.

Bagus Gran Cyber Cafe (Map p119, B3; ☎ 5428 3676; www.bagus-99.com/netcafé in Japanese; 6F, 28-6 Udagawachō, Shibuya-ku; 8 hours ¥1500; 🕐 24hr; 🚉 JR Yamanote line to Shibuya, Hachikō exit) This popular chain has branches all over Tokyo.

USEFUL WEBSITES

The LP website (www.lonelyplanet.com) offers a speedy link to many of Tokyo's websites. Other excellent sites include the following:

Metropolis (http://metropolis.co.jp)
Superfuture (www.superfuture.com/city/city /city.cfm?city=1)
Tokyo Food Page (www.bento.com/tokyo food.html)
Tokyo Journal (www.tokyo.to)
Tokyo Qool (http://tokyoq.com)

LANGUAGE

Note: Letters in square brackets are not pronounced.

BASICS

Hello.	*konnichiwa.*
Goodbye.	*sayōnara.*
How are you?	*o-genki des[u]. ka?*
I'm fine.	*genki des[u].*
Excuse me.	*sumimasen.*
Yes.	*hai.*
No.	*iie.*
Thanks.	*dōmo (arigatō).*
You're welcome.	*dō itashimashite.*
Do you speak English?	*eigo ga hanase mas[u] ka?*
I don't understand.	*wakarimasen.*

EATING & DRINKING

That was delicious!	*oyshikatta*
I'm a vegetarian.	*watashi wa bejitarian des[u]*
Please bring the bill.	*(o-kanjō/o-aiso) o onegai shimas[u].*

Local dishes

kabayaki	skewers of grilled eel
katsu-don	fried pork cutlet with rice
okonomiyaki	Japanese-style pancake
tempura moriawase	a selection of tempura
zaru soba	cold buckwheat noodles with seaweed strips

SHOPPING

| How much is it? | ikura des[u] ka? |
| That's too expensive. | taka-sugi mas[u] |

EMERGENCIES

I'm sick.	kibun ga warui des[u]
Help!	tas[u]kete!
Call the police.	keisatsu o yonde kudasai!
Call an ambulance.	kyūkyūsha o yonde

DAYS & NUMBERS

today	kyō
tomorrow	ash[i]ta
yesterday	kinō

0	zero/rei
1	ichi
2	ni
3	san
4	yon/shi
5	go
6	roku
7	nana/shichi
8	hachi
9	kyū/ku
10	jū
11	jūichi
12	jūni
13	jūsan
14	jūyon/jūshi
20	nijū
21	nijūichi
30	sanjū
100	hyaku
1000	sen

MONEY

Despite its status as a top-tier, modern city, Tokyo still largely runs on a cash economy. Hotels and high-end restaurants will accept credit cards, but many less-exclusive shops and services do not. Since it's generally safe to carry around large amounts of cash in Tokyo, line your pockets with some money just for walking around. You'll burn through yen quickly in Tokyo; if you're not on a tight budget, plan on spending a daily average of around ¥5000 to ¥8000 for meals, train fares and admission costs.

CURRENCY

The currency in Japan is the yen (¥). Coins come in denominations of ¥1, ¥5, ¥10, ¥50, ¥100 and ¥500; notes in denominations of ¥1000, ¥2000, ¥5000 and ¥10,000. Newer-issue ¥500 coins aren't accepted by some vending machines.

TRAVELLERS CHEQUES

There's little difference in commission charged by banks and big hotels. All major brands are acceptable, but cheques in yen or US dollars are preferred over other currencies.

CREDIT CARDS

Visa, MasterCard, Amex and Diners Club are widely accepted…where credit cards are accepted. For 24-

hour card cancellations or assistance, call:

Amex ☎ 0120-020 120
Diners Club ☎ 0120-074 024
JCB (☎ 0120-500 544
MasterCard (☎ 0053-111 3886
Visa ☎ 0120-133 173

ATMS

Tokyo post offices have ATMs that accept foreign-issued cash or credit cards, 9am to 5pm Monday to Friday. Some banks and department stores have global ATMs which accept Visa, MasterCard and Cirrus. Citibank is your best bet, with many 24-hour global ATMs scattered around Tokyo, including Shinjuku, Ginza and Roppongi.

TELEPHONE

Local telephone calls cost ¥10 for the first three minutes, and then ¥10 for each minute thereafter. Phonecards are available from both newsstands and convenience stores starting in denominations of ¥500 and ¥1000 and are the most convenient way to call either locally or internationally.

Japan's mobile phone network runs on the CDMA standard – incompatible with the widespread GSM system used in Europe, Australia and the rest of Asia (South Korea being the exception). However, several companies in Japan offer short-term mobile phone rentals at reasonable rates, from

around ¥3000 per week. Many even have pick-up and drop-off counters at Narita airport. Try one of the following:

DoCoMo (☎ 5911 3968; www.docomosentu
.co.jp/Web/english/rental)
GoMobile (www.gomobile.co.jp)
PuPuRu (☎ 052-957 1801; www.pupuru
.com/en/index_en.html)
Rentafone (☎ 0909-621 7318; www.renta
fonejapan.com)
Softbank (☎ 3560 7730; www.softbank
-rental.jp)

COUNTRY & CITY CODES

Japan ☎ 81
Tokyo ☎ 03

USEFUL PHONE NUMBERS

International directory assistance ☎ 0057
International operator ☎ 0051
Local directory assistance ☎ 104
Reverse-charge (collect) ☎ 0039

TIPPING

Tipping is not standard practice in Japan. Expect to pay a service charge (10% to 20%) at upper-end restaurants and hotels.

TOILETS

Public toilets can be found everywhere, but the most luxurious are in the big department stores. They also tend to be high tech, outfitted with bidet, dryer and rushing-water sound effects to mask unseemly noise. Japanese-style squat toilets are also still an option at most public toilets.

TOURIST INFORMATION

JNTO Tokyo TIC (Map pp46-7, E6; ☎ 3216 1901; www.jnto.go.jp; 10F, Kōtsū Kaikan Bldg, 2-10-1 Yūraku-chō, Chiyoda-ku; 🕑 9am-5pm Mon-Fri, 9am-noon Sat; 🚇 JR Yamanote line to Yūrakuchō) The JNTO provides excellent, up-to-date information on Tokyo and can make reservations for ryokan (Japanese inns).

Narita Airport TIC (☎ 0476-303 383, 0476-345 877; Terminals 1 & 2, Narita International Airport; 🕑 8am-8pm) These TICs are located in both arrivals terminals and can help with hotel bookings.

Tokyo Tourist Information Center (Map p89, A3; ☎ 5321 3077; 1F, Tokyo Metropolitan Government Bldg No 1, 2-8-1 Nishi-Shinjuku, Shinjuku-ku; 🕑 9.30am-6.30pm; 🚇 Toei Ōedo line to Tochōmae, exit A4) is a good place to pick up a Grutt Pass (¥2000; p71), free tourist map and information in English.

TRAVELLERS WITH DISABILITIES

Tokyo's size and complexity make it challenging for the mobility impaired, as well as the visually and hearing impaired. The upside is that attitudes to people with disabilities have vastly improved in the last two decades, and newer buildings tend to have excellent facilities. Advance planning is the key to a successful trip.

The 👩‍🦽 icon throughout this guidebook denotes listings that are wheelchair-accessible, have toilets accommodating wheelchairs and are otherwise navigable for those with ambulatory challenges.

>INDEX

See also separate subindexes for See (p212), Shop (p213), Eat (p214), Drink (p215) and Play (p215).

000 map pages

000 map pages

000 map pages